Professor of D...

JAMES P. MACKEY
Thomas Chalmers Professor of Theology,
University of

The Case for Wo

D0244919

BIBLICAL FOUNDATIONS IN THEOLOGY

General Editors
James D. G. Dunn   James P. Mackey

New Testament Theology in Dialogue
James D. G. Dunn and James P. Mackey

Jesus and the Ethics of the Kingdom
Bruce Chilton and J. I. H. McDonald

Meaning and Truth in 2 Corinthians
Frances Young and David F. Ford

The Case for Women's Ministry
Ruth B. Edwards

Liberating Exegesis
The Challenge of Liberation Theology to Biblical Studies
Christopher Rowland and Mark Corner

Reading in Communion
Scripture and Ethics in Christian Life
Stephen E. Fowl and L. Gregory Jones

Biblical Foundations in Theology

General Editors

JAMES D. G. DUNN   JAMES P. MACKEY

THE CASE FOR
WOMEN'S MINISTRY

Ruth B. Edwards

First published in Great Britain 1989
SPCK
Holy Trinity Church
Marylebone Road
London NW1 4DU

Second impression 1991

Unless otherwise stated, biblical quotations are from the
New Jerusalem Bible, © 1985 by Darton, Longman
& Todd Ltd and Doubleday and Company, Inc.,
and are used by permission.

British Library Cataloguing in Publication Data

Edwards, Ruth B.
The case for women's ministry.
1. Christian church. Women's ministry
I. Title II. Series
262′.14

ISBN 0-281-04389-2

Printed in Great Britain by
the University Press, Cambridge

Contents

EDITORS' FOREWORD   viii

PREFACE   ix

ABBREVIATIONS   xi

INTRODUCTION   I

PART ONE: FOUNDATIONS   II

I   WOMEN IN THE GRAECO-ROMAN WORLD   13
    The Greek contribution   14
    The Roman legacy   18

2   WOMEN IN THE OLD TESTAMENT AND EARLY
    JUDAISM   23
    Evidence for a subordinationist attitude   23
    Equalitarian texts and affirmations of women   30
    Conclusions and implications for methodology   34

3   JESUS AND WOMEN   39
    The nature of the evidence   39
    Jesus' relationship to women   40
    Jesus' teaching about women   47
    Possible masculine orientation in Jesus' teaching   48
    Conclusions   49

4   PAUL: MISOGYNIST OR FEMINIST?   54
    The enigma of Paul's attitudes   54
    Paul's fundamental theology   55
    Paul's acceptance of women as colleagues in ministry   57
    Paul's views on sexuality and marriage   59

Paul's views on women's roles in worship and
ministry   64
Conclusion   69

5 WOMEN AND MINISTRY IN THE NEW
   TESTAMENT   72
   Varieties of ministry in the New Testament   72
   Ministry as belonging to the whole people of God   74
   The significance of the male apostles   76
   Were there exclusively male bishops, priests and
   deacons?   80
   Women and the New Testament ideals of ministry   82

PART TWO: DEVELOPMENTS   87

6 WOMEN AND THE MINISTRY IN THE CHURCH
   FATHERS   89
   General attitudes to women   89
   Women and public ministry   95

7 WOMEN AND THE MINISTRY FROM THE MEDIEVAL
   PERIOD TO THE REFORMATION   104
   The medieval period   104
   The Reformation   111

8 WOMEN AND THE MINISTRY IN MODERN TIMES   117
   The changing climate   117
   The Church's response to change   122
   Women's ministry and contemporary challenges to
   the Churches   130

9 GOD AS FATHER AND MOTHER   133
   Male and female images of God in the biblical
   tradition   133
   The theological significance of the images   138
   Male-female imagery and the ordained ministry   141

10 MALE AND FEMALE: EQUAL BEFORE GOD?   144
   Arguments for the subordination of women from
   the Bible and Tradition   145
   Observation from human behaviour and the
   argument from 'Nature'   150
   Conclusions   156

11 WOMEN, AUTHORITY, AND PRIESTHOOD   159
    The functions of the ordained ministry   159
    Ontological and symbolic considerations   164
    Conclusions   173

12 WOMEN AND THE THREEFOLD MINISTRY   177
    The Episcopate   177
    The Presbyterate or Priesthood   179
    The Diaconate   180
    The Church's authority to make change   181

    CONCLUSION   185

    BIBLIOGRAPHY   202

    INDEXES   219

Editors' Foreword

The aim of this series is to bridge the gap between biblical scholarship and the larger enterprise of Christian theology. Whatever the theory or theology of the canon itself, Christian theologians have always seen in the Bible their ultimate court of appeal, and exegetes have rightly expected their work to contribute directly to a better theology for each succeeding century.

And yet the gap remains. Theologians from the beginning, the greatest as well as the least, have been guilty of forcing their preferred conclusions upon a biblical text which they could have better understood. And the more professional biblical scholars, too anxious perhaps for immediate theological impact, have often been tempted to produce Old or New Testament theologies which in the event owed too little to the rich variety of their authoritative texts, and too much to prevailing theological fashions. Co-operation between a critical scholar of the texts and a critical commentator on theological fashions was seldom evident, and few individuals have ever been able to combine both of these roles successfully.

Biblical Foundations in Theology attempts to address this problem by inviting authors from the disciplines of Biblical Studies or Systematic Theology to collaborate with a scholar from the other discipline, or to have their material reviewed in the course of composition, so that the resultant volumes may take sufficient account of the methods and insights of both areas of enquiry. In this way it is hoped that the series will come to be recognized as a distinctive and constructive contribution to current concerns about how, in the modern world, Christianity is to be lived as well as understood.

JAMES D. G. DUNN

JAMES P. MACKEY

Preface

This book is unusual in its series in that it has been written by a single author. Yet there is a real sense in which it represents a dialogue – between the data of the Bible and the historical developments both in Systematic Theology and in the life of the Church – concerning the ministry of women.

I should like to take this opportunity of thanking all who have contributed to its production: the academic editors, Professor J. D. G. Dunn and Professor J. P. Mackey, for accepting it in their series and for constructive criticisms and valuable comments during the course of writing; Mr Philip Law, Senior Editor at SPCK, for his enthusiastic support; the staff of Aberdeen University Library for their courtesy and help; and the many students, friends and academic colleagues who have supported me, discussed issues with me and provided offprints. I am particularly grateful to Dr Ruth Payne who cast a scientific eye over Chapter 10 and Mrs Elizabeth Johnstone for her expert advice on the Old Testament and Jewish material in Chapters 2 and 9.

Finally, I should like to thank my husband Patrick, who has discussed the work with me at all stages and given me enormous help with the proofs and indexes, and our two children, Hilary and Nicholas, who have shown unfailing patience and good humour as I wrestled with the issues debated here. It is not always easy, even in the late twentieth century, for a woman to combine family, profession, and Church ministry. I have therefore a very special debt of gratitude to all who have made this possible, including family, friends, and colleagues in both the University and the Church. Those who knew him will understand when I dedicate this book to the memory of a friend who first encouraged me to preach and to minister, the late Bob Allsopp, priest of the Scottish Episcopal Church, Rector of St James's, Aberdeen, and Canon of St Andrew's Cathedral, Diocese of Aberdeen and Orkney.

RUTH B. EDWARDS

King's College, Aberdeen
June 1989

I have taken advantage of the reprinting to make a few small corrections. I am very grateful to all who have responded so warmly to the book, and especially to Professor C. E. B. Cranfield and the Revd David R. Hall for sending me details of misprints and other comments.

R.B.E.
March 1991

Abbreviations

ACC	Anglican Consultative Council
ARCIC	Anglican-Roman Catholic International Commission
AV	Authorized Version (King James Version)
BCP	Book of Common Prayer
BEM	*Baptism, Eucharist and Ministry* (Lima Report, WCC), 1982.
CBQ	*Catholic Biblical Quarterly*
BMU	Board for Mission and Unity (C. of E.)
ET	English Translation
GNB	Good News Bible (Today's English Version)
GRU	*God's Reign and our Unity* (Anglican-Reformed International Commission), 1984.
IDB	*Interpreter's Dictionary of the Bible*, 1962–76.
ISBE	*International Standard Bible Encyclopaedia* (rev. edn)., 1979–88.
JB	Jerusalem Bible
LSJ	H. G. Liddell and R. Scott, *A Greek-English Lexicon*, 9th edn, 1940.
LXX	Septuagint (Greek Old Testament)
MOW	Movement for the Ordination of Women
NEB	New English Bible
NIV	New International Version
NJB	New Jerusalem Bible
NTS	*New Testament Studies*
par.	and parallel(s)
RSV	Revised Standard Version
RV	Revised Version
WCC	World Council of Churches
WIT	Women in Theology

Introduction

What are the proper roles of women and men in society today? This question is answered in different ways in different parts of the world. In Islamic countries some are seeking to reinstate the traditional seclusion and subordination of women; in parts of Africa the rights and wrongs of polygamy are still a live issue; in the sophisticated West professional opportunities for women and their role in the home and family are a subject of perpetual questioning and discussion.

Nowhere has the debate been more intense than in the Church. In recent years many denominations have opened their ordained ministry to women, or have greatly increased opportunities for other forms of ministry. Yet not all are happy about these developments: some Christians wonder whether the new freedom for women is really compatible with the teaching of the Bible, and have asked whether the ecclesial leadership has not just succumbed to secular values. A substantial part of the Church has, so far, felt unable to recognize the full ministry of women. In the Orthodox Churches the debate has barely begun; in Roman Catholicism it is still probably a concern of only a minority, though an increasingly vocal one, especially in the USA. In Anglicanism it has become a real controversy, seen by some as threatening division and schism, particularly when one Province goes ahead with the consecration of women bishops. Arguments have ranged over whether the Church has the authority to make the change; how the admission of women to 'Holy Orders' affects ecumenical relations; whether women priests would split the Church of England and even what financial compensation might be appropriate for clergy who found it necessary to resign their posts over the issue. Meanwhile 'Women's Studies' have burgeoned in universities and seminaries on both sides of the Atlantic, and books pour forth on feminist subjects. Yet with all the sociological, theological, and polemical works that have been published, there is still a need for a balanced discussion of the rationale for women's public ecclesial ministry that is not limited to the needs of any one tradition or denomination.[1] It is hoped that this book will help fill the gap.

One reason for the lack of an agreed theology of women's ministry is the current fluidity and uncertainty in many Churches over their doctrine of ministry as a whole. This is partly caused by changing social attitudes and roles and is partly the result of new theological developments. To take the social situation first: the days are long gone when the village schoolmaster, squire and parson were the only educated people in a parish; when the clergy were regarded as 'gentry'; and when only the ordained were perceived as having religious authority or professional expertise.[2] Western society is now for the most part democratic and egalitarian. Many lay people are as well educated as their clergy; many have their own professional skills; some may even have greater expertise than the ordained in theology, education, pastoral care and other areas once seen as the special preserve of clergy. In many denominations unordained members are now recognized as competent to preach, counsel, lead worship, take part in synodical government, and serve on doctrinal commissions. There has been a proliferation of new ministries – or fresh forms of old ministries: elders, readers, counsellors, chaplains, 'extraordinary ministers of the sacraments', lay pastors and missioners, as well as non-stipendiary priests, deacons and other ministers, who, though ordained, may continue in their regular secular employment.

Within these new and revived ministries women are expecting to play their part. Educated now similarly, if not identically, to men, with their legal and political equality officially recognized, and with the vast majority of professions open to them, with potential freedom from domestic drudgery and the continual round of child-bearing, they are offering themselves to the Church in increasing numbers, and are sometimes deeply disappointed at their rejection. At the same time men, who have traditionally been brought up to regard themselves as leaders, protectors and initiators, and who for centuries have taught, guided and ruled women, are often perplexed at these developments. While some have gladly accepted and even fostered them, others have felt threatened by them, and have sought to find new ways of asserting the traditional male domination. The emotional tone of some writings against women's ordination may in part be caused by a threat to male adequacy perceived in women's new roles in society.

Added to this has been the revolution that has taken place in theological thinking, occasioned partly by the modern critical approach to biblical study and partly by a new readiness to recognize that the Holy Spirit operates in people's lives without restriction to official Church channels. No longer is it possible, if it ever was, for any denomination to look back to the New Testament and claim quite simply that here is the source and pattern of its ministry. Modern scholarship has acknowledged the variety of ministries within the New Testament and the complexity of its relationship to the Old Testament and to the society in which it took shape. This has meant a severe shaking for the authority of the Bible. While some still affirm it as the infallible and inerrant word of God, others treat it virtually as a secular book, feeling free to accept or reject whatever parts may or may not appeal to them. Between these two extremes lie those who accept in principle its inspiration and centrality for Christian doctrine, but recognize that it must be studied critically and in context, and that its teachings cannot simply be removed from their original settings and mechanically applied to very different circumstances. In recent years biblical scholarship has become increasingly specialized, complex and elaborate. To the older disciplines of textual and literary criticism have been added form, source, and redaction criticism, rhetorical, narrative, and canonical criticism, as well as the broader work of theological and historical criticism.[3] Even those who have received a theological training often feel confused, while lay people unsuspectingly entering into the field may become thoroughly bewildered. Can we trust the Bible for giving us the teaching of Jesus? Does it support the equality of women and men? What is the relevance of its teaching for women's ordination? How do we handle ambiguous texts? Are we bound to accept traditional interpretations which first became promulgated in the patristic and medieval periods? Are we free to seek fresh understandings and applications for our own age?

This challenge to biblical authority has been accompanied by a challenge to the authority of the Church to pronounce on matters of doctrine or to enforce rules of behaviour. With the accessibility of the Scriptures in readable and readily intelligible translations, with the modern educational and social ethos which refuses to respect teaching merely given on authority without understanding the reason for it, and with the freedom that many Christians feel under the Spirit to think for themselves, to study, pray and worship without the guidance of professional clergy, has come a major crisis in perception of the nature of ministry. What actually is the difference between lay and ordained ministry? Are there psychological or theological reasons why women should be admitted to one form of ministry and not to another? In what sense is God male or female, and how does our doctrine of God affect our perception of ministry? Do the sexual distinctions between women and men imply different types of ministry for each? In Churches which uphold the threefold ministry of bishops, priests and deacons, is it right to admit women to the diaconate, but not to the presbyterate and episcopate?

In what follows we may not be able to answer all these questions, but we shall bear them in mind as we study the broad issues of the theology of women's ministry, paying special attention to those areas where controversy has been strongest.

SOME QUESTIONS OF METHOD

But how does one set about constructing a theology of women's ministry? It is important that this should not be done merely by emotional and personal *ad hoc* reactions to the present situation in the Churches (the 'gut' response), nor by the selective citation of biblical texts or patristic and other ecclesiastical documents out of their historical context (the 'pepper-pot' response). What is needed is a logical and systematic approach, adopting the same method as has been used to work out the Church's theological understanding of any significant issue, namely by the use of a combination of sources each of which is given its due weight.

For a long time it has been customary, especially within Anglicanism, to distinguish three such main sources: (a) Scripture, the foundation of Christian truth; (b) Tradition, the Church's continuing and developing perception of the truth; and (c) reason, which, together with conscience, can be understood as the individual's or the community's understanding of the truth, reached through intellectual, moral, and social processes.[4] In all three areas Christians have perceived the power of God at work – in Scripture through divine inspiration; in the Church through the continuing presence of Christ; and in reason through the enlightening work of the Spirit. At the same time it has to be recognized that none of these sources offers tidy, clear-cut guidelines which can be applied in an objective or clinical way. The perception of divine inspiration, whether in Scripture, Tradition, or reason, is itself to some degree subjective: what one Christian may regard as the activity of the Holy Spirit, another may see as the work of the Devil.

Moreover, different Churches, and even different groups within individual denominations, give varying weight to each of these three elements. For example, Protestant Churches and other 'Evangelical' and biblically-orientated groups tend to ascribe primary authority to the Bible (i.e. the shorter Protestant canon), against which they assess the testimony of other sources, seen as definitely subsidiary. Yet even they have to use reason to interpret the Bible, and in practice accept as matters of faith doctrinal developments which were only fully worked out in post-biblical times (e.g. developed doctrines of the Trinity, incarnation, or sacraments). Others, especially Orthodox, Roman Catholics, and 'high' Anglicans, give more weight to Tradition as such, and especially to the early Creeds, councils, and Fathers, being reluctant to depart from any article of faith which appears to rest on their united testimony.[5] Still others, especially those of 'liberal' outlook, see the ultimate source of authority as lying in conscience, governed by reason. This group includes not only free-thinking denominations such as the Quakers (Society of Friends) and Unitarians, but also many intellectuals from mainstream denominations, including perhaps especially Anglicans.

The position is further complicated by the fact that these three sources which we have been discussing are not really separate at all, but overlap with one another. Thus Tradition develops from Scripture, and it is sometimes hard to decide whether or not a particular practice or doctrine is a legitimate development from it. Scripture itself both embodies Tradition and relies on human reason, and it is a matter of wide debate what aspects of biblical teaching should be seen as divine revelation, valid for all time, and what as culturally-related human perceptions, applicable in only limited contexts. Even what is understood as divinely given may be geared to a particular social or historical situation. As for conscience and reason, these do not exist in a vacuum, but are shaped by personal experience, including our interactions with the Church, the Bible, other people, and the particular society in which we live.

Thus the extent to which each of these three may be used as a source depends to a considerable degree on personal and collective experience. This is why some Christians today are suggesting that experience should be seen as the key to 'doing theology', which should be allowed to develop in a free and untrammelled way. Those adopting this approach usually have a weaker sense of community with the historic past and the organized Church, and a strong sense of the present power of the Spirit in their midst. Unrestricted by convention they are especially open to creative theological thinking, and innovative, bold experimentation in liturgy and ministry, including women's ministry. Such groups have effected a spectacular renewal within the Roman Catholic Church in parts of Latin America.[6] A similar approach is adopted by some feminist sisterhood-groups, who also place the highest value on personal experience and interpersonal relationships and feel free to re-express biblical images and theology in modern terms through 'inclusive' language, feminist prayers, and an understanding of God as Mother.[7]

But many are cautious about too drastic a loosening from the Church's historical moorings. There must be continuity between the present and the past, and it is patently obvious that not all ideas and practices attributed to the Spirit are in fact the work of the Holy Spirit of God. The evidence of present experience, whether of the individual or of the group, must be balanced against the other sources of authority, namely the Bible, Tradition, and reason.

There is one further aspect of experience which must be taken into account. It should not be imagined that all human insight comes exclusively through the communities of Christian faith. Anyone who has thought seriously about history, or the social sciences, or the teachings of non-Christian religions, will be aware of how much good has come out of the intellectual, moral, and spiritual endeavours of philosophers and scientists, humanists and agnostics, and other men and women of integrity with and without religious faith who have worked for a better understanding of what it is to be human, and for human rights and the betterment of the world in which we all live. Such activity, where it is for good, may also be interpreted as the work of the Holy Spirit leading into truth. In the particular area in which we are interested, namely the theology of women's ministry, it is to be expected that we should be able to learn not only from secular historical study and methodology, but also from advances in the scientific understanding of human biology and personality, including the physiological and psychological differences between women and men, and from the insights of social anthropology and sociology into the workings of relationships between men and women in community. Any study of the theology of women's ministry must take account of these factors. (Methodology will be considered further at the end of Chapter 2.)

THE APPROACH OF THE PRESENT WORK

In view of all these considerations the best approach would appear to be a 'dialectical' one,[8] which takes account of all these sources of authority – Scripture, Tradition, reason, and experience – allowing them to interact with and on one another. In other words there must be a 'dialogue' between present and past, twentieth century and first century (and the intervening ones), between Bible and Systematic (or Dogmatic) Theology, and between the faith as confessed in the Churches and the social and other sciences.

Scripture will be taken as foundational, the biblical documents being our only real source for the teachings of Jesus and being recognized by Christians of a very wide variety of background as bearing witness not only to the human search for God, but also to God's revelation to humankind. This evidence of both Old and New Testaments will need to be listened to sympathetically and openly, without reading back into the documents later doctrinal developments or ecclesiastical positions, but giving priority to the authors' original intentions, as recoverable to us by study of their cultural, literary and theological contexts.[9] The main aim of Part One of this investigation will be to see whether biblical teaching as a whole contains any permanent principles relevant to women's roles and ministry which might be considered decisive for the debate on women's ordination (Chapters 2–5). To facilitate this study we shall need to begin by looking at the position of women in the wider Graeco-Roman world (Chapter 1).

In Part Two we will begin by considering historical developments in the Church's doctrine and practice of ministry, as they affect the role of women, reflecting on their relationship to the biblical witness and to social and ecclesial situations which gave rise to them (Chapters 6–8). Only when we have done this will we seek to adumbrate a theology of women's ministry, using the evidence of all four sources and paying special attention to the arguments of those who have found in Scripture, Tradition, or the social and behavioural sciences fundamental objections to women's ordination. Finally, we will draw some specific conclusions for the Churches where women's roles are a matter of debate and controversy today.

NOTES

1 The author readily acknowledges her debt to earlier writing from a wide range of traditions, including the pioneer studies of Raven (1928); Thrall (1958); Hannon (1967); and the notable series of Church of England Reports, the latest of which was published when this book was already in draft form (see Bibliography).

2 Russell (1980).

3 See, for example, Perrin (1970); Marshall (1977b); Stroup (1981); Childs (1984).
4 cf. Whale (1957), esp. p. 19; Dodd (1960); Sykes, (1978), chs. 5–7; Sedgwick (1988); and the collected essays in Jeffery (1987) and Sykes (1987), (on the Anglican position); also Drewery and Bauckham (1988).
5 See, for example, *ARCIC: The Final Report*, esp. p. 61.
6 See Boff (1986), chs 1–3 (on Latin American base-communities) and Spiceland in Toon and Spiceland (1980), pp. 133–57 (on Process Theology).
7 e.g. Ruether (1985); Morley and Ward (1986); Morley (1988).
8 cf. Baelz in Baelz and Jacob (1985), pp. 2f.
9 cf. Dunn and Mackey (1977), esp. ch. 1, stressing the need for dialogue between New Testament and Systematic Theology.

PART ONE

Foundations

1

Women in the Graeco-Roman World

'By the time of Jesus, Palestine had already been under "Hellenistic" rule and its resultant cultural influence for some 360 years.' So wrote Martin Hengel in his magisterial *Judaism and Hellenism*,[1] reminding the scholarly world of the long period of encounter, conflict, and interaction between Jew and Greek in the centuries before the birth of Jesus. When Jesus lived and died, Palestine was also under strong Roman influence and domination: Pompey had taken Jerusalem and set up his standards there (63 BC); Herod 'the Great' had ruled as a Roman nominee and puppet king (37–4 BC); first Judea (AD 6), then all Palestine (AD 44) became a Roman province, part of a vast empire liable to Roman taxation and military occupation, under continual pressure to adopt Roman values and ways of thought.

The New Testament books were probably all written in the half-century or so immediately after that last event. During this period Christianity emerged as a faith distinct from Judaism, and began to spread both informally and through the missionary strategy of Paul and his colleagues to many cities and villages of the Graeco-Roman world. Externally the formative period of the New Testament was one of constant upheaval and unrest. It witnessed the principate of the murderous and eccentric Nero, and the great fire of Rome, which occasioned the first persecution of Christians. It included the famous 'Year of the four Emperors' (AD 68–69), and the Jewish revolt, with the terrible siege and destruction of Jerusalem and the heroic stand at Masada (AD 66–73); it saw also a more general persecution of Christians under Domitian, whose principate ended in a 'reign of terror' (AD 93–96) marked by ruthless bloodshed. None of these external events are directly described in the New Testament texts, but they are part of the environment within which its books were composed, and they undoubtedly coloured the writers' attitudes towards social issues. It was clearly in the interests of the nascent Christian Church to keep on good terms with its Roman masters, and this meant working with the existing social order: any attempt to introduce political or social revolution would have brought about strongly repressive action.

But how did the existing social order come into being and how firmly established was it? To answer these questions we need to explore more thoroughly the complex cultural and social world in which the New Testament took shape. We begin with the Graeco-Roman tradition, itself composed of two originally separate strands, which came together in the late Hellenistic Age.

THE GREEK CONTRIBUTION

Greek attitudes to women were, in fact, quite varied, in that ancient Greece was never a full cultural unity, being composed in archaic and classical times (seventh to fourth centuries BC) of separate and independent political communities, with distinct dialects, religious cults, social and legal systems, literary and artistic life. Most influential was Athens, which so dominated the cultural scene that its dialect became the basis of the *koinē*, i.e. 'common', Greek spoken throughout the Graeco-Roman world (including Judea), after the collapse of the city-state system.

The classical Athenians are frequently admired in the Western world for their love of liberty and practice of democracy. It is not always appreciated that this liberty and democracy were almost entirely confined to male citizens. Slaves, aliens, and above all women had only a small share in democratic privileges. None of these could vote or hold civic office. Women could not even legally dispose of property or conduct business. A woman was always under the guardianship of her husband or close male relative, who was known as her *kyrios*,[2] i.e. 'master' or 'lord' (the same word as is used of Jesus in the Gospels). Girls received little education except in the domestic arts, and were subject to arranged marriages to husbands usually much older than themselves – a custom which reinforces male domination. A girl could legally marry as young as twelve; her husband might be as old as thirty. Xenophon, writing on Household Management, advocates that a man should marry a woman much younger than himself so that he can teach and train her as he wishes.[3] A husband had the administration and enjoyment of his wife's dowry during her life-time, but if she predeceased him or left him it went to her children or new *kyrios*. A wife could be divorced for adultery simply in the presence of witnesses, but had to go through due legal processes to divorce her husband. Women could also be divorced against their will for financial reasons: for example, when a woman became an heiress, it was possible for her nearest male relative to divorce his own wife to marry her and thus keep the property in the family.

Once married, Greek women were expected to be concerned with housekeeping and bearing children. Domestic tasks were much more time-consuming than today, involving grinding corn for baking, fetching and carrying water for washing and cooking, spinning, weaving and making clothes. Even wealthy women found their time occupied with supervising slaves. Athenian society expected women to remain indoors as much as possible. In Sophocles' tragedy, the *Antigone* (578f.), two princesses argue with the king about the burial of their brother. He simply tells his servants to take them indoors: 'From now on they must be women and not roam at large'.

Such words reflect an attitude to women which must have been common in classical Athens. It can be seen again in Pericles' famous funeral oration in which he praises at length the men who fell in the first year of the Peloponnesian War, and then turns briefly to their widows and says: 'If I must say something on a woman's excellence, I will signify everything in a short word of advice: your great glory is not to be worse than you are by nature, and to be the subject of talk among males as little as possible, either for praise or blame' (Thucydides 2.45). Xenophon similarly uses an argument from nature to advocate the seclusion of women: 'God from the first adapted woman's nature to the indoor tasks and cares (and man's to the outdoor)'

(*Oec.* 7.22), words echoed in patristic times by John Chrysostom (see below p. 99).

Such was the ideal. In practice, poor women had to go out, to fetch water, to work in the fields, or even to sell their goods in the market. But the better-off could confine outside trips to attendance at festivals and social gatherings with other women (usually of their own family). Even shopping was considered a man's task.[4] Respectable women did not take part in the philosophical discussions of the *agora*, such as we read about in Acts 17.17 and in classical writers, nor did they attend the lively *symposia* (drinking-parties), which often included philosophical discussion. Intellectual conversation with men seems to have been the preserve of the courtesans (*hetairai*), with whom wives had to compete for their husbands' affection. The comments of Demosthenes on this subject are notorious: 'We keep *hetairai* for the sake of pleasure; concubines for our day-to-day personal care; and wives for us to beget children legitimately and to have a trustworthy guardian of all that is in the house' (*Against Neaira* 122). The sexual standards implied by this speech are striking: in common with many others in the ancient world the speaker regards it as acceptable for a man to seek sexual gratification with a variety of partners, while a married woman is expected to remain faithful to one husband.[5] It is difficult also to estimate the effects on the role and status of women of the widespread practice of homosexuality among the Greeks, homosexual love being openly prized by some above heterosexual.[6]

However, even at Athens, attitudes to women were not totally negative. Tomb reliefs and inscriptions testify to the affection and esteem of many husbands for their wives and there were more enlightened thinkers who affirmed the value of women as people in their own right. The poet Euripides depicted women with sympathy in his tragedies.[7] Plato advocated equal opportunities for their education in his ideal 'Republic', though it is doubtful if he really saw them as equal to men: in another dialogue, when discussing the creation of the human race, he suggests that 'men who were cowards or led wicked lives may with reason be supposed in the second generation to have changed into women' (*Timaeus* 90E). Aristotle openly asserted the inequality of the sexes: 'The male is by nature superior, the

female inferior, the male the ruler, the female the subject'
(*Politics* 1.2.12). He grudgingly admitted that a woman might
have 'virtue' (1.5.5), but saw the male as the true human being.
We shall see later what long-lasting effects his views had
through their adoption by Aquinas; they are still echoed in
some discussions of women's ordination today.

Our knowledge about the position of women in the Greek
world is fullest for Athens because so much of surviving Greek
literature comes from that city. But the picture which emerges
needs to be balanced by literary and archaeological evidence
from other Greek communities, and by the testimony of the
numerous inscriptions and non-literary papyri. The celebrated
Law Code from the Doric town of Gortyn in Crete attests that
there free women could possess, control and inherit property. In
classical Sparta (another Dorian community) girls were
educated alongside boys, and took part in athletics and outdoor
pursuits (though in other respects their lot was less enviable).[8]
In the sixth century BC the woman poet Sappho on the Aeolic
island of Lesbos taught music and poetry to a group of girls; the
philosopher Pythagoras (active in Greek cities in southern
Italy) admitted women pupils. Women officiated in many
religious cults, including those of male as well as female deities.[9]
The Delphic prophetess and the priestess of Demeter Chamyne
(the only married woman allowed to watch the Olympic Games)
were held in especially high esteem. But the general pattern
throughout the classical age was of the political, legal, economic
and social subordination of women to men: almost without
exception the great philosophers, poets, artists and statesmen of
the classical world were male.

In the fourth century, and in the Hellenistic Age following the
death of Alexander in 323 BC, the lot of some women improved.
Royal women were politically influential in Macedonia and in
parts of Asia Minor: Artemisia reigned in Caria with her
brother-husband Mausolus, and on his death in 353 BC
succeeded him in her own right. In Egypt the wives of some of
the Ptolemies wielded considerable power: Arsinoe II (d. 270
BC), the sister-wife of Ptolemy II, was worshipped as divine
within her life-time, and Cleopatra VII has achieved worldwide fame for her relationships with Julius Caesar and Mark
Antony. At a more mundane level, women's rights to buy, sell

and lease property increased; some even became liable to taxation. Papyri reveal that women were sometimes treated as equal partners in marriage-contracts.[10]

Outside Egypt a slow improvement can also be detected. In the second and first centuries we hear for the first time of a woman magistrate.[11] Epicurus (341–270 BC), founder of the Epicurean school of philosophy, admitted women as pupils on the same terms as men; Hipparchia, wife of the Cynic philosopher Crates, is said to have appeared in public with her husband, to have attended dinner-parties, and even written philosophical treatises. She was regarded as an eccentric. Stoic, Peripatetic, and Neopythagorean philosophers all re-inforced traditional roles of subjection and obedience for women, and even their acceptance as philosophical students did not bring equality. The Neopythagorean treatise attributed to 'Perictione', and written for female pupils, says that 'a woman must live for her husband according to law and in actuality, thinking no private thoughts of her own...a woman must preserve the law and not emulate men. And she must endure her husband's temper, stinginess, complaining, jealousy, abuse, and anything else peculiar to his nature' (including drunkenness and sleeping with other women).[12] The same treatise also urges women to avoid gold jewellery, braided hair, or fine clothes, for it is the beauty that comes from wisdom which is to be treasured (cf. 1 Pet. 3.1–5; 1 Tim. 2.9).

THE ROMAN LEGACY

Rome began as a small agricultural community, which rapidly expanded economically, politically, and militarily until it dominated first all Italy and then the Mediterranean world. Roman culture and religion were thus originally distinct and separate from Greek, but her expansion into the eastern Mediterranean and eventual conquest of Greece meant that during the period from the third to first centuries BC Rome came under massive cultural influence from Greece. By the time of Christ we may appropriately speak of a Graeco-Roman attitude to women, while recognizing that there existed many local variations in their legal and social positions. But it is worth glancing back a little further to observe how this attitude originated and developed on the Roman side.

In Republican Rome women in general enjoyed a higher status than in classical Greece, being honoured in the home and having greater freedom to mix socially with men. Cornelia, mother of the Gracchi (second century BC), was an excellent example of the traditional Roman *matrona*, accomplished and educated, and famous for the virtuous upbringing of her distinguished sons. Unlike Greek women, who had separate quarters from the male members of the household in the inner part of the house, Roman women regularly sat in the *atrium*, accessible to visitors of both sexes. Their regular occupations were similar to those of Greek women, bringing up children and domestic work, especially spinning and weaving. A well-known inscription praises Claudia, a cherished wife: 'She loved her husband with her whole heart. She bore two sons... she was charming in converse, yet proper in bearing. She kept house, she made wool.'[13]

Yet in Roman society also women were legally subordinate to men, being continually under the tutelage of their father, husband, or other male relative. The older jurists explained that this was because of the weakness of their sex, their shallowness of mind, and ignorance of forensic matters; but some recognized the speciousness of these arguments.[14] Theoretically the *paterfamilias* had the power of life and death over his family, with the right to take up or reject a new born child (in both Greek and Roman society unwanted baby girls were often exposed). Women could be married as young as twelve years old. Forms of marriage varied from the elaborate religious ceremony known as the *confarreatio* (literally, 'sharing of spelt') to the simpler *coemptio* (a notional sale) and mere *usus* (continuous cohabitation for a year). Marriage could be either with *manus* (literally 'hand'), i.e. the woman transferred from her father's to her husband's authority, or without *manus*, in which case she remained under her father's tutelage. In theory a woman could not conduct even private business without the authorization of her *tutor* or 'guardian'. A free Roman woman had equal rights with a man to initiate divorce, but, as at Athens, could be divorced against her will on the initiative of her husband, or even of her father for financial or political reasons, or in order to safeguard property or produce an heir. Slave women could not contract legal marriages.[15]

Under the Empire women's independence increased. Laws on male guardianship were evaded through sham 'tutors' and fictitious marriages. Wealthy women, such as Eumachia at Pompeii, patronized trade-guilds and erected public buildings. Some women received honorific titles and had their statues erected in public places. Fulvia, the first wife of Mark Antony, actually followed her husband on his military campaigns. Gradually the legal position of women improved. Augustus abolished the *manus* requirement for mothers of three or four children, as part of a policy of social reform designed to encourage marriage at a time when divorce and sexual licence were rife and many men were not bothering to marry at all. He also introduced legal penalties for women who had not married by the age of twenty and men who remained unmarried at twenty-five. Claudius abolished the automatic guardianship of the *agnatus* (nearest male relative) over a woman whose father had died. Antoninus Pius abolished a father's right to compel a happily married adult daughter to divorce. But inequalities remained: for example, under Augustan law adultery was a public offence for a married woman, but not for a married man, who could legally consort with prostitutes. Such laws were not, of course, uniformly enforced throughout the Empire. In general, Rome allowed its subject peoples to continue to observe their own local laws and customs, except when they interfered with administrative interests.

As regards their religious role, Roman women participated in both the domestic and state religion. Several cults, including those of Venus and the Bona Dea, had priestesses. The goddess Fortuna (under various titles) was venerated as the patron of women's physical maturation and sexual fulfilment. Vestal Virgins tended the state cult of Vesta, goddess of the hearth: they were held in high honour (and their public and private lives were strictly regulated). Nevertheless, the chief religious offices, including those of *pontifex maximus*, the sixteen other *pontifices*, the *augurs*, *haruspices*, and other senior religious positions were confined to males, being often linked with political office. One gets the impression that women were particularly prone to become involved in magical rites, like those of Hecate, goddess of witchcraft and the underworld, and in the more emotional 'mystery' religions, such as the cults of Bacchus, Isis, and Cybele, which came in from Greece and the East, and which the Senate sought in vain to regulate.[16] Women also attended public games and gladiatorial shows.

As for education, Roman women, at least of the wealthier classes, seem to have had more opportunities than their Greek counterparts, studying literature, both Greek and Latin, with private tutors. Juvenal lampooned learned women: 'Worse still is the woman who as soon as she has begun her dinner praises Virgil, pardons the dying Dido, and compares the poets' (*Satires* 6.434–6). Juvenal adds that he hates a woman who is expert in grammar and presumes to correct her husband's mistakes. Such women were exceptional: normally women were neither expected to discourse on learned matters nor to take part in politics. Some women, particularly in imperial circles, exercised great power and influence – one thinks of Livia, wife of Augustus, Agrippina, mother of Nero, and Plotina, wife of Trajan – but most would have found their days occupied with domestic tasks and the maintenance of their families.

Even under the Empire there would have been many ready to agree with the sentiments attributed to the old moralist Cato, whose speech on the subject in 195 BC is reported by Livy (34.2–4): the Senate were about to repeal the Oppian Law regulating women's dress and the amount of jewellery they might wear. The patrician women, naturally interested in matters of such close concern to themselves, flocked round the Senate entrance. Cato indignantly demanded: 'What do you mean by rushing out in public, blocking the streets and shouting to men who are not your husbands? Could you not have each asked your questions from your husbands at home?' (cf. 1 Cor. 14.35). He went on to refer to womankind as 'an untamed animal', arguing that if men give women the reins they must expect them to kick over the traces. He warned the senators: 'As soon as they become your equals, they will become your superiors'. The speech reveals a masculine fear and distrust of women which we shall meet again in different contexts.

Thus, in both Greece and Rome women were regarded as legally and socially subordinate to men. They had only limited educational and professional opportunities. Their position varied from place to place and from one period to another, but at no time did they ever enjoy anything remotely resembling the freedom available to modern Western women. It should perhaps be added that similar patterns existed for women among Israel's other neighbours, including Assyria, Babylon, the Hittites and Egypt.[17]

NOTES

1 Hengel (1974), vol. I, p. 1.
2 Schaps (1979), esp. ch. 4.
3 Xenophon, *Oec.* 7.5 (using his character Ischomachus as mouthpiece). For the same idea in Hesiod, Plato, Epictetus, etc. see West (1978), p. 327.
4 See Pomeroy (1975), p. 72; Schaps (1979), p. 52.
5 In Homer's *Odyssey* (still influential in Hellenistic times) the male hero Odysseus goes uncriticized when he has sexual relations with Circe and Calypso, whereas his wife, Penelope, is expected to remain faithful even through twenty years' separation.
6 Dover (1978). See further Cosby (1984), pp. 154–66.
7 See his *Hecuba, Hippolytus, Ion, Medea, Trojan Women.* It is ironical that some have seen Euripides as a misogynist – perhaps precisely because of his unconventional images of women.
8 For Gortyn and Sparta see Pomeroy (1975), pp. 35–42.
9 On the role of Greek women as priests, prophets, sacred virgins, and sacred prostitutes, see Farnell (1904).
10 See further Pomeroy (1984).
11 At Istria on the Black Sea and at Priene in Asia Minor.
12 Trs. F. R. Levin in Pomeroy (1975), pp. 134–6.
13 Trs. Warmington (1940), no. 18 (c. 135–120 BC).
14 See Gaius, *Inst.* I. 144 and 190f. (disagreeing with the traditional view of women's *animi levitas*), and Ulpian, *Tit.* 11.1 on the *infirmitas sexus*; see further Raming (1976), ch. 2; Gardner (1987), chs. 2–3, esp. p. 21. As late as the fifth century AD Justinian's *Digest* commented on the many legal disabilities women suffered under Roman law compared with men.
15 On Roman women in general see Balsdon (1962); Pomeroy (1975), chs. 8–9.
16 On the religious role of Roman women see Farnell (1904); Pomeroy (1975), ch. 10; on State cults open only to males, see Ogilvie (1969), pp. 106–11.
17 On the wider background see further Edwards (1988), esp. pp. 1089f.

2

Women in the Old Testament and Early Judaism

The books which make up our Old Testament incorporate material which originated over many hundreds of years, during which time the Hebrew people changed from being wandering nomads to settled agriculturalists and town-dwellers; they experienced tribal government, near-slavery in Egypt, independent monarchy, deportation and Babylonian exile, restoration, domination by Hellenistic rulers, a measure of political independence under Maccabean and Hasmonean kings, and finally incorporation into the Roman Empire. Naturally documents composed in such changing social and political conditions exhibit varying attitudes to women, especially since they embrace a wide variety of literary forms, involving both poetry and prose, prophecy and history, law-giving and love-songs. Many texts were also edited for dogmatic or other purposes in the course of their transmission. All this makes a description of Old Testament attitudes very complex, and one must guard against over-simplification.

EVIDENCE FOR A SUBORDINATIONIST ATTITUDE

In essence Hebrew and Jewish society was patriarchal in structure and outlook, with men exercising political, religious and social leadership and women having supportive and domestic roles. As in most ancient societies, descent was reckoned in the male line. According to legislation attributed to Moses, women could inherit property only where male heirs were lacking (Num. 27.1–11). As in ancient Greece and Rome, women were married young (often aged only twelve to thirteen years) to men older than themselves. A woman's husband was known as her *ba^{c}al* or lord (cf. the Athenian *kyrios*). Throughout her life a woman was expected to be subject to a man, first her father, and then her husband or some other close male relative (cf. above Ch. 1 on Greece and Rome). In early times a father had absolute power over his children: Jephtha, in the familiar story, acted within his paternal rights when he sacrificed his own daughter (Judg. 11.30–40), just as in Roman legend Verginia was killed quite legally by her father, supposedly to protect her from outrage. Genesis 19.6–8 narrates in a quite matter-of-fact way how Lot offered his own daughters to be raped in order to protect male guests from homosexual abuse (cf. the similar barbaric story in Judg. 19). Fathers and husbands could annul religious vows made by women, and a father could sell his daughter into various forms of slavery (Exod. 21.7; Neh. 5.4).

The Old Testament contains many examples of a woman being treated as a man's possession rather than as a person in her own right.[1] Even within marriage the two partners were also far from equal. A man was permitted several wives (both polygyny and concubinage were legal), but a woman could have only one husband. Under the institution of levirate marriage, if a woman was left a widow without children she had to marry her brother-in-law or other close male relative. (The system was primarily designed to ensure the continuation of the male line.) The man had the option of declining such a marriage if it was not in his interest, but the woman had no comparable right (cf. Ruth 4 and the pitiful tale of Tamar, daughter-in-law of Judah, in Gen. 38). According to Genesis 21, to appease the jealousy of Sarah, Abraham sent Hagar, his slave-concubine, with their child out into the desert to die of thirst; the narrative contains no condemnation of his act, but Hagar and the baby are saved by divine intervention. If a husband suspected his wife of adultery, he could subject her to a humiliating ordeal (Num. 5.11–31); no equivalent right existed for a woman and she received no compensation if proved innocent. If an unbetrothed virgin were violated, a sum of money was paid to her father; she personally received no compensation, but was forced to marry her rapist

(Deut. 22.28f.). This provision was presumably intended to be humanitarian, as she would otherwise have no hope of marriage, but it must have caused untold suffering to the women concerned.

Only a man could legally initiate divorce: interpreters differed over the precise meaning of the Mosaic law (Deut. 24.1) which permitted divorce if a husband found 'something indecent' in his wife: some took this as referring to sexual misdemeanour, others in a broader sense to include any conduct displeasing to him. Dowries were customary and helped provide some support in the event of divorce; but social custom and financial need regularly required a divorced woman to remarry or return to her father.

Early marriage and the commitment to time-consuming domestic duties meant that very few professions could be open to women. In early times, in addition to raising children and looking after the home, they assisted with flocks and herds (cf. Rachel); at all times peasant women helped with agriculture, especially with the harvest (cf. Ruth), and engaged in spinning and weaving, and making garments for sale; a husband might allow his wife a share in the profit (Prov. 31.13–24; Tobit 2.11). When Hebrew society became literate, women rarely received more than rudimentary education. The command to teach God's judgements and statutes to 'thy sons and thy sons' sons' (Deut. 4.9 AV) was all too easily restricted to males, although the original meaning may well have been inclusive (Heb. *banim* can mean children or descendants of either sex; cf. Neh. 8.3). Some scholars believe that the later Jewish custom of exempting women from the study of the Law (and from daily prayers at fixed times and from attendance at all but three major festivals in the year) arose out of consideration for their domestic commitments, but it had the effect of making them second-class members of the religious community. It meant also that women lacked the devotional and spiritual benefits of the activities from which they were so excused. Excusal soon grows into positive exclusion: some rabbis taught that it was better to burn the Law than teach it to a woman.[2]

Women were not expected to take part in public affairs, and even their social life was limited. Early narratives describe men receiving company without their wives (cf. Gen. 18, where

Sarah listens at the tent door while Abraham entertains the three strangers). As in Greece and early Rome, women were expected to remain within the house as much as possible: 'Your wife (shall be) a fruitful vine in the inner places of your house' (Ps. 128.3). Their social life centred on agricultural and religious festivities and other family occasions – and conversation with other women. To have children was a woman's greatest joy; to be 'barren' her greatest sorrow (it was never imagined that childlessness might be due to the husband). Apart from beauty and fecundity, the qualities most admired in women were prudence, industriousness, silence, modesty, and marital fidelity (e.g. Prov. 19.14; Ecclus. 26.1–4; 14–18). Loquacious women are frequently censured; the Old Testament hardly ever criticizes talkative men. Proverbs' picture (31.10–31) of a 'virtuous woman' (more correctly 'ideal wife') is justly famous: she is skilled and industrious, charming, wise and provident – and she brings credit to her husband.

In their religious life women were regarded as subordinate to their husbands in every way. In early times a responsible male represented the household or clan, making sacrifices and offerings on their behalf (e.g. Gen. 31.54; 46.1). A striking example is Abraham's attempted sacrifice of Isaac (Gen. 22), undertaken in obedience to what he believed to be God's command: he does not discuss the matter with his wife, even though it involved the loss of their only child; Sarah is just ignored. When a specialized priesthood evolved, it is only to be expected that it was exclusively male. Priests, i.e. ritually acceptable men who could claim to be descendants of Aaron, offered sacrifices on behalf of the other men, and of the women and children (e.g. Lev. 12.6f.; 15.29f.). Women were allowed to take part in worship (though not to enter the sanctuary). Sometimes we hear of them singing and dancing (e.g. Exod. 15.20; 1 Sam. 18.6f.; Judith 15.12–16.17), but there is no evidence that they did this regularly in the cult. In Herod's later temple the court where women worshipped was separated from the men's by a wall and stepped gateway; women must have found it hard to participate in what they could neither see nor hear properly. It is generally believed that in the synagogue also women were segregated from the men, but the evidence for this is not conclusive, and it has recently been argued that initially the two sexes worshipped together.[3]

Women were greatly hampered in their active religious life by the so-called 'purity laws', which were in effect taboos concerning bodily secretions, childbirth, and other matters (see esp. Lev. 12.1–5; 15.19–33). While men were also regarded as 'unclean' at certain times, for example until the following evening after seminal emissions and for seven days after any venereal discharge (Lev. 15.1–18), the laws concerning women were more far-reaching, affecting them for a large proportion of their adult lives. They were considered 'unclean' during menstruation and any other discharge of blood and for seven days afterwards, as well as for forty days after the birth of a boy and eighty days after that of a girl. At these times everything and everybody that a woman touched was also 'unclean' and in need of purification. This concept that menstruation and childbirth cause 'uncleanness' persisted into the patristic and later Church, to the detriment of women's ministry and leadership roles (see below Ch. 6, with n. 15). It still affects Christian attitudes today.

Other customs and conventions further limited opportunities for women's religious leadership in Judaism. Circumcision – the special sign and symbol of Yahweh's covenant relationship with Israel – was for men only: there was no comparable rite for women. Under Mosaic legislation only males had to 'appear' three times a year before the Lord (Exod. 23.17); in later times only boys had the special coming-of-age ceremony known as *Bar Mitzvah*. Various items of the Law suggested women were worth less than men, notably in the special vows of persons (Lev. 27.1–8), in which the value of a girl or woman was around half that of a boy or man. Sons were normally esteemed far more highly than daughters.

Many Old Testament texts are so worded as to apply directly to men, and only by implication to women. Psalms and other texts extol the blessings of the man (Heb. *ʾish*)[4] who puts his trust in God. The Decalogue forbids coveting one's neighbour's wife (Exod. 20.17); there is no parallel provision about coveting somebody else's husband.[5] A wife (*ʾishshah*) is spoken of as if she were part of a man's property like his house, his ox and his ass.

Female leadership, whether political or religious (and the two were often inseparable) was generally considered unnatural and undesirable: in the course of Israel's long history, kings, judges, prophets, scribes, elders, and members of the Sanhedrin were almost exclusively male (we shall mention a few exceptions later); so too were the authors of all scriptural texts (except possibly the Song of Songs), as well as extracanonical and rabbinic writings. Women were seen as weaker than men and in need of protection (e.g. Jer. 51.30; cf. 1 Pet. 3.7). To compare a man to a woman was an insult (Isa. 19.16; Nahum 3.13); to compare a woman to a man was a compliment – the mother of the Maccabean martyrs is praised for her 'masculine' courage (2 Macc. 7.21). (Similar sentiments are found in classical authors.) It was a particular shame for a man to be killed by a woman (Judg. 9.53f.; cf. 4.9; 5.24–7; Judith 14.18).

In intertestamental and early rabbinic Judaism (c. second century BC to second century AD) limitations on women's public roles seem to have become even more stringent, perhaps in reaction to growing freedom (and laxity) in the Graeco-Roman world. Women did not count as part of the *minyan* (quorum) for synagogue worship; by convention they were not called upon to read lessons; they were discouraged from pronouncing the blessing on behalf of men at meals. They could not legally bear witness. Men acted as local elders and synagogue rulers (at least in Palestine).[6] Rabbis were always men, and did not accept female pupils. The social life of respectable women became, if anything, even more restricted than earlier. Philo, an Alexandrian Jew much influenced by Greek thought, urged them to stay indoors, and 'not meddle with affairs outside the home'; he recommended that even when going out to pray they should choose times when few men were about (*De Spec. Leg.* 3.169–71). They were expected to be veiled outside the home. Some rabbis regarded it as shameful for a man to talk to a woman in a public place, even if she were a member of his own family. Some discouraged any talk with women: one is said to have advised, 'Talk not much with womankind' (or 'the wife'); for this could lead to Gehenna (Hell).[7] Pious Jews thanked God daily that they were not created a Gentile, a woman, or an ignoramus (or slave).[8]

The rabbis are often criticized by Christian scholars for their negative attitudes to women, and misogynist statements are indeed not difficult to find. For example, women are described as 'light-headed' and as having no wisdom except with the distaff; one Tanna (rabbi living before c. AD 200) is said to have taught that 'though a woman be as a pitcher of filth and her mouth be full of blood', yet all speed after her.[9] But distasteful as these references are, when looked at in their contexts they will be found to be essentially warnings to *men* not to be promiscuous or indiscreet. Even the much-quoted dictum of R. Eliezer, 'If any man gives his daughter a knowledge of the Law, it is as though he taught her lechery', seems to be not so much a general prohibition of women's study as a warning to fathers not to give their daughters the opportunity of learning how to avoid or postpone the unpleasant Sotah ordeal in cases of suspected adultery.[10] Many rabbis speak warmly of what a good wife means to a man, even going so far as to say that 'a man who has no wife lives without joy, blessing and good';[11] but one cannot help observing that it is as wives and as mothers of sons that women are appreciated, rather than for their own sake.

Some Old Testament pseudepigrapha are even more openly misogynistic than the rabbis. The *Testament of Reuben* (? second century BC) states unequivocally: 'Women are evil, my children: for not having authority or power over men, they scheme how they may attract them to themselves by their appearance ... for the angel of the Lord spoke to me about them and taught me that women are more easily overcome by the spirit of fornication than men' (5.1–3). The *Letter of Aristeas* (§250) approves the view that women are 'rash, energetic in pursuing what they want, prone to sudden changes of mind through false reasoning, and by nature weak'. We shall encounter similar ideas among the Church Fathers. Some texts accorded deuterocanonical authority in parts of the Church (but regarded as apocrypha by others) contain harsh attacks on women as a class. For example, Ben Sirach comments in the book known as Ecclesiasticus (i.e. 'belonging to the Church'): 'From garments comes the moth, and from woman comes woman's wickedness. Better is the wickedness of a man than a woman who does good; and it is a woman who brings shame and disgrace' (*Ecclus.* 42.12–14 RSV; cf. 25.16–26; 26.6–12). Even texts accepted as fully canonical by all the Churches can be very negative towards women. Qoheleth (i.e. Ecclesiastes or 'the preacher') writes: 'I find woman more bitter than Death, she is a snare, her heart is a net, her arms are chains. The man who is

pleasing to God eludes her, but the sinner is captured by her'
(Eccles. 7.26). The condemnation here seems to apply to all
women.

EQUALITARIAN TEXTS AND AFFIRMATIONS
OF WOMEN

The Old Testament also contains positive affirmations of
women, examples of their initiative and leadership, and passages
implying their equality with men in the eyes of God. Most
significant is the creation narrative of Genesis 1, believed by
scholars to stem from the Priestly tradition ('P'). This describes
how God created 'Adam', i.e. mankind or humanity, in the
divine image, as the crown of creation and to rule over the
animals. The text makes it absolutely plain that both male and
female are made in God's image and likeness (Gen. 1.26–8).
Even the more 'primitive' Creation narrative of Genesis 2,
attributed to the earlier Yahwist source ('J'), is much more
positive towards women than often assumed. For example, the
Hebrew word ʿezer, 'helper' used in connection with woman's
creation (Gen. 2.20), far from implying subordination, is
regularly used in the Old Testament of the assistance afforded
by a superior to an inferior, and is quite frequently applied to
God as the one who comes to the aid of those in need (e.g. Exod.
18.4; Deut. 33.7, etc.).[12] The creation of woman from man's rib,
repeatedly used in the argument that women have a secondary
or supportive role in God's creation, is in fact a vivid symbol of
the unity of male and female – they are, quite literally, 'of the
same substance' (bone and flesh), that is to say ontologically
identical.

Again, although women were excluded from many features of
Israel's religious life, they were still regarded as an integral part
of Yahweh's holy people: hence their subjection to the 'purity
laws', and their obligation to keep all the negative precepts of
the Law, as well as its positive ordinances not tied to particular
times and seasons. The blessings for those who kept the
Covenant applied to women as well as to men, as did the
penalties for disobedience. The custom – so barbaric to us – of
sometimes including a man's family in his punishment illus-

trates this strong sense of corporate solidarity, which the Hebrews shared with other Semitic peoples (see Josh. 7.24f.; Dan. 6.24; but note also Deut. 24.16).

Apart from general affirmations of women as part of God's people, there are also many instances where the Old Testament depicts individual women with sympathy and understanding. In the patriarchal narratives Sarah, Rebekah, and Rachel all have well-rounded personalities and minds of their own; their initiatives, even though exercised through ruses, help to fulfil a divine purpose (e.g. Gen. 27; 31). In 1 Samuel 1 Hannah's unhappiness at her childlessness is vividly portrayed, as is her husband's love for her despite this. She acts with independence in proposing that their special son should be dedicated to God's service in the Shiloh temple, and she – not her husband – is said to have prayed the deeply spiritual and radical song (1 Sam. 2.1–10) which became the model for Mary's Magnificat. Manoah's unnamed wife shows far more religious sensitivity than her husband (Judg. 13.2–22); Abigail's intelligence and good sense are directly contrasted with her husband's boorish behaviour (1 Sam. 25.3, 23–5, 33). Ruth, a Moabite woman, appears as an exemplar of loyalty and faithfulness in the book of that name. The Book of Esther dramatically illustrates the courage and fortitude of the queen whose heroism was regularly commemorated at the Jewish feast of Purim. Judith, the apocryphal slayer of Holofernes, is praised for her intelligence and piety, as well as for her beauty (Judith 8.6–8, 28–31); she is represented as a widow controlling her own property, and we are told that, though many men desired to marry her, of her own choice she remained independent. In the Greek version of Daniel (ch. 13) Susannah serves as an outstanding example of a virtuous woman who is wrongly accused, and her innocence is vindicated to the shame of her male accusers.

At all times in Israel's history there were women who proved exceptions to the general pattern of subjection and submissiveness, or who at least are represented as such. Miriam, in the familiar story of Exodus 2 (attributed to the Elohist or 'E' source), uses her ready wits to save Moses from destruction; after the escape from Egypt she takes a timbrel in her hand and leads the women in dance, singing the 'Song of the Sea' (Exod. 15.21). She is described as a prophet (15.20[13] capable of joining her brother Aaron in rebuking Moses when she thought he had acted wrongly (Num. 12; but she is smitten with leprosy as a punishment, while Aaron remains unscathed). The prophet Micah (6.4) later celebrated her as sent by God, along with Moses and Aaron, to be a national leader.

In the period of the Judges Deborah, a married woman and mother, exercised civic, religious and military leadership. Called a prophet like Miriam, she 'judges' Israel – precisely the same term (Heb. *shaphat*) is used of her as of men. She takes the initiative in summoning Barak in the name of the Lord to muster troops against Sisera, and her strength and courage make a striking contrast with the feebleness of that male leader of Israel. Her heroism, and that of Jael (the woman who killed Sisera), is celebrated in the magnificent 'Song of Deborah' (Judg. 5), one of the earliest surviving pieces of Hebrew poetry.

During the monarchy, Huldah, another woman prophet, was held in high standing, being consulted by the High Priest and Secretary and other male leaders on behalf of the king. Her outspoken words to Josiah may have encouraged him to initiate his reforms (seventh century BC). It is remarkable that Huldah, like Deborah, does not hesitate to say: 'Thus says the Lord...' (2 Kings 22.15,18), a formula showing that her message was believed to be directly from God. Other female prophets are the wife of Isaiah (Isa. 8.3) and Noadiah, denounced by Nehemiah along with the male prophets (Neh. 6.14).

In spite of the ideal that women's concern should be family and home, there were some exceptional women, usually of royal blood, who exercised political power and influence. In the early monarchy (tenth-ninth centuries BC) Bathsheba, wife of David, wielded power from behind the throne (e.g. 1 Kings 1.11-40); Jezebel (1 Kings 18-21; 2 Kings 8.18) and Athaliah, who reigned both as Jehoram's consort and as queen regnant (2 Kings 11.1-16), were both very powerful women, though one can hardly hold them up as models of good conduct. In later times Salome Alexandra reigned as queen (76-67 BC) and other women of the Hasmonean and Herodian court circles exercised considerable political power and influence (e.g. Mariamne). Perhaps one sees here influence of the increased freedom for some women in the Graeco-Roman world.

In a more general way, negative sentiments about evil women

need to be balanced by more positive appreciations of their value. The love of husband for wife is more than once mentioned (e.g. Isaac's love for Rebekah, and Jacob's for Rachel). Ecclesiastes bids a man enjoy life with the wife whom he loves (9.9); and although Proverbs' praise of the 'perfect housewife' (discussed above) lays special stress on the woman's industriousness and usefulness to her husband, it also mentions other virtues such as her care for the needy, her kindness, and wisdom of speech (Prov. 31.20, 26). In a poetic passage Proverbs also refers to the physical pleasures of marital love: 'May your fountain be blessed, and may you rejoice in the wife of your youth. A loving doe, a graceful deer – may her breasts satisfy you always, may you be captivated by her love' (5.18f. NIV).

Sometimes feminists have complained that the Old Testament values women chiefly as mothers, capable of bringing male heirs into the world; yet Canticles (Song of Songs) also affirms very positively the joy of heterosexual love for its own sake. Substantial sections of this exquisite collection of love poems are written from the woman's viewpoint, as can be seen even in the opening words:

> Let him kiss me with the kisses of his mouth,
> for your love-making is sweeter than wine.

The woman's beauty is described in the first person: 'I am the rose of Sharon' (2.1). The poem tells of her initiative in seeking out her lover, catching him, and refusing to let him go. She brings him to her *mother's* house (3.1–4). His loving actions are described with delightful frankness:

> His left arm is under my head
> and his right embraces me (8.3).

Scholars have commented on the remarkable freedom of this text from patriarchy and male chauvinism, and its almost matriarchal colouring (the lovers speak seven times of mother, but father is never mentioned). It is striking that there is no reference to the hope of children – deemed by some Christian thinkers to be an essential accompaniment to marital relations. In fact, the text does not even make it clear that the couple are married (though the Song's traditional association with Solomon shows that it was thought to imply this):[14] the physical expression of heterosexual love is valued for its own sake. The Song of Songs was preserved as Jewish and Christian Scripture because it was interpreted allegorically. Viewed as love-poetry, which it originally was, it acts as an important corrective to the male orientation and negative view of female sexuality found in some Jewish (and later Christian) texts.

CONCLUSIONS AND IMPLICATIONS FOR METHODOLOGY

The significance for women's ministry of this survey of Old Testament and Jewish attitudes needs to be carefully assessed. It is clear that there are two strands in the Old Testament – subordinationist and equalitarian. This raises a fundamental question of how one copes when some parts of an authoritative text differ from others in their teaching or perceptions.

Some Christians suggest that in ambiguous cases Scripture should be interpreted according to the Church's tradition (cf. the Roman Catholic concept of the Church's 'magisterium' or teaching authority). The problem here is that those to whom the Church has traditionally looked for guidance are by no means unanimous on many key issues. 'Tradition' itself contains tensions and varying attitudes. And one must acknowledge that what has become 'authoritative' teaching for many Christians is sometimes merely a consensus of fallible leaders who were as limited by the social and intellectual conditions of their day as we are by ours. The contemporary Church must be free to take account of fresh evidence and new insights in biblical interpretation – not to mention the continuing work of the Spirit – as has indeed begun to happen even in those denominations which attach great importance to traditional teaching.[15]

A more modern approach is to examine the biblical sources critically, studying carefully their literary and cultural settings, with scrupulous attention to the *purpose* for which each was written. But while much can be gained from this method, it too can only take us so far. It is not always possible to determine the original purpose of some texts, or they may have been re-interpreted or misinterpreted within Scripture (or Tradition) in ways contrary to the authors' original intentions.

We therefore need to make a distinction between general *scriptural principles* and more detailed *culture-related prescriptions*. For example, Old Testament rules about ritual 'purity' and such matters as not wearing garments of mixed cloth, or not cooking goatmeat in milk, could be regarded as superseded for Christians, while the general principle of the need for moral sanctity among God's people might be confirmed. Similarly the provision that a woman should have to marry her rapist, while unacceptable today as a precept, nevertheless can be seen as enjoining the principle of care for the injured. But even this method has its limitations, as critics will differ as to what is ceremonial and time-related or moral and permanent.

Another approach is to seek to assess the Old Testament in the light of the New Testament, looking especially for what comes closest to Jesus' teaching. Long ago Luther understood Scripture in this way, arguing (even of the New Testament): 'That which does not teach Christ is not apostolic, even if a Peter or Paul taught it'.[16] The advantage of this method is that it allows for development of doctrine in Scripture, and for the reinterpretation of 'problematic' Old Testament teaching (e.g. on war and vengeance) in the light of the New Testament. Difficulties here include knowing precisely what Jesus did teach and what formed the centre of his message (see below Ch. 3), and the diversity of developing theological insights in the New Testament writings. Even the authors of the New Testament were influenced by their cultural environment, which was much closer to that of the Old Testament than to our own.[17]

Similar problems arise with Mary Hayter's recent suggestion (made in the context of the use and abuse of the Bible in the debate about women's ministry) that in handling seemingly contradictory texts, one should ask: 'Which view lies nearer to the centre of Christian doctrine?' and 'Which comes closest to expressing the highest ideals of the Christian faith?'. She proposes that in applying biblical teaching the central concern should be 'the interdependent objectives of glorifying God and edifying the whole congregation' and 'the proclamation of the Gospel'.[18] From a devotional point of view few could quarrel with these criteria. But they suffer from the fact that Christians of different traditions are bound to interpret them differently. For some, the proper subordination of women – as apparently enjoined in certain texts – works for the glory of God and the edifying of worshippers: for such people an exclusively male ordained ministry may be at the heart of the Christian faith. For others, the exact opposite is true: for them the full participation of women in worship affirms the biblical principles of the essential equality of women and men, and of God's justice and impartiality; for these it is vital that women should be recognized as equal to men if the Church is to be effective in spreading the Gospel in the contemporary world.[19] More objective criteria are necessary.

One method which deserves fuller consideration and which is rarely explicitly followed is that of *comparative study*. Where a particular custom or command is paralleled in non-biblical cultures, and where it seems particularly orientated to the physical or social needs of those communities, then the possibility should seriously be considered that the command is culturally conditioned and not necessarily applicable to other times and places. This is where our study of women in the Graeco-Roman world is so important because it shows how deeply Old Testament teaching on women was grounded in the socio-economic conditions of the ancient world. There is no point in pretending that a majority of Old Testament documents support the social, legal or religious equality of women. Subordinationist texts far outnumber equalitarian ones. In spite of exceptional women, like Miriam, Deborah, and Huldah who exercised real leadership, women were regularly regarded as legally and socially subordinate to men. But so they were in the Graeco-Roman world and in the Near East generally. The very fact that so many of the Hebrew limitations on the role of women were held in common with contemporary peoples of very different religious commitment strongly suggests that this subordination is part and parcel of an ancient way of life, influenced by such factors as the need (at an early period) to preserve a warrior governing-class in the face of military and political insecurity and the sheer struggle for economic survival which still dominates so many societies.

But the mere fact that a biblical custom such as regarding women as permanent minors is paralleled elsewhere would not mean in itself that this was not the will of God. To come to a balanced judgement one must use the whole range of available criteria, considering whether there are any other grounds in reason or experience for regarding a particular teaching as of temporary or permanent value. In the case of the subordination of women to men, one could ask: are there any physiological or psychological reasons why this should be regarded as part of God's plan for humanity? This is something which will concern us later in this book. Meanwhile a central question remains: how far does the New Testament supersede, for Christians, the Old Testament? What did Jesus and Paul teach about women and men? How do the New Testament doctrines of incarnation, redemption, and the gifts of the Spirit affect our understanding of the subordinationist and equalitarian views we have noted? How does the New Testament understand ministry, and does it perpetuate religious inequalities we observed in the Old Testament and Judaism?

NOTES

1 cf., for example, Saul's attitude to his daughter Michal (1 Sam. 18.21); the abuse of royal concubines by claimants to the throne (2 Sam. 3.7; 16.21f.); Amnon's treatment of Tamar, daughter of David (2 Sam. 13.1–20); and the raping or forced marriage of women captured in raid and war (Judg. 5.30; 21.14–23).

2 See Swidler (1976), p. 94; also Loewe (1966), esp. p. 23f., pp. 42–6. On women's exemption from 'affirmative precepts limited to time' see *b. Kidd.* 34a–35a (ed. Epstein).

3 No biblical or rabbinic text prescribes the separation of women and men in worship. Brooten (1982), pp. 103–38, argues that archaeological remains from early synagogues show no evidence (such as galleries) for it. However, separation eventually became customary. See further Swidler (1976), ch. 4, and Edwards (1988), pp. 1093f.

4 Hebrew has three common words for man – ʾadam, 'human being', ʾish, 'male', and geber, 'strong man', 'warrior'. But they are not always used consistently, (e.g. ʾish may be generic: see Ch. 6, n.6), nor are translations always reliable: in Pss. 84.12; 1.1; 34.8 AV renders all three words indifferently as 'man'.

5 In Exod. 20.17, NJB wrongly renders ʾishshah, 'wife', as 'spouse', implying that the commandment was phrased inclusively.

6 But see Brooten (1982) on epigraphic evidence for women elders and synagogue leaders in the Diaspora.

7 *Abot* 1.5 (ed. Danby, p. 446) – saying ascribed to Jose b. Johanan.

8 e.g, *t. Berakot* 7.18, ed. Rengstorf; ET in Williams (1921), p. 84, on which see Fiorenza (1983), pp. 217f. and Bruce (1982), p. 187 (with further references).

9   See *b. Kidd.* 80b; *b. Yoma* 66b; *b. Shab.* 152a (ed. Epstein) with the
     rather negative appraisal in Swidler (1976), p. 80.
10 See *Sotah* 3.4 (ed. Danby, p. 296).
11 Saying ascribed to R. Hanilai: see further Montefiore and Loewe
     (1938), pp. 507–15. After the destruction of the Temple (AD 70)
     women were especially valued for their scrupulous observance of the
     food-laws in the home, thus ensuring the 'purity' of the table.
12 Prohl (1957), pp. 35–7 claims that out of 21 occurrences of *ᶜezer* 16 are
     for a 'superior' and 5 are without hierarchical sense.
13 Hebrew *nᵉbiᵓah*, the feminine form of the regular OT term for a
     prophet.
14 Interpretations vary from allegory to royal wedding-song, manifesto
     for women's liberation to funerary text. Canticles is now generally
     recognized as a collection of love-poetry, including references to
     courtship and premarital love: see Gottwald in *IDB* 4, 420–6; GNB, *ad
     loc.*; also Pope (1977), pp. 89–229, esp. pp. 205–10.
15 See, for example, Wijngaards (1977), (esp. pp. 11f. on changing RC
     attitudes to NT textual criticism); Rahner (1968), p. 6 (on post-
     Vatican II concepts of ministry); Brown (1985), (on modern RC
     biblical exegesis).
16 Cited in Blackman (1957), p. 123; fuller details in Greenslade (1963),
     p. 7.
17 See Dunn (1977); Dunn and Mackey (1987), esp. pp. 9f.
18 Hayter (1987), ch. 8. esp. pp. 149–54.
19 cf. the differences of opinion in the C. of E. Bishops' Report, *The
     Ordination of Women to the Priesthood: A Second Report* (1988).

3

Jesus and Women

THE NATURE OF THE EVIDENCE

In the next three chapters our task will be to examine the New Testament evidence relevant to the theology of women's ministry. A central element in the discussion is obviously the attitude of Jesus himself to women. But how do we know what Jesus taught about women or how he treated them? Independent, 'objective' sources for his life are lacking:[1] the Gospels, as is well known, are products of faith, designed to lead others to faith. The aim of the evangelists was not to write biographies, but to present their Lord as they experienced him through their own faith and that of the Christian communities in which they lived. But there is reason to believe that they all used and adapted sources (including eye-witness testimony), to which they added fresh insights through their selection of materials, manner of presentation, personal interpretations and the addition of new matter. Ancient literary conventions allowed considerable freedom in the handling of sources, and the risen Christ was very much alive for these early writers, who had a strong sense of the Spirit's presence to guide them into truth. This means that in our Gospels the historical teaching of Jesus of Nazareth has become closely meshed with the Church's developing understanding of Christ the Lord.

Nevertheless, modern scholarship has established some methods for distinguishing Jesus' original teaching from later developments. We have four Gospels, which may be compared with one another and set against the background of Judaism and early Christianity. Such study, combined with literary analysis of forms and structure, enables individual sources to be identified, as well as the evangelists' distinctive contributions.[2] The likely form of the historical Jesus' teaching may thus be recovered through the application of such criteria as 'multiple attestation' (does a saying appear in more than one source?); 'dissimilarity' (is it distinctive from traditional Judaism or later Church teaching?); 'coherence' (is it consistent with the rest of Jesus' teaching as recovered?); and 'formal analysis' (e.g. does it involve poetic parallelism, word-play, or other signs of a Semitic original?). These criteria are not infallible,[3] but they remain our best method for distinguishing a probable core of Jesus' own teaching.

It was not, of course, such hypothetical reconstructions of Jesus' words which the Church accepted as authoritative for doctrinal purposes, but the finished form of the Gospels. For the purposes of our study, therefore, we need to be concerned with the *totality* of Gospel witness as well as those elements which seem reasonably certain to go back to Jesus himself.

JESUS' RELATIONSHIP TO WOMEN

His Caring for those in Trouble. All four Gospels represent Jesus as accepting women to an astonishing degree, and in ways which contrast sharply with some of his Jewish contemporaries. From the beginning of his active ministry Jesus healed women just as he healed men. Examples from Mark, almost certainly the first Gospel to be written,[4] are Peter's mother-in-law (1.29–31), the woman with the haemorrhage (5.24–34), and the Syro-Phoenician woman's daughter (7.24–30), as well as the raising of Jairus' daughter (5.35–43), episodes all attested in Matthew and mostly also in Luke. The narratives depict Jesus as unfailingly courteous and compassionate towards those concerned. He interrupts his journey to the house of a synagogue official to heal an unknown woman in a crowd: he addresses her affectionately as 'daughter'; he touches her, although she must have been ritually 'unclean'. He also touches Peter's mother-in-law and Jairus' little girl, showing his practical concern by asking that she be given something to eat. He responds to the faith and ready wit of the Syro-Phoenician woman, even though she was a Gentile.

Other healing miracles which feature women prominently come from Luke's special material (known as 'L').[5] We note the reference to Jesus' compassion for the widow of Nain, whose son he raises (7.13), and his affirmation of the woman with a spinal deformation, as a 'daughter of Abraham', i.e. one of God's chosen people (13.10–17).

John describes no healings of women in his highly selective account of Jesus' miracles. Some manuscripts and versions contain a narrative which became associated with his Gospel (John 7.53–8.11), in which Jesus encounters a woman caught in the act of adultery. The scribes and Pharisees accuse the woman, quoting the Mosaic law that adulterers should be stoned, and ask Jesus what should be done (one notes the sexism whereby only the woman is accused, and not her male lover!). The question is an obvious trap, which Jesus meets with skilful repartee. His attitude to the adulterous woman is significant: calm and relaxed, he shows no inhibitions about speaking alone to her, but simply says that he does not condemn her; she is to go and sin no more. Although this episode is an intrusion into John's Gospel, there are good reasons for regarding it as embodying genuine early tradition.[6]

Jesus' Acceptance of Women's Service. Other passages illustrate how Jesus accepted the personal service of women without fear of impropriety or ritual contamination. We have already mentioned Peter's mother-in-law, who after her cure served Jesus at table (Mark 1.31 par.). Her action is a sign of the completeness of her cure; it also affirms Jesus' open attitude to her, since some rabbis disapproved of women serving men at table.[7] Martha similarly 'welcomed Jesus into her house' and served him a meal (Luke 10.38–42; cf. John 12.2).

Jesus also accepted the more intimate service of the anointing of his person. All four Gospels contain accounts of such an episode, but it is unclear whether they all represent the same occasion. In Luke 7.36–50 the incident occurs early in Jesus' ministry. A woman described as a 'sinner' (probably a prostitute) intrudes on him when he is dining at the house of Simon the Pharisee. Weeping and full of emotion, with her long hair let down (something no respectable woman would do in male company), she wets Jesus' *feet* with her tears and dries them with her hair; she smothers them with kisses, and anoints them. Simon criticizes him for allowing such a woman to touch him; Jesus replies by referring to what matters most – her love. By contrast the anointing described in the other Gospels occurs only a few days before Jesus' death (Mark 14.3–9; Matt. 26.6–13; John 12.1–8). It takes place at Bethany, according to Matthew and Mark, in the house of 'Simon the leper'. As Jesus is eating a woman breaks a jar of expensive perfume, and pours it over Jesus' *head*. Some of those present are indignant at the waste, but Jesus replies: 'Leave her alone. Why are you bothering her? She has done a beautiful thing to me.... she poured perfume on my body beforehand to prepare for my burial' (Mark 14.6–8 NIV).

The critical problems involved in interpreting these stories are complex.[8] From our point of view the significance of the incidents is not 'what happened', but the use to which they are put by the evangelists. For Luke, the heartfelt repentance and impetuous devotion of the sinful woman contrasts with the cold, ungracious self-righteousness of her host. Thus the woman's great love serves to illustrate in a dramatic way the Gospel truth that Jesus is the 'friend of sinners'.

For Mark, the episode prepares the way for Jesus' passion. The totality of the woman's devotion (the perfume was worth nearly a year's wages) contrasts sharply with the small-mindedness of her critics. By her generous action she displays prophetic insight as well as love. Elisabeth Moltmann-Wendel has commented on the way this woman goes against accepted manners to do something good for Jesus, anointing him in the same way as in ancient Israel a male prophet anointed a king: 'Here is the proclamation of a new age in which old values will be turned upside down'.[9]

It is an irony that this woman should be anonymous, of whom Jesus said 'Wherever the gospel is preached in the whole world, what she has done will be told in memory of her' (Mark 14.9 RSV). Elisabeth Schüssler Fiorenza, another leading feminist theologian, comments rather acidly: 'The woman's prophetic sign-action did not become a part of the gospel knowledge of Christians. Even... the name of the faithful disciple is forgotten because she was a woman'.[10] But this is unfair to Mark. Many early traditions are about anonymous people. Mark must be given due credit for preserving this story, and for using the woman's action as a foil both to the male disciples who so often misunderstood Jesus and to the Jewish religious leaders.

Women as Disciples. How far did Jesus actually teach women alongside men? Women were much more tied to their homes than in the West today; indeed, for them to leave their children to follow an itinerant preacher might be irresponsible. Even to be the wife of a fully committed disciple was tough for a Palestinian woman. J. Jeremias has pointed out: 'If the father of the house decided to enter Jesus' company, his wife and children would have no choice but to return to her parents' house, although that was felt to be a stigma'.[11] But although discipleship meant putting first the call of the Gospel (Matt. 10.37; Luke 14.26), this did not involve for all the leaving of home and possessions. G. Lohfink and others have shown that there were two groups of people who accepted Jesus, those like Lazarus, Zacchaeus and possibly Joseph of Arimathea, who remained in their towns and villages, patiently waiting for the reign of God; and those who were 'disciples' (Greek *mathētai*, lit. 'learners') in a more technical sense, like the Twelve, who abandoned home and profession to 'follow' Jesus quite literally, learning from him (as a rabbinic pupil learned from his master), in preparation for being sent out by him in mission.[12]

Women belonged to both these categories, though naturally there were likely to be more in the first group than the second. The evidence has to be gleaned by a careful examination of the sources, since the evangelists, being men of the first century AD, were not particularly interested in women's issues, and mention women only casually. For example, Matthew, in his accounts of the two feeding miracles, says the numbers of those fed were, respectively, five and four thousand men, *besides women and children* (14.21; 15.38); the other evangelists ignore the women completely. His words show that women were among the crowds listening to Jesus even during the three days of teaching before the second feeding miracle (Matt. 15.32). Jesus' celebrated blessing of the children (told by all three synoptists) also presupposes the presence of mothers in the crowds (Mark 10.13–16 par.; cf. Luke's reference to 'babies').

Luke tells us that on another occasion, as Jesus was teaching, a woman called out: 'Blessed is the womb that bore you and the breasts that you sucked'. Jesus replied: 'Blessed rather are those that hear the word of God and keep it' (Luke 11.27f. RSV). This incident is interesting, not only for mentioning a woman in the crowd, but even more for showing that Jesus was not prepared to affirm the primary role of biological motherhood, either for Mary, his own mother, or for any other woman. The strong adversative particle in the Greek (*menoun*, 'nay rather') shows that the blessing is for those – both men and women – who are obedient to God's will.

An equally significant episode is Jesus' meeting with a Samaritan woman, described in John 4. In contrast to the rabbis, many of whom were reluctant to speak of God's law to women, Jesus directly teaches this woman about spiritual things – the nature of God, of worship, of himself as the giver of 'living water'. The woman comes to faith, recognizing Jesus as the *Ta'eb* (Samaritan equivalent of Messiah), and eagerly passes on the good news to the people of her village. John adds: 'Many Samaritans of that town believed in him on the strength of the woman's words of testimony' (4.39). His use here of the Greek word *martyreō* ('testify') is especially important, because a woman's witness was not acceptable in a Jewish court of law. The historicity of the episode has been challenged, because the dialogue clearly owes much to the evangelist himself; but it also contains many details of 'local colour', and the attitude of Jesus towards the woman is fully consistent with that shown in the Synoptics. The episode shows a woman as a paradigm of faith; she learns from Jesus and becomes an effective missionary.

Another instance where Jesus teaches a woman occurs in a passage already mentioned (Luke 10.38–42). Jesus was dining at the house of Martha and Mary. Mary 'sat at the Lord's feet listening to what he said' (v.39 NIV), while her sister Martha was harassed with the catering. Martha asked Jesus to tell her sister to help her. Jesus replied: 'Mary has chosen what is better, and it will not be taken away from her' (v.42 NIV). To sit at a teacher's feet was the traditional role of a pupil.[13] Jesus here is clearly affirming a woman's right to be a disciple and not to be solely concerned with domestic affairs. It is hard to think of a greater contrast with contemporary Jewish attitudes (cf. above pp. 27f. Some scholars consider this episode to be an 'ideal scene', i.e. basically fiction (so Bultmann); but others have argued that it represents an 'old tradition', with a possible historical basis (so Marshall; Witherington).

Martha and Mary reappear in John's Gospel, in an episode where Martha is now the chief character. She meets Jesus outside the house, and he talks to her about spiritual truths – resurrection and eternal life. In responding Martha, like the Samaritan woman, recognizes Jesus as the Messiah: 'I believe that you are the Christ, the Son of God, the one who was to come into this world' (John 11.27; cf. 4.29). Martha's strong profession of faith contrasts with the unbelief and hostility of 'the Jews', so prominent in John's Gospel, and closely parallels Peter's famous 'confession' (Mark 8.29 par.). But why is Martha's acknowledgement of Jesus so little-known compared with Peter's? It may be partly because of scholarly doubts over the historicity of the episode; but why did John choose Martha, a woman, for this role unless it is to affirm that women too may learn from Jesus and show spiritual insight?[14]

In all these passages the evangelists depict women as among those taught by Jesus, i.e. they demonstrate that the early Church considered them disciples in at least the broad sense of the term.

There is also evidence that some women belonged to that narrower group of disciples who left their homes to follow Jesus. Luke 8.1–3 describes how, as Jesus made his way with the Twelve through towns and villages preaching the good news, certain women whom he had healed went with them, including Mary Magdalene, Joanna, the wife of Herod's steward Chuza, and Susanna, and many others, who supported them financially (the Greek word used is *diakoneō*, usually rendered 'minister', on which see below pp. 80 f.). Presumably these women were well off and were able also to provide for their families. A similar group of women is mentioned by Mark in his Passion narrative: 'There were also women looking on from afar, among whom were Mary Magdalene, and Mary the mother of James the younger and of Joses, and Salome, who, when he was in Galilee, *followed* him and ministered to him' (15.40f. RSV; cf. Matt. 27.55). The word used here for 'follow' (*akoloutheō*) is the one regularly used in the Gospels for discipleship in the fullest sense (e.g. Mark 2.14; Matt. 8.19–22). The 'ministry' of these women may well have included caring for Jesus' personal needs.

All three Synoptists mention that these women, who followed Jesus to Jerusalem and saw him crucified, also witnessed the place of his burial, and prepared the ointments for the body (Mark 15. 40f.; Matt. 27.61; Luke 23.49, 55f.). It is members of the same group who first find the tomb empty (Mark 16.1–8; Matt. 28.1–10; Luke 24.1–11; John 20.1, 11–18) and amaze the incredulous male disciples with reports of a 'vision of angels' (Luke 24.10f., 22f.). The contrast between their faith and the initial scepticism of the male apostles is marked. So too is the prominent role of Mary Magdalene, sent by Jesus as the *apostola apostolorum* with a message for his 'brethren' (John 20.17f.). Although these women do not preach in synagogues like the men (Luke 8.1), they are clearly disciples in a real sense of the word: they are taught by Jesus, they serve him personally, and they bear witness to him.

It is remarkable that, in spite of this evidence, some theologians have asserted that *there are no women disciples in the Gospels*, and, taking the New Testament pattern of discipleship as a model for the Christian priesthood, argue that because the original 'disciples' of Jesus were male, so too must be Christian ordained ministers. Thus Jean Galot, who rejects the possibility of the ordination of women in his influential book, *Theology of the Priesthood*, writes: 'In the language of the gospels the term "disciples" never refers to a woman'.[15] This claim deserves further consideration.

It is true that all the Gospel references to 'disciples' in the original Greek are in the masculine form, i.e. *mathētēs*.[16] But in Greek many masculine forms are used to refer to both men and women. It is a rule of grammar that where a noun, pronoun, adjective, or definite article refers to a group of both sexes, the masculine form is used – even if only one man is present among a hundred women! While the term 'disciples' is occasionally restricted to the Twelve (e.g. Matt. 10.1), it is mostly used of a wider group, to be sure predominantly men, but possibly including women (e.g. Matt. 10.42 on offering a person a cup of cold water because 'he' is a disciple). A particularly clear case is the incident when Jesus' mother and brothers come seeking him. He asks rhetorically, 'Who are my mother and my brothers?', and turning to the 'disciples' (so Matt.), or to 'those sitting in a circle round him' (so Mark), declares: 'Here are my mother and my brothers. Anyone who does the will of God, that person is my brother and sister and mother' (Mark 3.32–5; Matt. 12.49f.; cf. Luke 8.21).[17] Can it be doubted that women are here seen as men's equals in the matter of discipleship?

JESUS' TEACHING ABOUT WOMEN

Some Epistles contain special sections on 'household duties', including the submission of wives to husbands (see Ch. 4). Jesus' recorded teaching, on the other hand, while affirming the Decalogue's command to honour both father and mother, contains no specific advice to women about their roles as wives or mothers. Much of his teaching applies to them by implication, even if not specifically addressed to them (e.g. parables, ethical teaching, sayings about the Kingdom), and his proclamation of the Good News to the outcast and poor might well be seen as particularly relevant to women, living as they did on the fringes of Jewish society. A memorable saying affirms that prostitutes and tax-collectors (i.e. the social outcasts of his day) will enter the Kingdom of God before respected figures like the Jewish priests and elders (Matt. 21.31f.). Jesus also speaks sympathetically of widows (a particularly underprivileged group), condemning the Pharisees for consuming their property (Mark 12.40 par.); he commends a poor widow for her generous giving (Mark 12.41–4); he grieves for the 'daughters of Jerusalem' at the prospect of the destruction of the city (Luke 23.28), expressing special compassion for expectant and nursing mothers (Mark 13.17).

Jesus draws on women's activities in his parables: Luke records that he compared the Kingdom of God first to a man sowing seed, and then to a woman baking bread. Both her action and the man's are analogies for God's action. A woman's search for a lost coin similarly parallels the parable of a shepherd's search for a lost sheep (Luke 15.8–10). In both stories the human search illustrates God's care for 'lost' sinners. In another parable (also 'L' material) a widow's importuning of an unjust judge is used to encourage persistence in prayer.[18]

In contrast to certain Old Testament and non-canonical writers, Jesus never disparages women. If imprudent bridesmaids appear in Matthew 25.2, prudent women also feature in this parable, just as both sensible and foolish (male) house-builders appear in Matthew 7.24–7. What is significant, in view of the comparatively small number of references to women in the Gospels, is how often they are commended for their actions or are used as examples to be imitated.

POSSIBLE MASCULINE ORIENTATION IN JESUS' TEACHING

In describing Jesus' attitude to women, it is not enough simply to look at the places where he speaks directly of or to them. We also need to consider his teaching where women are not mentioned, but might have been. To the modern feminist some of Jesus' teaching might indeed seem male-orientated. In the parables male characters appear much more frequently than female. In that of the Prodigal Son all three central characters are male: how effective it might have been if Jesus had depicted a loving and forgiving *mother*! Similarly with the Good Samaritan: every character in the parable is male. Much is made of the fact that the leading character belonged to a people hated and despised by the Jews; would it not have been even more dramatic and unexpected if the person who showed kindness had been a Samaritan *woman*? But one must take into account the social background. The parables were stories based on real life; and in a society where men occupied the dominant roles, it is hardly surprising that Jesus' stories refer to male shepherds, farmers, servants, hired labourers, kings, and judges. What is remarkable is the presence of at least a modicum of parables reflecting women's activities.

A second area where male orientation might be noted is in Jesus' ethical teaching, e.g. the 'Sermon on the Mount', where the peacemakers are called the 'sons of God' (Matt. 5.9 RSV) and Jesus refers to the 'men of old' (5.21) and one's 'brother' (5.22, 24; 7.4f.). The teaching on adultery and divorce also seems androcentric: 'Every one who looks at a woman lustfully has already committed adultery with her in his heart' (5.28 RSV) – there are no corresponding words about lustful women, though Mark's Gospel contains a more 'inclusive' phrasing of the teaching on divorce.[19]

The masculine emphasis of such passages can often be alleviated by judicious translation. Some of the terms rendered in older versions as 'man' or 'men' are in fact inclusive. Thus 'men of old' (*tois archaiois*) might reasonably be translated 'our ancestors' (so NJB); 'brother' may well also imply 'sister' (cf. Ch. 4, n.6). But there are limits as to how far one can go with this. Is it right to change 'sons of God' in Matthew 5.9 to 'children of God' (so NJB)? Sometimes there are reasons for believing that masculine orientation is due to the evangelist rather than Jesus himself: for example, Luke 14.25–7 speaks of a 'disciple' needing to 'hate' father, mother, *wife*, children, etc., from which it might be assumed that the 'Jesus movement' was one of itinerant charismatic men.[20] But, as E. Fiorenza has ably shown, the words 'and wife' are here redactional and are not found in the more primitive forms of the saying (cf. Mark 10.29; Matt. 10.37).[21] Similarly, the male-orientated formulation of the teaching on divorce needs to be balanced by Mark's more 'inclusive' formulation (10.10–12). A certain male-orientation is almost inevitable in texts stemming from the ancient world in which men were society's leaders. What is important is whether this maleness is theologically significant or simply part of the ancient way of thinking and writing. For example, do Jesus' references to God as 'Father' (e.g. Matt. 5.16, 6.9, etc.) teach some theological truth which could not be conveyed if God were thought of as 'Mother'? We shall return to this question and to the apparently exclusive choice of males for the Seventy (Luke 10.1)[22] and the Twelve in more detail in later chapters.

CONCLUSIONS

To sum up: Jesus' attitude to women seems to have been unusually positive for a Jew of his period. The Gospels present him as accepting them as individuals, and affirming their right to be disciples; he receives their personal service, speaks to them of spiritual matters, and recognizes them as participants in mission. The first resurrection appearance, according to Matthew and John, was to a woman.[23] At the same time, the evangelists present some of Jesus' teaching as androcentric and the evidence suggests that he relied on men for public preaching and healing.

How historical is this picture? There are good reasons for believing that it is soundly-based. It is attested in a multiplicity of sources, in that all four Gospels contain narratives and teaching in which Jesus affirms women. This picture makes a consistent whole, in harmony with his attitudes to other underprivileged members of society, and in contrast to the attitudes of many of his Jewish contemporaries. It also differs, as we shall see, from the attitudes of some of his later followers. A saying so radical as that in which he affirms that tax-collectors and harlots will precede priests and elders in the Kingdom is most unlikely to have been invented by either Matthew or any other Christian who was eager to present the early Church as socially respectable. The material as a whole contains many incidents which accurately reflect details of Palestinian daily life, as well as semitisms and actual Aramaic phrases (e.g. Mark 5.41; Luke 13.21), the occurrence of which is generally taken as a mark of 'authenticity'.

What about the evangelists themselves? F. J. Moloney has observed how frequently Mark depicts women in 'a situation of primacy':[24] Jesus' raising of Jairus' daughter, for example, forms the climax to a series of miracles which demonstrate the active reign of God realized in his person. The Syro-Phoenician woman is the first Gentile recorded in any Gospel as coming to faith. The insight of the woman who anoints Jesus at the start of his Passion is heightened by the lack of understanding of Jesus' male host. The faithful women who follow him from Galilee to the cross serve as a foil to the male disciples who 'all deserted him and ran away' (Mark 14.50).

Matthew adds some 'feminine' details of his own (e.g. the appearance of the risen Jesus to the two Marys at the tomb), but his presentation of Jesus' teaching seems to be more androcentric than Mark's, possibly because of its strongly Jewish character. In 20.20 he transfers the odium of an inappropriate request for 'chief places' in the Kingdom from James and John to their mother (not mentioned by name, but identified by reference to her sons and husband). Matthew also tells the birth-narrative very much from a man's viewpoint, but contrary to Jewish custom includes women in his genealogy of Jesus.[25]

Luke seems generally supportive of women. He tells his

birth-story from Mary's view-point, portraying both Mary and her relative Elizabeth with understanding. Mary's prompt and positive acceptance of God's will contrasts with Zacharias' sceptical reception of his angelic revelation. Elizabeth displays profound insight in recognizing Mary as the mother of the Messiah and is said to have been filled with the Holy Spirit (1.41–5). The exquisite song of praise which we know as the 'Magnificat' is attributed to a woman. Luke also tells of the prophetess Anna in the temple, whose recognition of Jesus parallels that of Simeon (2.36–8). He includes more healings of women than Mark, and may have deliberately incorporated parables with central female characters as a counterpart to those involving men. Luke is also the unique source for Jesus' affirmation of Mary of Bethany's right to learn from him.

John's Gospel is well-known for its sympathetic portrayals of women, including the Samaritan woman, Martha and Mary at Bethany, and Mary Magdalene, as well as Jesus' own mother. Raymond Brown has suggested that this is evidence for women's leadership roles in the Johannine community,[26] but this must remain conjectural.

Finally, we need to consider the implications of all this for women's ministry today. Jesus' radical and loving acceptance of women contrasts strongly with much Jewish teaching of his time. He treated them as disciples, healed them, accepted their service, used them to spread the good news of the Kingdom. Though the Twelve were all men, he is never recorded as affirming any principle of 'male headship' or as explicitly excluding women from future ministry, while the evangelists portray women as models of receptiveness, faith, and religious perception. All this suggests that *prima facie* the Gospels point to the acceptability of women in ministry.

NOTES

1 Non-biblical sources supply background information, but add nothing of substance to the Gospels on Jesus' actual life and teaching: see Bruce (1960), esp. chs. 8–10.

2 On form, source, and redaction criticism see above p. 3.

3 For example, a genuine saying might be preserved in only one source, while one attested in several might be apocryphal; teaching might be closely paralleled in Jewish sources or applicable to a later church

situation, and yet still be authentically spoken by Jesus; conversely it might involve underlying Semitic speech-forms, and still be the work of the Aramaic-speaking Church. See Barbour (1972); Marshall (1977a).

4   See, for example, Anderson (1976), pp. 2–32; Fitzmyer (1981), pp. 3–40.

5   The label 'L' for material not found also in Mark or 'Q' (a postulated common source for Matt. and Luke) does not imply a single, unified document: cf. Marshall (1978), p. 31; Fitzmyer (1981–85), pp. 63–106.

6   See the commentaries of Brown, Barrett, and Schnackenburg ad loc.

7   See Schweizer (1971), p. 53, suggesting that the service of Peter's mother-in-law may be intended by Mark as a model for female disciples. From a feminist point of view this is ambivalent: it affirms the presence of women with Jesus beside the men, but in a supportive capacity.

8   If all the stories go back to one historical episode, then it is likely that Mark represents the more original form: so Schweizer (1971), pp. 288f. but see also Dodd (1963), pp. 162–73; alternatively there may have been two separate incidents, one featuring a penitent sinner who wets Jesus' feet with her tears and dries them with her hair, the other a symbolic anointing by a respectable woman, whom John identifies with Mary of Bethany. See Brown (1971), vol. I, pp. 449–54; Marshall (1978), pp. 304–7.

9   Moltmann-Wendel (1982), p. 98.

10 Fiorenza (1983), p. xiii, whose book *In Memory of Her* takes its title from this episode. On the authenticity of the saying see Taylor (1966), pp. 533f.; Anderson (1976), p. 306.

11 Jeremias (1971), p. 224.

12 Lohfink (1985), pp. 31–3; Hengel (1981), vol. I, pp. 61–3 (who, however, argues that Jesus was not a 'rabbi' in the technical sense of the term).

13 Witherington (1984), p. 101.

14 Schnackenburg (1980–82), vol. II, p. 332, is among those who stresses Martha as a faith model for the Christian community.

15 Galot (1985), p. 255.

16 But the corresponding fem. *mathētria* occurs in Acts 9.36 of a woman.

17 Rawlinson (1949), p. 46, comments: 'The mention of "sisters" is due to the presence of women in Jesus' audience'. Others suggest that the phrase 'and sister' was added by the evangelist in v.35 to 'reflect the Church's recognition of women disciples' (so Anderson (1976), p. 125).

18 On women in the parables see Witherington (1984), pp. 35–44.

19 Mark 10.28–30. Some see this as evidence for Jesus' acceptance of women as equal partners with men in marriage; but the formulation may be an adaptation of his teaching for a Gentile audience (under Roman law a woman could initiate divorce). See Edwards (1988), p. 1096, and, in more detail, Witherington (1984), pp. 23–8.

20 cf. Theissen (1978), pp. 11f.

21 Fiorenza (1983), pp. 145f.
22 Their names are not recorded, but it would be unprecedented to send out women on such a mission.
23 cf. Mark 16.9 (an addition to the original Gospel).
24 Moloney (1985), pp. 13, 18–22; cf. Fiorenza (1983), pp. 315–34. See also Witherington (1984), p. 97, on the special role of Mary, the mother of Jesus, as a model for female discipleship.
25 On this see Brown (1979a), pp. 71–4.
26 Brown (1979b), pp. 183–98. On women in the Churches of the evangelists see now Witherington (1988), chs. 4–5.

4

Paul: Misogynist or Feminist?

THE ENIGMA OF PAUL'S ATTITUDES

The apostle Paul has been interpreted in an astonishing variety
of ways by those concerned with women's ministry. On the one
hand he has been castigated as a male chauvinist and misogynist;
on the other, he has been hailed as a herald of women's
liberation. Some critics have seen him as divided within himself,
a 'half-liberated legalist' who could not quite break away from
his Pharisaic background; others have argued that his writings
display a consistent teaching, either affirmative of women or
otherwise.[1] Part of the problem lies in determining how much of
the corpus ascribed in the New Testament to Paul is by the
apostle himself, and part in the detailed interpretation of
difficult or ambiguous texts. In what follows we will make use
of the whole Pauline corpus, but note that many of the
problematic passages occur in texts widely believed to be
deutero-Pauline, i.e. written under Paul's name by followers
and admirers (these include Colossians, Ephesians, the Pastoral
Epistles, and certain verses of 1 Corinthians).[2] We will also
adopt the general principle of seeking to interpret specific
references to women in the light of Paul's broader theology,
since all too often attention has focused on a small number of
disputed passages rather than his teaching as a whole.

PAUL'S FUNDAMENTAL THEOLOGY

The starting-point of Paul's theology is the love of God shown to sinners. The universality of sin is a major theme of his letter to the Romans, in which he teaches that all human beings – Jew and Gentile alike – share in the same sinful nature in solidarity with Adam, seen as the progenitor of the human race and the prefigurement of the 'One who is to come', i.e. Jesus Christ (Rom. 5.14). It is noticeable that Paul here makes no reference to the sinfulness of Eve, or of women in general, but sees 'Adam' as bringing condemnation to all.[3] He goes on to proclaim that God, in love and patience, freely offers forgiveness to *all*, through the obedience and sacrificial death of Jesus Christ, seen as the new 'Adam' or humanity (Rom. 5.12–21) – teaching echoed in 1 Cor. 15.22: 'Just as all die in Adam, so in Christ all will be brought to life.' This unmerited divine acceptance of sinners is described by a variety of metaphors, which include redemption, like a slave's liberation from bondage (Rom. 3.24), justification or acquittal, as in a court of law (Rom. 5.1), restoration from death to life or rebirth (Rom. 6.4), reclothing or 'putting on' Christ (Gal. 3.27). Colossians and Ephesians speak of putting on a new self, renewed in the image of its Creator, and called to a life of holiness (Col. 3.10; Eph. 4.24; cf. 2 Cor. 5.17).

At no point is there any hint that these central theological affirmations apply only to the male sex; several key passages use inclusive language, such as *Adam* (mankind) or *anthrōpos*. In a justly famous passage of Galatians, which has been described as the 'Magna Carta of humanity',[4] he solemnly affirms: 'There is neither Jew nor Greek, there is neither slave nor free, there is neither male nor female: for you are all one in Christ Jesus' (3.28 RSV). It is widely thought that he is here quoting a primitive Christian baptismal formula. Whether or not that is the case, the expression 'male and female' (*arsen kai thēlu*) – an unusual term in the New Testament for 'man and woman' – recalls the same phrase in Genesis 1.27, where male and female are both said to be made in the image of God. His words contrast strikingly with the traditional Jewish prayer in which a man thanked God daily that he was not made a Gentile, a woman, or a slave (cf. above p. 28). Paul here recognizes that the old religious distinctions between men and women were now abolished, just as the early Church by baptizing both men and women (Acts 8.12, etc.) proclaimed its difference from Judaism where only men were circumcised as members of God's covenantal community.[5]

In 1 Corinthians, one of his earliest epistles and written probably c. AD 55, Paul speaks of the gifts of the Spirit, emphasizing their variety and the fact that they are given to *each individual* (1 Cor. 12.4–11). He then develops the analogy of the Christian community as a body with different members (e.g. hands or feet), each with a different and complementary part to play. Neither here nor in Rom. 12.4–8, where he also speaks of varieties of gifts and service, does he imply any distinction between male and female members of the community in the exercise of these gifts. This would have been a golden opportunity to suggest that the male members represent the head, and the female members the less distinguished parts. But there is no hint of this. Paul affirms that *all*, no matter how humble, contribute to the whole. Eph. 4.11–13 similarly speaks of Christ giving a variety of spiritual gifts to humanity (*anthrōpois*), for the building up of his 'body', the Church.

A remarkable feature of Paul's theology is his emphasis on liberty. In Galatians, possibly his earliest letter, he teaches justification by faith and Christian freedom from the Jewish Law, reproaching the Galatians for reverting to conditions of 'slavery' by accepting the imposition of Jewish circumcision and ritualist observances. In an elaborate allegory (Gal. 4.21–31), he compares Christians to the children of Sarah, the free woman, as opposed to Hagar, the bond-woman. He continues: 'For freedom Christ has set us free; stand fast therefore, and do not submit again to a yoke of slavery' (Gal. 5.1 RSV). He urges Christians to live by the Spirit in freedom (Gal. 5.13–25; cf. 2 Cor. 3.17). Paul is also deeply moved by the concept of God's grace, freely bestowed on those who do not merit it. He reminds the Romans that through baptism they have died to sin, and are now living 'not under law, but under grace' (Rom. 6.14). He compares Christians to a married woman, bound by law under her husband's control as long as he lives, but set free by his death: 'In the same way you, my brothers,[6] through the body of Christ have become dead to the

Law and so you are able to belong to someone else... and so we are in a new service, that of the Spirit, and not in the old service of a written code' (Rom. 7.1–6). It is vital that we remember these fundamental theological affirmations when we come to consider more problematic passages about women's roles.

PAUL'S ACCEPTANCE OF WOMEN AS COLLEAGUES IN MINISTRY

Paul's references to individual women in his letters bear out the general picture of full acceptance which we have so far gained. Several times he refers to Christian women as 'sisters' (Rom. 16.1; 1 Cor. 7.15, 9.5; Philem. 2; cf. 1 Tim. 5.2), sometimes expressing warm affection for individuals: note 'my dear friend Persis' (Rom. 16.12), and Rufus' mother, 'a mother to me too' (Rom. 16.13 NIV), as well as the mention of 'Chloe's people' (1 Cor. 1.11), 'Nympha and the church which meets in her house' (Col. 4.15), Tryphaena and Tryphosa, 'who work hard in the Lord' (Rom. 16.12), Julia and Nereus' sister, who are among the Christian men and women bidden to 'greet each other with a holy kiss' (Rom. 16.15f.). It is striking that Paul treats such women as *colleagues*, not as subordinates. In Philippians (4.2f.) he writes that Euodia and Syntyche 'have struggled hard for the gospel with me, along with Clement and all my other fellow-workers' (*synergoi*). In Romans 16 he commends the hard work of Mary and Persis, using the same verb (*kopiaō*) of their ministry as of his own (Rom. 16.6, 12; cf. 1 Cor. 15.10). He describes Prisca (Priscilla) and her husband Aquila as colleagues (*synergoi*), saying that they risked their lives for him (Rom. 16.3f.). Priscilla and Aquila shared Paul's ministry and tent-making at Corinth, and travelled with him to Ephesus, where they instructed in the Christian faith an Alexandrian Jew named Apollos, described as 'an eloquent man, with a sound knowledge of the scriptures' (Acts 18.24–6). This passage, in which Priscilla's name appears first in reference to the instructing, constitutes important evidence for the fact that women did, on occasion, teach men, and the manner of Paul's references to Priscilla suggests no reservation on his part. Some of the later scribes transmitting the text were not so happy, and inverted the order of the names. Priscilla is named before her husband in four out of the six references to her, which is about as odd as speaking of Mrs and Mr Smith would be today. The best explanation seems to be that she was 'the more active Christian' or 'more capable than her husband'.[7]

In another significant passage Paul mentions a woman apostle, Junia. She and Andronicus – presumably her husband – are commended as 'outstanding (*episēmoi*) among the apostles' (Rom. 16.7). Modern translators often render this name as a masculine, Junias (contrast AV), but the masculine form never occurs in any ancient source and has to be postulated specially for this context. As far back as the fourth century John Chrysostom, who can hardly be accused of prejudice in favour of women's liberation, recognized Junia as female when he wrote: 'To be apostles is something great. But to be outstanding among them – just think what a wonderful encomium that is! How great this woman's devotion to learning (*philosophia*) must have been that she was deemed worthy of the title apostle'.[8] Andronicus and Junia are described as Paul's kinsfolk (either relatives or fellow-Jews) and fellow-prisoners with him, who were 'in Christ' before him, that is to say, they were senior in standing to Paul himself.[9] It is clear that the term 'apostle' (*apostolos*) is used here in a broad sense, rather than with reference to the Twelve; nevertheless, it is patently a term of honour, and its application to Junia once again alerts us to the fact that many Greek nouns of this type are common in gender and can refer to male or female.

This leads us to Phoebe (Rom. 16.1f.), modestly described in the New International Version as a 'servant of the Church in Cenchreae...(who) has been a great help to many people, including me'. One might be forgiven for thinking from this and similar translations (cf. GNB) that Phoebe was a subordinate assistant. But the Greek describes her as a *diakonos* of the congregation, using exactly the same term as is used elsewhere of men, such as Epaphras and Tychicus (Col. 1.7; 4.7; Eph. 6.21), and even of Paul himself (Col. 1.23, 25). The difference is that, whereas in those passages the addition of phrases like 'of Christ' or 'in the Lord' seems to indicate a general sense, here the additional phrase 'of the congregation' (or 'Church') suggests ecclesial office. Some translations render *diakonos* as 'deaconess' (so RSV, NJB), but the use of this special feminine formation tends to suggest something different from, or inferior to, the male office. The New Testament never uses the feminine *diakonissa*, which first occurs in post-biblical times.

Paul's respect for Phoebe is further illustrated by his commendation of her and the way in which he bids his readers to assist her in whatever she requires. It is reinforced by his description of her as the '*prostatis*' of himself and of many others. This term derives from the verb *proistēmi* meaning 'set over.' When the corresponding masculine, *prostatēs*, occurs in classical sources or the Greek Old Testament, it is rendered 'chief, president, champion, or patron' – Church Fathers use it of bishops, angels and God![10] But when the feminine appears in the New Testament, then the translations suddenly become a little humbler. Is this because exegetes are not prepared to admit that a woman might be in a senior position? Some scribes softened the implication that a woman held high office by substituting *parastatis*, 'helper', 'right-hand woman'.

Paul's frequent mention of women in his closing greetings (including around one third of those named in Romans 16), as well as his other references to women leaders, clearly indicates that he accepted women as colleagues.[11] This is indeed the logical implication of his doctrine of the Spirit, and of God's impartial acceptance, by grace through faith, of men and women, Jew and Gentile, slave and free.

PAUL'S VIEWS ON SEXUALITY AND MARRIAGE

In contrast with this material some passages in the Pauline corpus seem to suggest negative attitudes to women and sexuality, or have been understood as teaching the permanent subordination of women to men in marriage and in the Chrstian community. Since these have played a prominent part in debates on women's ordination, it is important to give them fair consideration.

1 Corinthians 7

Paul writes: 'It is a good thing for a man not to touch a woman', and suggests that a prime motive for having a wife is avoidance of fornication (vv.1f.). He wishes that all were as himself (v.7), a phrase usually taken as meaning that all should be single; he advises the unmarried to remain as they are: 'but if they cannot control themselves, they should marry, for it is better to marry than to burn' (vv.8f. NIV). He even recommends that those who have wives should live as if they had none (vv.29f.). To the modern reader this suggests an unbalanced and low view of marriage.

But here, as always, it is important to set Paul's teaching in context. He is not giving a full theology of marriage, but rather answering a series of questions raised by the Corinthians. The chapter opens with the words, 'Now for the questions about which you wrote', and the first main sentence, 'It is a good thing for a man not to touch a woman' may well be not Paul's own words, but a quotation from the Corinthians' own views.[12] The implication of v.1 that sexual relations within marriage are not desirable is inconsistent with traditional Jewish attitudes, symbolized by the command to 'be fruitful and multiply' (Gen. 1.28) and God's words in Gen. 2.18, 'It is not right that the man should be alone' (cf. Tobit 8.6). There is evidence that some Christians at Corinth were adopting negative, 'gnostic' attitudes to sexuality. In contrast, Paul by his words 'every one has his own gift from God' (v.7) affirms that marriage is good; at the same time he expresses a preference for the state of virginity (vv.37f.).

It is important to look at his reasons for so doing, which are not hostility to the body, but rather the urgency of the situation. He evidently expects an imminent consummation of all things, as can be seen from his words, 'the time has become limited' and 'this world as we know it is passing away' (vv.29, 31; cf. 1 Thess. 4.15; Rom. 13.11f.). He therefore advises all to stay in their present state, whether married or single, circumcised or uncircumcised, slave or free, 'because of the stress which is weighing upon us' (vv.24, 26). If Paul had not expected a prompt 'second coming', he could never have given such advice, for the world needs to be peopled, and the Church needs new generations of members. The paradoxical advice to husbands to act as if they had no wives must also be seen in the context of Paul's further injunctions that those who have possessions are to act as if they had none. This urgency with which Paul views the work of mission may be compared to that of Jesus when he bids the Twelve provide themselves with no money, bag, staff, or spare clothes and shoes (Matt. 10.9f.), and his command to the Seventy not to greet anyone on the road (Luke 10.4). Paul's words reveal the same sense of urgent dedication.

A prime motive for his advice is the idea that marriage brings cares and distractions from 'the Lord's work'; he himself had utterly dedicated his life to mission, which involved hazardous journeys, beatings, stoning and imprisonment. His wife (if he were married) would have had many trials. He wants the Corinthians to be free from worries, so that they can devote themselves to the task in hand. Even the wish that all should be like himself, probably refers to the dedication that consecrated celibacy implies rather than the unmarried state as such.

For Paul does not disparage the physical side of marriage. He affirms its value: 'the husband must give to his wife what she has the right to expect' and the wife likewise; they are not to deprive one another of sexual intercourse, except by mutual consent for a limited time to leave themselves free for prayer (7.3–5). The mutuality of the marriage relationship is further emphasized by his suggestion that each partner has 'authority' over the other's body (7.4); and by his earlier affirmation (when denouncing prostitution) that the body is the temple of the Holy Spirit, and that in intercourse the partners become one flesh (6.14–20).

1 Corinthians 7, perhaps more than any other writing of Paul, gave rise to the ascetic ideal, favoured in the patristic and medieval Church and still current in some quarters today, that virginity is preferable to marriage. Historically it encouraged negative attitudes to women and sexuality (cf. Chapter 6) and thus indirectly hindered women's ministry. It underestimates the companionship and help that a happy marriage can bring; Paul fails to appreciate how fully and faithfully married people can serve God in their partnership. But it would be unfair to call him here either chauvinistic or misogynistic.[13]

The 'Household Codes'

1 Corinthians 7 is universally recognized as Paul's own composition, and is striking for the way in which it treats husband and wife as equals in regard to such matters as sexual intercourse or separation from marriage. However, two passages (Eph. 5.22–6.9 and Col. 3.18–4.1) in what are often considered 'deutero-Pauline' writings directly enjoin the subjection of wives to husbands, and seem to imply a rather different attitude. They occur in passages known as 'Household Codes' (German *Haustafeln*) since they are concerned with domestic relationships. Similar material is also found in 1 Pet. 2.18–3.7, and, less formally organized, in 1 Tim. 5.1–2, 6.1–2 and Titus 2.2–10. The pattern of the teaching can be seen most clearly in Eph. 5.22ff., which follows a general injunction to Christians to submit themselves to one another out of reverence for Christ. It may be formulated: 'Wives be subject to your husbands...husbands love your wives. Children obey your parents...fathers do not anger your children. Slaves obey your earthly masters...masters treat slaves fairly.' It is striking that in each case where a class of people is asked to submit themselves to another group, there is a reciprocal demand. But the duties are by no means exactly parallel: wives are told to *be subject to* husbands; husbands to *love* wives, and so on. In some instances the reciprocal duty is omitted: thus Colossians and 1 Peter omit the injunction to masters to treat slaves fairly.

These passages could, if taken out of their social context, be interpreted as enjoining a permanent subjection for women, as for slaves and children.[14] But when they are studied against their cultural background, it becomes clear that their purpose is to endorse current social morality. The Household Codes are closely related to Greek philosophical teaching – with parallels in Platonic, Aristotelian, Stoic and Neopythagorean sources. Aristotle, for example, treated these same three pairs of relationships (master-slave, husband-wife, parent-child) in his discussion on 'household management', enjoining a similar submission. The thought was also well-established in Hellenistic Judaism: both Philo and Josephus taught that wives must be subject to husbands, and children to parents. Most philosophical writers accepted slavery as part of the *status quo*.

Because of the precarious position of Christianity as a *religio licita* in the Roman Empire, the New Testament authors were wary of challenging current social structures: they enjoined payment of taxes, and submission to the Emperor and civil authorities (Rom. 13.1–7; 1 Pet. 2.13–17; Titus 3.1). In a convincing study entitled *Let Wives be Submissive* D. L. Balch has argued that the primary purpose of the Household Codes was apologetic and missionary – to commend Christianity to unbelievers, who might be put off if they thought it was revolutionary, and to convert unbelieving husbands and masters through socially acceptable submissive behaviour (cf. Titus 2.7f.; 1 Pet. 3.1f.).

In the medieval period the fact that the Household Codes endorsed the submission of wives to husbands was used to argue that women are in a state of subjection and should not be ordained. But the Codes also endorse slavery, and were, for many centuries, used to justify that institution. Today, almost universally, slavery is rejected as contrary both to 'human rights' and to the biblical teaching that human beings are made in the image of God, who makes no distinctions of persons. Thus the Household Codes need to be reinterpreted in each new age: it is a mistake to see them as laying down permanent rules, when what they are seeking to do is to enjoin mutual consideration and civilized behaviour according to the lights of their day. They exemplify Paul's injunction to regard others as more important than oneself (cf. esp. Rom. 12.10). They should not be taken as enjoining sex and class distinctions; rather in the modern context, they may be interpreted as urging that nothing be done to upset the currently acceptable civilized *mores* – which for most people today means accepting social and sexual equality.

The Ephesians passage is striking for its concern for the 'subject' groups, and especially for its very positive advice to husbands to love their wives as their own bodies (v.28) – there is no hint of 'gnostic' hatred of the flesh here. It is also remarkable for the analogy which it draws between the husband's love for his wife, and Christ's love of the Church, personified, following Jewish tradition, as a woman or glorious bride (cf. Rev. 21.2). It has sometimes been suggested that clergy must be male because they represent Christ the bridegroom; but what Ephesians is teaching is that both male and female members of the Church should relate to Christ as a submissive bride to her loving husband. The passage, whether by Paul or not, accepts the social situation where women are in fact subject to their husbands (cf. Rom. 7.2; 1 Cor. 7.39), but transforms this subjection by its injunction to husbands to love their wives as Christ loved the Church. In a society where men and women are legally and socially equals, this love will surely involve treating the wife as an equal.

PAUL'S VIEWS ON WOMEN'S ROLES IN WORSHIP AND MINISTRY

Three important, but difficult, passages refer explicitly to women's roles in the ecclesial community, and merit close attention.

1 Corinthians 11.2–16

As in 1 Corinthians 7, Paul is responding to a specific problem. It is clear that the Corinthians, under a sense of direct prompting from the Spirit, were indulging in very free, disorganized worship, so much so that Paul twice advises them to speak one at a time (14.27, 31). They so much overvalued *glōssolalia* (speaking with tongues) that Paul needs to remind them that other spiritual gifts are more important, especially love (chs. 12–14). In particular, it seems as if 'charismatic' women, convinced that sexual distinctions no longer mattered, were acting with unacceptable freedom by quite literally letting their hair down. Paul's response is to urge decorum in worship, and a proper respect for traditional ways of marking sexual differences.

The passage contains a number of difficulties and ambiguities.

(1) Is Paul enjoining the regular veiling of women in worship? The word 'veil' (*kalymma*) nowhere occurs in the Greek and some scholars have argued that Paul is merely insisting on women wearing their hair long (to distinguish them from men who wear theirs short) or put up tidily and not dishevelled (in contrast to some orgiastic cults where women

wore it loose).[15] But Church Fathers (e.g. Tertullian and Ambrosiaster) understood this passage as prescribing head-covering, as was customary for married women in both Judaism and the Graeco-Roman world. The Greek words (*akatakalyptos* and *kalyptomai*) normally refer to head-covering rather than hair-styles.[16] It seems therefore probable that Paul is here arguing both for women to cover their heads (vv.5–10), and for them to wear their hair long (v.14).

(2) But is the head-covering a sign of men's authority over women or of the woman's own authority? Traditionally Paul has been understood as arguing the former (cf. v.10 NJB: 'as a sign of the authority over her'). But the Greek does not say 'over her'; it simply states that women must wear 'an authority' (*exousia*) on or over their heads. Morna Hooker has strongly argued that the veil is worn as a sign of the woman's 'own authority to pray and prophesy in the new order of the Christian community'.[17] She also suggests that the phrase 'because of the angels', commonly interpreted as referring to the danger that angels might be attracted sexually by unveiled women (cf. Gen. 6.1–4; *Test. Reub.* 5.6; Tert., *Virg. Vel.* 7) may simply refer to their role as guardians of the created order and participants in God's worship. Whichever view we adopt, the veil should be seen as a sign of women's modesty, dignity, and the respect due to them.[18]

(3) A third ambiguity lies in the meaning of the term *kephalē*, 'head' in the phrase, 'the head of a woman [or wife] is man [or her husband]' (v.1). Does it mean 'chief', with the idea that a husband has authority over his wife, or 'source' with the idea that woman was made from man (cf. v.9 and Gen. 2)? A long controversy has raged over this point.[19] Some theologians, relying on the interpretation 'chief', have argued that Paul is here teaching a hierarchical view of creation in which women are created subordinate to men and stand in a different relation to God from them.[20] But even if they are right on the meaning of *kephalē*, they are still reading too much into the text. Paul is not here enunciating a fundamental theological principle, but rather supporting his argument for the proper headdress of women by the use of a rabbinic-style argument based on Jewish exegesis of Genesis 2.[21] His whole theology presupposes that women and men are equally accepted before God in baptism,

and that women have access to God through the mediation of
Jesus Christ (Rom. 5.1–2; cf. Eph. 2.18); to suggest, as did
some Church Fathers, that women are only in the image of God
through their husbands is to go well beyond Paul's meaning.
Even within this passage he seeks to avert a hierarchical
understanding of male-female relationships when he says,
'However, in the Lord, though woman is nothing without man,
man is nothing without woman; and though woman came from
man, so does every man come from a woman, and everything
comes from God' (vv.11f.). This statement, which some believe
to be the climax of the passage, affirms the *mutual* dependence
of women and men and must strongly modify any hierarchical
implications of his earlier argument.[22]

To sum up, the whole passage must be read in its literary and
cultural context. Paul speaks from the perspective of one who
accepts some kind of male headship, as was customary in the
Greek, Roman and Jewish worlds, and adduces a somewhat
weak theological argument. But his central concern is the proper
conduct of worship. His injunctions on women's headgear seem
to be motivated by missionary zeal and perhaps excessive
sensitivity to the religious and social conventions of his day (cf.
his concern for 'weaker brethren' over the issue of meat offered
to idols: 1 Cor. 8.7–13; 10.23–33).

1 Corinthians 14.26–40

Once again Paul is concerned with orderly conduct in the
congregation. He urges that only two or three 'prophets' speak
on each occasion, and those one at a time, stressing that 'God is
a God not of disorder but of peace' (14.26–33). With bitter
irony he asks the 'prophets': 'Do you really think that you are
the source of the word of God? Or that you are the only people
to whom it has come?', and he finishes by saying: 'Make sure
that everything is done in a proper and orderly fashion'
(vv.36–40).

The problem comes with two verses (34f.) which stand
between these two sections and state that women must remain
quiet, 'since they have no permission to speak. Theirs is a
subordinate part, as the Law itself says'. These seem to
contradict 1 Cor. 11.5, where properly attired women are

envisaged as praying and prophesying in the congregation. The whole tone seems much more legalistic than Paul's normal style, with an un-Pauline word *epitrepetai* ('it is permitted'); it assumes that all the women are married (contrast ch. 7, where Paul encourages virgins to remain single), and it makes an uncharacteristic appeal to the Law. Nowhere else does Paul refer to the Jewish Law in this absolute way as if it were binding on Christians, and it is hard to see to which part he is appealing. Moreover, a number of manuscripts place these verses in a different position after v.40, indicating textual uncertainty. If the verses are removed, the argument proceeds fluently. A good many scholars have, therefore, argued that vv.34f. are not by Paul himself, but are an early gloss by a hard-line interpreter, (probably of Jewish background), who felt that women should be kept in their place.[23]

Other commentators retain the text, and seek to explain it in various ways. Some believe that the tension with ch. 11 can be resolved by limiting the reference to women's speaking there to *private* prophecy: but the distinction between private and public prophecy is artificial, and the context shows that 1 Corinthians 11 is also about congregational worship. Others suggest that women (or wives) are being forbidden to interpret prophetic utterances, or simply that women should not chatter and disturb the congregation with questions, noting the words, 'If they want to inquire about anything, they should ask their husbands at home' (v.35 NIV). None of these explanations is fully satisfactory. If we retain the text, then we have to assume that, provoked by the disturbing behaviour of some women, Paul is, for the meantime, banning women's vocal leadership in congregations. He could not have intended this ban as either permanent or universal without contradicting the whole thrust of the rest of his theology.

1 Timothy 2.8–14

The Pastoral Epistles stand apart from the majority of Paul's letters in that they are written to individual Christian leaders (Timothy and Titus), and in their concern for Church ministry. They display differences in language and theology from other Pauline writings, and seem to presuppose a more settled Church life. They are widely thought to be post-Pauline compositions, dating from towards the end of the first century.[24] In 1 Timothy 2 the author writes on public prayer, urging that it be made for rulers and those in authority, so that 'we may be able to live peaceful and quiet lives with all devotion and propriety' (vv.1–2). He explains that he wants the men to pray with their hands lifted up reverently; and women to dress modestly, without braided hair, jewellery, or expensive clothing, and to learn quietly and submissively. He adds: 'I do not permit a woman to teach or to have authority over a man; she must be silent. For Adam was formed first, then Eve. And Adam was not the one deceived; it was the woman who was deceived and became a sinner' (vv.13f. NIV).

There are a number of ambiguities: it is unclear whether all women's teaching is forbidden, or only their teaching of their husbands (or possibly men in general). The meaning of *authenteō* (here usually rendered 'have or usurp authority') is also uncertain. Some think the primary aim was to stop 'liberated' Christian women 'lording it' over their husbands by teaching them domineeringly.[25]

Whatever the precise details, the main point is clear: the author, in common with many writers of the ancient world, is enjoining the submission of women or wives (cf. the Household Codes), and limiting their leadership roles in some way. The 'theological' reason given is once again based on Jewish exegesis of Genesis 2–3, in which Eve, not Adam, is blamed for the 'Fall', and Adam's priority in the order of creation is taken as indicating men's pre-eminence over women. We shall return in Chapter 10 to the problems with this line of reasoning; we have already noted (above p. 55) that elsewhere Paul uses *Adam*, not Eve, as the type of sinful humanity. The author continues: 'Nevertheless, she (i.e. a woman/wife) will be saved by child-bearing, provided she lives a sensible (or modest) life and is constant in faith and love and holiness' (v.15). It is hard to reconcile this last statement with Paul's central teaching about justification by faith through God's grace. Possibly child-bearing is mentioned to counter 'gnostic' views that marriage and childbirth are evil; cf. the advice to young widows to remarry and rear children (5.14; contrast 1 Cor. 7). One gains the impression that the author sets great store by respectability and takes a rather low view of women – or at least of those to whom he is relating in these epistles. The dependence of the passage on its cultural background is obvious: possibly it was necessitated by particular circumstances, such as the leading astray of gullible and uneducated women by heretical teachers (cf. 2 Tim. 3.6; Titus 1.10f.).[26]

CONCLUSION

It will be apparent that there is no easy answer to the question: Was Paul a male chauvinist or a feminist? In fact, to put the question in that way is unfair, since no ancient writers would have thought in those terms. It is evident that, for the most part, Paul was affirmative of women, seeing them as full members of the Christian community, and accepting them as fellow-labourers in the work of the Gospel. It is clear also that he wrote within the framework of ancient ways of thinking, which took for granted women's social and religious subordination. Some passages seem to see the new life in Christ as superseding that subordination – at least in its religious aspects (e.g. Gal. 3.28); but others appear to endorse it, notably the 'Household Codes' of Ephesians and Colossians, the disputed verses in 1 Corinthians 14, and certain passages of the Pastorals. Doubts have been expressed about the Pauline authorship of all these passages: if none of them were by Paul, then the evidence for his positive affirmation of women would be very strong indeed. But even within the writings accepted as Pauline there is an inevitable androcentricity (e.g. in 1 Cor. 7), which makes Paul appear to the modern reader as ambivalent towards women, and 1 Corinthians 11, while affirming the right of women to speak in the assembly, contains a theological argument which some scholars believe implies female inferiority. But it must be stressed that these passages have to be understood in relation to the situations for which they were written. All too often they have been hooked out of their contexts, and applied to totally different social situations, or to issues which lie beyond their concern. To assess their relevance to the theology of women's ministry, we need to read them in the light of the whole New Testament teaching about the nature of ministry, which forms the subject of our next chapter.

NOTES

1   For a range of views see Williams (1977); Terrien (1985), p. 163; Daly (1986), p. 5; Armstrong (1986), pp. 12–18. In what follows I develop ideas first sketched in Edwards (1987), pp. 423f. and (1988), pp. 1095f.

2   On questions of Pauline authorship see Kümmel (1975), pp. 250–387.

3   In 2 Cor. 11.3, he uses Eve as a warning to both men and women; on 1 Tim. 2.13 see above pp. 68f.

4   Jewett (1975), p. 142.

5   See Bruce (1982), pp. 187–91. For criticisms of the view that the Galatians formula seeks also to abolish social and biological differences between the sexes see Fiorenza (1983), pp. 211–14.

6   *Adelphoi*, 'brothers', includes *adelphai*, 'sisters', following Greek grammar (cf. above p. 46) and Jewish idiom. This 'inclusive' use of 'brother(s)' is common in both Gospels and Epistles (e.g. Matt. 5.22–4, 18.15; Luke 22.32; Rom. 1.13, 12.1; 1 Cor. 1.10). See further Ch. 5, n. 3.

7   So Kapp, in *ISBE* 1 and Shroyer in *IDB* 1, both *s.v.* Aquila (thus acknowledging Priscilla's leadership while still discussing her under her husband's name!).

8   *Hom. in Rom.*, *ad loc.*; cf. Cranfield (1975–79), pp. 788f. Brooten (1977), pp. 141–4, notes that Origen, Jerome, Theophylact and Abelard all understood this name as feminine; it was not until Aegidius of Rome (1245–1316) that it was taken as masculine.

9   Barrett (1962), p. 284 (who, however, assumed the name to be masculine).

10 See Lampe (1961), and the other standard lexicons *s.v.* On Phoebe's senior role cf. also Prohl (1957), pp. 70f.; Cranfield (1975–79), pp. 780–3; Horsley (1981–87), vol. IV pp. 239–44 (on a fourth century epitaph of 'a second Phoebe').

11 Some scholars believe that Rom. 16 is displaced and may refer to another phase of Paul's ministry (e.g. at Ephesus): see Barrett (1962), pp. 281f. (criticizing the view); but this would not affect our argument.

12 So Barrett (1971), pp. 154f.

13 cf. Williams (1977), pp. 52–62, 145; Fee (1987), pp. 266–357.

14 The verb used of women, *hypotassomai*, 'subject yourselves', is weaker than *hypakouō*, 'obey', used of children and slaves.

15 Murphy-O'Connor (1980), pp. 482–500, suggests homosexuality may have been a problem; Fiorenza (1983), pp. 227f. sees a possible relation to mystery cults; see further Murphy-O'Connor (1976); Fee (1987), p. 492, discussing the possibility that 11.2–14 may be non-Pauline.

16 The idea that *akatakalyptos* might mean 'with loosed hair' has been

supported from Num. 5.18; but whatever the original Hebrew meant, the Greek version was taken by both Josephus, *Ant.* 3.270 and Philo, *De Spec. Leg.* 3.56 to mean with bared head. For evidence that respectable married women normally covered their heads in public see Jeremias (1969) pp. 359f. (on Judaism); Conzelmann (1975), pp. 184f. (on Graeco-Roman customs). Paul probably intended a kerchief or shawl, rather than a full-scale veil.

17 Hayter (1987), p. 123; Hooker (1963–4), pp. 410–16; Barrett (1971), pp. 253–5.

18 cf. Williams (1977), p. 64, quoting Sir William Ramsay.

19 See Bedale (1954) (arguing for 'source'); Grudem (1985) (arguing for 'head'); Kroeger (1986a), adducing fresh evidence from the Greek OT and Church Fathers for 'source'. But the basic thrust of the passage is not dependent on the precise translation of this word: see further the varying interpretations of 'source' in Mickelsen (ed.), (1986), pp. 97–132.

20 See Hurley (1981), esp. pp. 160f.; Saward (1978), p. 7; see further below pp. 144f.

21 See Jewett (1975), pp. 119–28; Raming (1976), pp. 111f.; Gibson (1981), vol. I, p. 86 suggesting that Paul is bringing 'a huge theological hammer to crack a tiny social nut'.

22 So Hayter (1987), p. 124, and many others. Padgett (1984) argues that vv.10–12 not only modify but contradict vv.4–7. He suggests that in vv.4–7 Paul is summarizing the Corinthians' own ideas, and in the later verses giving his own views, which involve both the equality of men and women and the right of women to decide how they dress their heads. But his explanation strains the text, and involves a number of novel interpretations.

23 cf. Barrett (1971), pp. 330f.; Conzelmann (1974), p. 246; Fee (1987), pp. 699–705.

24 See, for example, Hanson (1982); Kelly (1963), still maintains Pauline authorship.

25 So Payne (1986), noting Chrysostom's use of *authenteō* to mean 'play the despot'; Knight (1984), pp. 143–57, argued for a neutral meaning. See also Kroeger (1979), and (1986b) (with the Response there). The verb occurs here only in the NT.

26 On the social context see further Padgett (1987).

5

Women and Ministry in the New Testament

'There is no such thing as *the* New Testament Church Order'. These words from Eduard Schweizer in his seminal work on this subject[1] serve as a warning to anyone seeking to extract from the New Testament any single principle of how the Christian Church should be organized. Numerous scholars have commented on the dangers of Christians looking at the New Testament and finding their own denomination's ecclesial organization. The reason for this does not lie entirely in the ability of interpreters to deceive themselves. Modern scholarship has shown that there were within the New Testament communities different forms of ministry, some free and charismatic, others more formal and structured. Organization clearly varied from place to place: what was true for the Church at Corinth was not necessarily true for the Church at Jerusalem. Nor did ministry remain static during the period from Jesus' first call of the disciples to the expansion of the Church into the Gentile world. The purpose of this chapter is to consider the broad patterns of New Testament ministry, the ideals which inspired them, and their significance for women.

VARIETIES OF MINISTRY IN THE NEW TESTAMENT

In the Gospels there are references to disciples and apostles, including groups known as 'the Twelve' and 'the Seventy'. These are not 'ministers' in the modern sense of the term, but rather companions of Jesus, who learn from him and are sent out by him. It is Jesus himself who is the minister *par excellence*, combining qualities of teacher, prophet, servant, and king. The Twelve (all men) stand especially close to him: according to Mark 3.13–19 they are called 'to be with him' and are sent out with authority to preach the Gospel and to cast out demons. They witness his healing miracles, are present at the Last Supper, and receive a special commission from the risen Christ (Luke 24.36–49; Matt. 28.16–20; John 20.19–23). The Seventy (or Seventy-two – the manuscripts vary) are mentioned once only (Luke 10.1–20); they too are sent out to heal and to preach with a 'mission charge' closely similar to that of the Twelve.[2] Among the Twelve Peter acts as spokesman, and receives special charges to 'bind and to loose' (Matt. 16.17–19), to 'strengthen his brothers' (Luke 22.31f.), and to 'feed Christ's sheep' (John 21.15–17).

Acts also refers to apostles and disciples (note the woman disciple at 9.36), to 'the Seven' who assist the Twelve, to prophets, teachers, elders, and many informal leaders, both men and women, in whose houses the early Church met. It is striking that while Acts mentions women who 'prophesy' (21.9) and one woman who teaches (18.24–8), the Church's public leaders appear to be men. In addressing the assembled Christian body (1.16; 2.14) Peter says '*andres adelphoi*' (Christian men) rather than simply *adelphoi*.[3]

The Pauline letters use a very varied vocabulary for those who minister, ranging from general expressions like 'those who admonish you' (1 Thess. 5.12) to more specific terms such as 'overseers' (*episkopoi*) and 'deacons' (*diakonoi*) (Phil. 1.1). These last reappear in the Pastorals, which presuppose the most developed structure of ministry in the New Testament; the Pastorals also mention 'elders' (*presbyteroi*), without making it clear how they relate to the 'overseers'. 1 Peter (5.1) and 2 and 3 John both use the title 'elder'; James mentions both teachers and elders (3.1; 5.14).

Ephesians makes it clear that ministry arises from the gifts of the ascended Christ. It says specifically (4.11) that he gave some to be apostles, some prophets, some evangelists, some shepherds and teachers. 1 Corinthians 12 and Romans 12 also emphasize the importance of spiritual gifts, referring to their exercise by members of the community in many different ways, including prophecy, service, encouragement, teaching, administration, and miracle-working. Romans 16 mentions by name a large number of leading Christians, calling them 'fellow-labourers', 'servants of Christ', 'brother', 'sister', or simply those who 'work hard in the Lord' (cf. above pp. 57f.)

MINISTRY AS BELONGING TO THE WHOLE PEOPLE OF GOD

A remarkable feature of New Testament Church organization is the lack of any distinction between *clergy* and *laity*. Paul sees the gifts of the Spirit as given to the whole community. 1 Peter likewise stresses that all Christians are part of the people of God, describing them as a 'holy priesthood' (*hierateuma hagion*), called to offer spiritual sacrifices (1 Pet. 2.5; cf. also Heb. 13.15; Rev. 1.6; 5.10). In stirring words addressed to women and men, Gentiles and Jews, slaves and free, the author proclaims: 'You are a chosen race, a royal priesthood, a holy nation, God's own people, that you may declare the wonderful deeds of him who called you out of darkness into his marvellous light' (1 Pet. 2.9f. RSV). It is worth stressing that the title *hiereus* (used of pagan as well as Jewish priests) is never applied in the New Testament to any Christian minister: it is reserved for Christ, the only High Priest of the Christian profession, who gave himself as a perfect and unrepeatable sacrifice for sin (Heb. 4.14–10.22, esp. 7.27; 9.12; cf. Rom. 6.10, etc.). It follows that the Jewish priesthood, with its elaborate sacrificial system, is superseded for Christians. This is the central theme of the Epistle to the Hebrews, and there is no reason to think that other New Testament writers took different views. This fulfilment and supersession of Jewish priesthood in Christ is bound to have important repercussions for Christian women.

But although all receive spiritual gifts, not all perform the same tasks. Some are commissioned for particular functions. Again one notes the wide variety of call and commission. The Twelve were called by Jesus himself in his human life-time. Paul encountered the risen Christ in a visionary experience: three days later he was baptized, healed and endowed with the Spirit through the laying on of hands by a 'disciple' named Ananias (Acts 9.1–22). He immediately started preaching in

Damascus. Later Paul had hands laid on him again, together with Barnabas, to set him apart for his first missionary journey (Acts 13.2f.). This commissioning, for a particular function, was carried out, after prayer and fasting, by the *prophets* and *teachers* of Antioch.

In Acts 6.1–6 seven men are appointed by the apostles in Jerusalem to provide for the material needs of the Greek-speaking widows. There is no hint that this is a permanent 'ordination' resulting in ontological change, but rather the giving of authority for a particular task. Only two of the Seven are mentioned again – Stephen and Philip – who are found, not administering food or finance, but working miracles, preaching, and baptizing; Acts later refers to Philip as 'the evangelist' (Acts 6–8; 21.8). In Acts 14.23 Paul and Barnabas appoint elders in the Churches they visit. In 1 Tim. 4.14 Timothy is reminded of the spiritual gift he received when the *prophets* spoke and the *body of elders* laid their hands on him.

All this suggests fluidity in the theology of ministry and flexibility in its practice: the New Testament nowhere prescribes who should baptize, or preside at the Lord's Supper, or lay on hands. It is evident that these activities are not restricted to 'apostles': Paul indicates that he does not regard baptism as central to his apostolic ministry (1 Cor. 1.14–17). He nowhere mentions his presiding at the Lord's Supper, and in dealing with abuses at Corinth addresses his remarks to the congregation there rather than to any specific leaders. Luke, in a generalized and perhaps idealized picture of the early Jerusalem Church, speaks of the new converts as devoting themselves 'to the apostles' teaching and fellowship, to the breaking of bread and the prayers' (Acts 2.42f. RSV). But one should not assume from this that all teaching was carried out by the apostles or that they alone presided at the Lord's Supper. Just before this, Luke says that 3000 people had been converted and baptized. Luke also mentions (Acts 2.46) that the first Christians 'broke bread' in private houses (which would be unable to accommodate very large gatherings). It has recently been suggested[4] that the most natural 'president' at these early gatherings might be the host or hostess in whose house the Church met (see Philem. 2; Col. 4.15; Rom. 16.5; 1 Cor. 16.19, referring to Philemon, Nympha, and Prisca and Aquila), though this remains conjectural.

Within this broad pattern of shared ministry certain functions seem to have been restricted wholly or mostly to men. We have already noted that there were no women among the Twelve (when Judas died, he was replaced by another male), nor among the Seven (often seen as the first 'deacons'), nor, it is generally believed, among the *presbyteroi* and *episkopoi*, the precursors of the later priests and bishops. For those who emphasize the continuity of the present Church with its New Testament antecedents, these are important points, and we need to consider them carefully.

THE SIGNIFICANCE OF THE MALE APOSTLES

The role of the Twelve Apostles is crucial for the debate. Thus the Roman Catholic scholar J. Galot claims that only men were present with Jesus at the Last Supper, and that it is 'to the Twelve and to them alone that he willed to impart the power to offer the Eucharist in his memory'.[5] Galot also insists that Jesus entrusted only men with the mission to evangelize the nations (Matt. 28.16–20), thus revealing his will to establish 'the definitive structure of pastoral authority in the Church'. The Reformed theologian J.-J. von Allmen, arguing against women's ordination to the pastoral ministry, similarly claims: 'To no woman does he [Jesus] make the promise to ratify in heaven what she has bound or loosed on earth'.[6]

But such views may be challenged on several grounds. First, how can we be sure that historically no women were present on the occasions in question? If the Last Supper was a Passover meal, then it is likely that Jesus' mother was there, and possibly other women; for the Jewish Passover was a family occasion.[7] It is also possible that women were present at the resurrection appearance when Jesus authorized his followers to declare the forgiveness of sins (John 20.19–23). John nowhere indicates that these words were confined to Apostles, but speaks of the *disciples* being gathered together (20.19); Luke's parallel passage relates how the two to whom Jesus had revealed himself at Emmaus returned to Jerusalem and 'found the Eleven assembled together *with their companions*' (Luke 24.33). These 'companions' might well have included Mary and some of the other women, who, we are told in Acts 1.14, gathered with the apostles in prayer.

Secondly, as a general point, caution needs to be exercised in building theological conclusions on the precise wording of these important Gospel events. There are considerable differences in the New Testament accounts of Jesus' 'words of institution' at the Last Supper, and major problems over the chronology, locations, and nature of his resurrection appearances and the form of his final mission charge. One may reasonably assume that Jesus intended to found a community and to make provision for its future activities; but did he intend a hierarchical organization? Traditionally in Roman Catholicism (and elsewhere) Jesus' words at the Last Supper have been seen as inaugurating a priestly ministry, just as his words in John 20.22 have been seen as instituting the sacrament of penance, or at least the authority of future bishops and priests to forgive and retain sins.[8] New Testament exegetes have problems with such views. The bulk of the evidence suggests that Jesus was not interested in founding a hierarchy, but rather something more akin to a family, whose members serve one another. Teaching on servanthood occurs at least six times in the Gospels, ascribed to some four separate occasions: Jesus rebuked those who sought 'chief places' or disputed who was the greatest: 'the kings of the Gentiles lord it over them; and those who exercise authority over them call themselves Benefactors. But you are not to be like that' (Luke 22.24–6 NIV). Lohfink has drawn attention to the solemnity with which he speaks of his disciples as brothers and sisters (Mark 3.32–5) and tells them that they must not be called 'rabbi' or 'teacher' or address anyone on earth as 'father' (Matt. 23.8–12).[9] These sayings on servanthood and the family of believers are widely recognized by New Testament scholars as an authentic core of Jesus' teaching.[10]

What then are we to make of Jesus' references to the authority of Peter and the Twelve? Assuming that these commissions also go back to a historical core, did he intend them to stand for future bishops and clergy, or for the Church as a whole? It is here that denominational allegiance can so easily colour exegesis. To determine Jesus' intentions, we need to look as objectively as we can at the key passages in their contexts.

The words of John 20.23: 'Whose soever sins ye forgive, they are forgiven unto them; whose soever sins ye retain, they are retained' (RV) are closely paralleled by Jesus' words to Peter in Matthew 16.19: 'Whatsoever thou shalt bind on earth shall be bound in heaven; and whatsoever thou shalt loose on earth shall be loosed in heaven' (RV). They are also very similar to some solemn words spoken to a wider group of disciples with reference to dealing with a 'brother' who has sinned: 'What things soever ye shall bind on earth shall be bound in heaven; and what things soever ye shall loose on earth shall be loosed in heaven' (Matt. 18.18 RV). These sayings all contain the same poetic parallelism and Semitic idiom; many scholars believe that all three go back to the same original saying based on Isa. 22.22: 'I will place on his shoulder the key of the house of David; he shall open, and none shall shut; and he shall shut, and none shall open' (RSV). They also have striking parallels in rabbinic terminology. Some have doubted whether the historical Jesus would ever have spoken in this way and believe that all the sayings arose in the post-Easter Church.[11] But they are paralleled by further, surely authentic, sayings in which Jesus speaks of the authority of those whom he sends or who are received in his name (e.g. John 13.20; Matt. 10.40; Mark 9.37; Luke 10.16). They can be seen as a special instance of the power of prayer, recalling Jesus' more general teaching, especially 'if you have faith, everything you ask for in prayer you will receive' (Matt. 21.22; cf. Mark 11.24f., where the saying is linked with teaching on forgiveness).[12] Compare also the continuation of Jesus' words in Matthew 18.19: 'If two of you on earth agree about anything you ask for, it will be done for you by my Father in heaven' (NIV).

The most plausible interpretation of this complex evidence is that Jesus intended those commissioned to symbolize the whole Church or community of believers, bidden by their Lord to continue the fellowship meal which he instituted, and empowered by the gift of the Spirit to proclaim the forgiveness of sins (cf. Luke 24.47; Acts 1.8f.). In a real sense John 20.22f. is the Johannine equivalent of both Pentecost, when the Spirit fell on women as well as men (Acts 2.17f.), and Matthew's 'Great Commission' (28.16–20), which has inspired Christian missionaries of both sexes throughout the centuries (Galot and others are surely mistaken in restricting the application of this to the Eleven). The view that the Twelve stand for the future Church as the new, or restored, Israel is further supported by their symbolic number, corresponding to the twelve tribes, and the saying in Matthew 19.28 and Luke 22.30 (where their eschatological role, sitting on thrones and judging, should be compared with that of all the 'saints', i.e. people of God, in 1 Cor. 6.2 and Rev. 5.10). This representative role of the Twelve as the nucleus of the new Israel might in itself have been sufficient to deter Jesus from choosing females, though it is likely that there were also practical reasons.

To say all this is not to deny that the Twelve became important leaders, or that in them, and especially in Peter, we have models for future pastoral ministry. But one needs to guard against an over-simplified view, in which the Apostles are seen as the direct source of all ordained ministry. The New Testament recognizes their significance for the foundation of the Church (cf. Eph. 2.20; Rev. 21.14), but they were not its unique ministers nor its only missionaries. The popular picture of the Twelve as travelling to all the quarters of the earth is largely the product of apocryphal works.[13] The canonical Acts recounts in detail activities of only two of them (Peter and John), preferring to tell of other leaders, especially Paul. It is noteworthy that when Herod executed James, the son of Zebedee (one of the original Twelve) he was not replaced (Acts 12.2).

In this context it is worth saying a little more about the title 'apostle', which was applied to others (including possibly a woman) besides the Twelve (see above p. 58). The name means literally 'one sent'.[14] In John the word occurs only once, in a general sense (John 13.16); Mark too has only one certain occurrence (6.30), and here too the meaning may not be technical.[15] Matthew also only once calls the Twelve 'apostles' (10.2), like Mark and John preferring the term 'disciples'. It is Luke who stresses the importance of the apostles, using the title six times in his Gospel and twenty-eight times in Acts, and he may have idealized their role. But he nowhere grounds their significance in their maleness; it is something he simply takes for granted as part of the church organization of his day.

WERE THERE EXCLUSIVELY MALE BISHOPS, PRIESTS AND DEACONS?

The second group of New Testament ministries in which it is claimed that women are significantly absent is that of *episkopoi*, *presbyteroi*, and *diakonoi*. It needs to be said at once that these ministries do not form a separate and distinct group from apostleship or other New Testament ministries. The word *episkopos* (from which English 'bishop' is etymologically derived) simply means 'one who oversees or superintends', and it may have been adopted into the Church from the Graeco-Roman world.[16] It appears to be virtually synonymous with *presbyteros*, 'older man' or 'elder', though one should be wary of assuming that the terms were interchangeable.[17] The title *presbyteros* seems to have been taken over from Judaism, where it is used for elders in the Old Testament, for members of the Jerusalem Sanhedrin, and for local religious leaders. The *presbyteroi* and *episkopoi* of the Jewish and Graeco-Roman world were male, and it is likely that the early Christian leaders of the same name were also male. It is, however, worth remembering that grammatically these terms can include the feminine (cf. above p. 46), and in recent years fresh evidence has come to light for women synagogue-leaders in the Jewish dispersion (see above Ch. 2, n. 6). It is possible that some congregations might have had women elders (cf. the *presbytides* of Titus 2.3, though this text is perhaps more readily interpreted as referring to informal office).[18] The important point, however, is not whether there were occasionally women elders or overseers, but rather whether the New Testament gives any indication of theological reasons for excluding them. The only possible grounds would seem to be the Pauline limitations on women teaching and exercising authority, which we have already argued (in Ch. 4) were motivated by cultural and local considerations. It should be added that the New Testament nowhere prohibits women from baptizing, or presiding at the Lord's Supper, or pronouncing the forgiveness of sins, so that the apparent New Testament custom of having only male overseers and presbyters is rather less relevant than sometimes supposed to the ordination of women to these forms of ministry.

It remains to say a few words on deacons (*diakonoi*). The term is a regular one in secular literature for a servant, especially someone waiting at table. In the past the fact that the Seven appointed to 'serve tables' (Acts 6.1–6) were all male was used to argue against the ordination of women to the diaconate. But the New Testament never calls the Seven 'deacons',[19] whereas Phoebe in Romans 16.1f. is unequivocally described as a *diakonos* – the same term as is used elsewhere of men – and it is evident that she is in a position of leadership in the Church (cf. above pp. 58f.). As Lightfoot long ago observed, it is illogical to assume that Phil. 1.1 refers to office, but not Rom. 16.1. The *diakonoi* of Philippians may well have included women. It is now widely thought that 1 Timothy 3.11 also refers to women deacons.[20]

It is clear from this survey that the New Testament nowhere prescribes a uniform pattern for Church organization and government, but rather suggests variety and adaptability to the local situation. Even the Pastoral Epistles, which come closest to laying down guide-lines for the choice of ministers, are geared to a particular social and theological context, and we may doubt whether their seemingly twofold pattern of overseers/elders and deacons was intended as a model for all time. Churches practising episcopal, presbyteral, congregational, and charismatic forms of ministry can all find precedents in the New Testament; but none may fairly claim to preserve its *sole* pattern.

The real problem with searching the New Testament to find justification for any particular form of ministry, whether for men or for women, is the risk of imposing on it anachronistic views and modern categories of thought. This applies to all forms of ministry, but perhaps especially to that of the Apostles, who have so often been interpreted as models for future clergy. It needs to be emphasized that as companions to Jesus and witnesses to his resurrection they fulfilled a unique and unrepeatable ministry. Richard Hanson has rightly commented: 'to identify the apostles with bishops or priests, or to imagine that they instituted ministers of religion as we know them is to commit a grave historical error'.[21] This means that if the ordination of women to clerical ministry is to be justified in the present-day Churches, the grounds for it must lie not in historical precedents (e.g. the 'deacon' Phoebe or the 'apostle'

Junia or the possibility of women presidents at house-eucharists), but in the essential nature of New Testament ministry.

WOMEN AND THE NEW TESTAMENT IDEALS OF MINISTRY

The first, and perhaps the most important, feature of New Testament ministry is that it is a divine gift. Like the discipleship that arose in response to Jesus' summons, it is utterly dependent on the call of God, and its effectiveness comes from the gifts of the Spirit, imparted to different members of the community for the common good (cf. Rom. 12.4–13; 1 Cor. 12.4–11; Eph. 4.11f.). In none of these passages on spiritual gifts is any distinction made between men and women; throughout the New Testament women, as well as men, are called to discipleship and to witness to their faith.

Secondly, New Testament ministry is corporate, shared by the whole community – both women and men – called to be God's holy people. The Jerusalem apostles and elders act collegially with the whole Church (Acts 15.22; cf. 1.15ff.). When Paul perceives a problem over immoral behaviour at Corinth, he urges the whole Church to assemble together to take action (1 Cor. 5.4f.). He expresses appreciation of the work of fellow-labourers, both male and female (Rom. 16). It is true that some, like the apostles and elders, have special responsibilities for leadership, and that these leaders were normally men. But we should not read into their roles nor into such terms as *hoi hēgoumenoi*, 'those who lead' (Heb. 13.7, 17, 24), or the use of the verb *proistēmi*, 'be in charge' (Rom. 12.8; 1 Thess. 5.12; 1 Tim. 5.17), connotations of hierarchy and authoritarianism (note Rom. 16.2, where the noun *prostatis* is used of a woman). This collegial nature of ministry must surely go a long way towards removing difficulties felt by some about women exercising 'authority' over men, especially as all Christian authority is derived from Christ, and is not the individual's own.

This brings us to the third characteristic: all New Testament ministry is rooted in Jesus himself. He is described as the 'apostle and high-priest' of our confession (Heb. 3.1), the shepherd (pastor) and guardian (bishop) of our souls (1 Pet. 2.25), the true teacher (Matt. 23.10; cf. 1 John 2.27), and prophet and herald of the Gospel (Luke 4.18; Acts 3.22). Although roles of this kind were normally associated with men in the ancient world, nowhere is Jesus' fulfilment of them directly related to or dependent on his male sexuality. When Paul describes himself as Christ's ambassador (2 Cor. 5.20; Philem. 9; cf. Eph. 6.20), the picture brought to his readers' mind would no doubt be of a man; but there is no reason in principle why a woman should not be sent as an ambassador: compare Jesus' sending of Mary Magdalene to his 'brothers', or Paul's own commendation of Phoebe, who was possibly the bearer of his letter to the Romans. Many of Jesus' authoritative commissions have a wide application (cf. above pp. 78f., and n. 2 on Matt. 10, etc.).

Christ is also the Servant. Several different Greek words are involved here. (1) Sometimes (e.g. Acts 3.13; 4.27) Jesus is referred to as God's *pais*, a term which can also mean a child, but which here recalls the 'suffering servant' (*pais*) of Isa. 52.13. (2) In Phil. 2.7 Christ is described as taking the form of a servant (*doulos*), literally 'a slave' – a symbol for extreme humility. At Luke 22.27 Jesus refers to himself as *ho diakonōn*, 'the one who serves'. All of these words can ordinarily be used of both males and females. The New Testament never applies *pais* to a Christian minister as such, but apostles and other church leaders regularly use *doulos* as a title for themselves (e.g. Rom. 1.1; Jas. 1.1; 2 Pet. 1.1; Rev. 1.1), and the word is used in a religious sense of the Virgin Mary (Luke 1.38, 48) and of Christian men and women in general (Acts 2.18). The verb *diakoneō* and its cognate nouns are applied to women's service, both secular and religious (e.g. Matt. 8.15; Luke 8.3; John 12.2; Rom. 16.1). Jesus' own *diakonia* sets the pattern for Christian ministry, and we find the term used for preaching (Acts 6.4), reconciliation (2 Cor. 5.18), personal care of others (2 Tim. 4.11), and financial giving (Rom. 15.31; cf. Acts 6.2f.).

We conclude that there is nothing in the New Testament ideals and practice of ministry which in itself should exclude women from it, but rather many features which endorse and encourage their participation.[22] The barriers which have been

perceived stem from particular attitudes towards the male
apostolate and other ministries, and from developments in the
Church's understanding of ministry in post-biblical times, to
which we now turn.

NOTES

1 Schweizer (1961), p. 13.
2 cf. Matt. 10.1–15; Mark 6.7–13; Luke 9.1–6. Some scholars believe
   that the two charges are 'doublets' from a common source in 'Q' and
   reflect general instructions for Christian missionaries: see Marshall
   (1978), 412f.; Fitzmyer (1981–85), pp. 842–5.
3 Bruce (1952), p. 76, argues that *andres*, 'men', is 'otiose' and that in
   the original Aramaic Peter's words would have been inclusive (cf.
   Dalman (1902), p. 40). But although he may be right that *andres* was
   introduced by Luke here and elsewhere (e.g. Acts 1.11) as a touch of
   classical elegance, one does get the strong impression that Luke
   envisaged the Christian leaders in council as all male.
4 So Dunn and Mackey (1987), p. 135, writing: 'there is nothing in any
   of our texts to counter the most obvious implication: that when the
   Lord's Supper was celebrated, it would have been the host(ess) who in
   the course of the common meal reminded his or her guests of the words
   first said by Jesus on the night on which he was betrayed'. Cf. also
   Nunally-Cox (1981), p. 128; Best (1988), p. 155.
5 Galot (1985), pp. 255f., following RC tradition.; for a similar Orthodox
   view see Ware (1978), pp. 75f.
6 Von Allmen (1963), in Lutge, (n.d.) p. 35.
7 Note that Jesus requires a *large* room (Mark 14.15). On the nature of
   the Last Supper see Jeremias (1966), and Marshall (1980a).
8 cf. the Council of Trent and Vatican II, esp. *Lumen Gentium*, §§ 19–28
   (in Abbott and Gallagher (1966), pp. 38–55); also the BCP Ordinal
   (Consecration of Bishops). See further Brown (1971), pp. 1023–45.
9 Lohfink (1985), pp. 43–50.
10 See Mark 9.35 (par. Matt. 18.1–5; Luke 9.46–8) – teaching following
   the first dispute as to who is the greatest; Mark 10.45 (par. Matt.
   20.26–8) – following James' and John's request for 'chief places';
   Matt. 23.11 – following a denunciation of the ostentatious piety of the
   scribes and Pharisees; Luke 22.26f. – a response to another dispute
   about greatness; and John 13.4–16 – washing of the disciples' feet as an
   example of humble service. The sheer frequency with which this
   teaching has been recorded shows its centrality to Jesus' message.
11 cf. Schweizer (1976), p. 336; Barrett (1978), pp. 568–71; Beare
   (1981), p. 380. Many NT scholars believe that Matt.'s account of Jesus'
   committal of the 'power of the keys' to Peter originated in the
   Aramaic-speaking Church (see Hill (1972), pp. 259–62; Beare (1981),
   pp. 353f., and note Mark's and Luke's shorter and very different
   version.). See further Cullmann (1953), esp. pp. 155–238; also Barrett
   (1985), ch. 1.

12 cf. Hill (1972), pp. 276f.; see also Dodd (1963), pp. 343–52.

13 The role of the Apostles as teachers was also much enhanced in later times. See Hennecke (1965), chs 11–15.

14 cf. Greek: *apostellō*. Some derive the NT usage from the rabbinic *shaliach* (also literally 'one sent'), who acted as an authoritative agent (see Lampe (1949), pp. 9–14); but this is uncertain.

15 In Mark 3.14 the term is probably an addition from Luke; on this, and on 6.30, see Taylor (1966), pp. 230f., 318f.

16 In Greek literature and the papyri *episkopos* occurs for community officials (also as an epithet of male and female deities); in the LXX (Greek OT) it is used of military officers. The cognate abstract *episkopē* appears in Acts 1.20 (citing LXX) for the office of *apostle*. See further Moulton and Milligan (1930), and LSJ, *s.v. episkopos*.

17 See Lightfoot (1894), pp. 193f., and note Titus 1.5 beside 1.7; 1 Tim. 3.2 beside 4.14, 5.17; Acts 20.17 beside 28. Paul never uses *presbyteros* of Christian leaders in his central letters, which casts some doubt on the accuracy of Acts 14.23. In the papyri *presbyteros* is a title for both civic and religious officials (see Moulton and Milligan (1930), *s.v.*).

18 The *presbytides* teach other women; their epithet *hieroprepeis*, 'as fitting those engaged in sacred service', suggests either ecclesial office or their sharing in the 'royal' priesthood of the Church, but hardly 'the natural priesthood of matrons' (Hanson (1982), p. 180 – a concept alien to the NT). See further below p. 98.

19 The verb *diakoneō* is used: see Haenchen (1971), pp. 259–69, esp. pp. 265f. In the papyri *diakonos* is used for pagan cultic officials.

20 Some think that 'the women' in 1 Tim. 3.11 are Christian women in general; but this is awkward in the context. Others suggest it means 'wives' (*gynē* means both woman and wife); but the absence of the possessive pronoun and of any corresponding qualification for bishops' wives argues against this. See Kelly (1963), pp. 83f.; Hanson (1982), pp. 80f.

21 Hanson (1979), p. 12; cf. W. H. Vanstone in Carey (1954), pp. 23–40.

22 Similar conclusions have been reached by theologians from a wide range of church traditions, including Küng (1972), p. 59; Hanson (1979), pp. 111–15; Schillebeeckx (1981), pp. 96–9; Green (1983), pp. 83–95; Boff (1986), pp. 76–97.

PART TWO

Developments

6

Women and the Ministry in the Church Fathers

The Patristic Age, following immediately after the New Testament period (c. AD 100 to 800), was a time of immense importance for the formulation and development of Church doctrine. It derives it name from the great 'Fathers' (Greek *pateres*, Latin *patres*) of the Greek, Latin and Eastern Churches who are endowed with special authority in some parts of Christendom. During this period Christianity developed from being an offshoot or reform movement of Judaism into a distinct faith with its own organization – at first subject to persecution, but later, under Constantine, recognized as the official religion of the Roman Empire. It was also the period of the great 'Oecumenical Councils', responsible for formulating what became orthodox doctrine in the face of christological and other controversies. The patristic doctrines of ministry and sacraments, and patristic pronouncements on the role of women, shaped the attitudes of the medieval and later Church, and are still being cited in the debate over women's roles today. For this reason we need to give them careful attention.

GENERAL ATTITUDES TO WOMEN

The teaching of the Fathers on women is not to be found in systematic and consistent theological expositions, but rather scattered throughout a voluminous collection of writings – sermons, biblical commentaries, polemical works, doctrinal treatises on other topics – which, together with canons, synodical decrees and other constitutional documents, form the raw material for studying patristic thought. Attitudes to women and the ministries permitted to them were by no means identical in all parts of the Church. Individual Fathers often differed in their biblical interpretations, and even within the writings of a single author there are sometimes inconsistencies. This means that any outline of their views is bound to be simplified, but in what follows we will seek to summarize them fairly.

The most charitable assessment of patristic attitudes to women is that they were ambivalent.[1] The Fathers recognized that women are capable of receiving salvation. They acknowledged that they could be endowed with spiritual gifts, including theological understanding and – exceptionally – Biblical expertise. They praised and encouraged those who practised the virtue of 'continence', living ascetic lives as virgins or widows, and whose courageous faith sometimes led to death by martyrdom. But at the same time they saw women as weak in body and intellect, prone to sin and heresy, sexually provocative and potentially a danger to devout Christian men. While some 'heretical' groups allowed women considerable freedom and religious leadership, the doctrinally 'orthodox' seem to have assumed that they should be excluded from public teaching and almost all forms of religious leadership.

The reasons for these attitudes involve three factors.

(1) First, the Fathers were the products of a social system which regarded women as inherently lacking in authority and subordinate to men, both in marriage and in public life. In the fourth century BC Aristotle had accepted female subordination as in accordance with nature, and his views strongly influenced Christian thinkers, as did those of the Stoic, Neopythagorean and Neoplatonist philosophers (who regularly sought to reinforce the subjection of women). In spite of some progress towards 'liberation', women's subordination remained encoded in Roman civil law (cf. above p. 19 and n. 14, on Gaius, Ulpian, and Justinian). It is, therefore, hardly surprising that the Fathers accepted women's subjection to men as both natural and universal.[2] Sometimes they explicitly argued from the civil subjection of women to their spiritual subordination. Ambrosiaster (c. fourth century), for example, maintained that women are not even made in God's image in the same way as men: 'How can it be said of woman that she is the image of God when

she is manifestly subject to man as her master and has no authority? For she can neither teach, nor be a witness in court, nor take an oath, nor be a judge; how much more then is she incapable of ruling!'

(2) Secondly, the Fathers found support for their views from the subordinationist passages of Scripture, resorting to ingenious explanations of more equalitarian texts in order to harmonize the two. Naturally, in their exegesis they adopted the methodology and presuppositions of their age. For example, they understood the creation narratives of Genesis 1–3 as a unified account, written by a single author (Moses), and as literally true. Woman, being made from Adam's rib and as a 'helper' for him, was seen as designed by God to be subordinate to man. By being tempted first, Eve was the archetypal sinner, and sufficient reason for castigating all women as temptresses and a source of evil. Following Jewish intertestamental tradition, blame for the fall of humanity was laid squarely on *Eve*, rather than Adam, and her supposed conduct in the garden of Eden was used as a justification for both the general subjection of women to men and their enforced silence in church. It is in this context that we must understand Tertullian's bitter words to women: 'You are the Devil's gateway; you violated that tree; you first deserted the divine law; you it was who persuaded him whom the Devil could not assail; you willingly destroyed the man Adam, the image of God; because of the death which you deserved, the Son of God had to die'.[3] We shall see later (in Ch. 10) that such literal and misogynistic interpretations fail lamentably to do justice to the intentions of Genesis.

The Fathers not unnaturally also assumed that the Creation narratives must be read in the light of the Pauline Epistles, and some of them wrestled hard to harmonize the statement in Genesis 1.26f., that both male and female were created in God's image, with Paul's apparent teaching (1 Cor. 11.7) that women stand in a different relationship to God from men (see above pp. 65f.). The tension can be seen in Augustine's teaching on the nature of humanity, which he reaches by means of an allegorizing interpretation of Scripture. On the one hand, he argues that although Eve's body was made from Adam's, her soul was independent of his – a view which surely implies some kind of spiritual equality; yet at the same time he believed that the human soul has two elements, one masculine, devoting itself to eternal truths, and one feminine, providing for earthly needs. Just as the 'male' element of the soul guides the 'female', so in this life men must guide women. The corollary of this dualistic doctrine of the soul (quite unfounded in biblical teaching) is that men are by their nature more concerned with the spiritual, and women with the physical and sensual. This stereotyping of the sexes was to have a profound influence on later Christian thought to the detriment of women's spiritual leadership. It is summed up in the dictum of the medieval scholar Peter Lombard, in his exegesis of 1 Timothy: 'Woman is the type of the flesh, Adam (i.e. man) the type of understanding'.[4] Thus Augustine taught it is by 'natural law' that women serve men; he dealt with the tension between Gen. 1.26f. and 1 Cor. 11.7 by arguing that women stand in the image of God only through their husbands – in spite of the clear statement in Genesis that both male and female are created in the image of God.[5]

Sometimes dubious biblical exegesis was backed up with suspect philology or erroneous biology. Thus Ambrose derived the Latin word for woman, *mulier*, from *mollities mentis* (softness of mind), contrasting it with the derivation of *vir*, man, from *animi virtus*, meaning strength of soul. Along with Aristotle, he believed that the male was the norm and ideal of the human species, but argued that women who believe could progress to become like males. Alluding to Eph. 4.13 where Christians are promised they will become the 'perfect man' in knowledge of the Son of God, he writes: 'She who does not believe is a woman and is still designated by the name of her bodily sex, whereas she who believes progresses to perfect manhood (*occurrit in virum perfectum*), fully mature with the fulness of Christ; she now dispenses with her worldly name and her bodily sex, both the seductiveness of youth, and the talkativeness of old age'. What Ambrose fails to realize is that in the original Greek text the word for 'man' (*anēr*) is used generically, as a symbol of maturity, in contrast to *nēpios* ('infant', 'minor') in v.14, and without any specific reference to masculinity.[6] Augustine also had difficulty with this text, and put forward an ingenious explanation that in the resurrected state there would be no procreation; and so women – who he believed only *helped* men in begetting children – would be truly *homo* (human), and no longer ancillary and subordinate to males.[7] One is reminded of the episode in the apocryphal Gospel of Thomas, when Peter asks that Mary might leave them for 'women are not worthy of life'. Jesus replies: 'I myself shall lead her, in order to make her male, so that she too may become a living spirit resembling you males. For every woman who will make herself male will enter the Kingdom of Heaven'.[8] Traditionalist Christians are often critical of Gnostic distortions of the Christian faith; it is not always appreciated how perilously close some 'orthodox' Fathers come to misrepresenting it.

(3) A third major reason why the Fathers so strongly endorsed female subordination was their ascetic and generally negative attitude to the body and human sexuality. They interpreted the natural feminine functions of menstruation and childbirth as part of the curse on Eve for her sin. Many of them, under influence of the monastic movement, whereby both women and men took to the desert to escape from 'the world' and live as hermits or in strictly regulated communities, despised 'the flesh', seeing ordinary bodily desires of both male and female as something to be suppressed. They wore rough clothes, fasted extensively, and went without washing and anointing for long periods, denying themselves sleep, and abstaining from sexual relations or any close contact with the opposite sex. In contrast to the Old Testament attitude, which saw marriage and procreation as good, and children as a blessing from God, they treasured virginity above marriage. Drawing on Paul's advice in 1 Cor. 7 (written probably in expectation of an imminent 'second coming,' see above p. 60), they encouraged young girls to stay single, and married women to leave their husbands, or live with them 'in continence' as brother and sister. Both Augustine and Jerome were extremely negative towards feminine sexuality. At the time of his conversion Augustine wrote: 'There is nothing which I am more determined to avoid than relations with a woman. I feel that there is nothing which so degrades that high intelligence of a man than the embraces of a woman and the contact with her body, without which it is impossible to possess a wife'. It will be noted that Augustine's fear of the feminine extended even to relations within marriage; his ideal was procreation without

passion or the loss of female corporeal virginity, such as he postulated for the state of 'innocence' before the 'Fall'.[9]

Jerome thought that there was nothing more defiling than a woman with her monthly period (contrast Jesus' attitude to the haemorrhaging woman). He supported abstinence from sexual intercourse before receiving Holy Communion (implying belief in the uncleanness of the marital act), and taught that by withholding from sexual relations husbands 'honoured' their wives (despite 1 Cor. 7.5). He advised devout Christian men to keep away from even virtuous women; but he himself associated with a number of earnest Christian women, including his protegée Eustochium, whom he exhorted to fast daily, to rise at night to pray, to go rarely outside the house, and to mix with women pale and wan through fasting.[10] Marina Warner has observed that such rigorous fasting, which sometimes brought women to the verge of starvation, would have induced amenorrhea (absence of menstruation), thus eliminating completely the 'curse of Eve'.[11] By suppressing their feminine sexuality, virgins were seen as coming as close as possible to desirable masculinity, an idea summed up well in the words of Leander of Seville (c. 550–601): 'A virgin remains a woman, and yet knows nothing of the drives and compulsions of her sex. Forgetful of her feminine weakness, she lives in masculine strength; nor has she any need to become a slave to her body which by natural law should be subservient to a man.'[12]

To keep the balance, one must also record that some Fathers upheld marriage as good: Clement of Alexandria, though preferring celibacy, affirmed its relative goodness in the face of extreme Gnostic views that sexual relations were always evil. Elizabeth Clark describes his defence as 'the strongest argument for the goodness of marriage to be found in the writings of the first three Christian centuries'; but even she admits that it appears lukewarm.[13]

The Fathers also accorded high honour to Mary, the mother of Jesus; yet ironically their stress on her virginity and exceptional holiness served to emphasize the supposed frailty of ordinary women and to reinforce doubts about the acceptability before God of regular sexual relations in marriage.[14] However charitably one reads the Fathers, one cannot escape the conclusion that they regarded female sexuality as somehow sinful and degrading. The *Apostolic Constitutions* (6.27), a fourth-century compendium of church law, insisted that menstruating women are not devoid of the Holy Spirit, and that neither sexual intercourse, child-bearing nor menses defile. Pope Gregory the Great affirmed (in 601) that pregnant women could be baptized, and women allowed in church after childbirth and while menstruating; yet later in the same century Theodore of Tarsus, when Archbishop of Canterbury, insisted that menstruating women neither enter a church nor communicate, with a penalty of three days' fasting for offenders. A wide range of documents survives from the Latin Church, forbidding women to enter the sanctuary, touch sacred vessels or altar cloths (even to remove them for washing), or convey Communion to the sick, on the grounds that it was 'indecent and unfitting'. Thus, in spite of Gregory's affirmation, there is clear evidence that menstruation and childbirth were widely believed to be polluting and dangerous to the community, as they still are in some primal societies.[15] The idea that feminine bodily functions are a barrier to sacral service, or to handling the consecrated Elements, may be contrasted with Jesus' open attitude to women and ready acceptance of their anointing of his body (see above Ch. 3).

WOMEN AND PUBLIC MINISTRY

With such attitudes to women in general, it is not surprising that the Fathers denied them most forms of public ecclesial ministry. This was a natural corollary of their subordinate social status,[16] the prevalent views on feminine sexuality, and the patristic interpretations of Scripture. Their exclusion was further fostered by doctrinal developments affecting the priesthood and sacraments.

In Chapter 5 we drew attention to the wide variety of ministries and a diversity of practice in the New Testament communities. But such fluidity and informality were really only practicable as long as the Church remained small and uninstitutionalized. As it grew, it naturally became more tightly organized. In a highly structured and undemocratic society like the Roman Empire, ruled by a single autocratic ruler backed up by a bureaucracy, it is understandable that the Church should seek to imitate forms of authority familiar in the secular world.[17] The evolution of the 'monarchical' episcopate (i.e. single bishops as governors of individual dioceses with officially authorized clergy under them) and even the emergence of the papacy at Rome – the political capital of the Roman Empire – are readily explicable in historical terms. But they are hard to reconcile with the simplicity of the Gospel, its teaching about servanthood, and its understanding of the Christian community as a family of brothers and sisters who have only one 'father' in heaven.

Such changes did not happen overnight. In writings dating probably towards the end of the first century AD we can still observe varieties of practice. The *Didache* – a writing probably from Syria, pseudonymously attributed to the twelve Apostles – makes much of the ministry of teachers and prophets. This text also recognizes the existence of *episkopoi* and *diakonoi*, but suggests that *prophets* offered the Eucharistic Prayer (*Did.* 10.7; 13–15). Clement of Rome believed that the apostles established a *twofold* ministry of bishops and deacons, and contrived by use of a 'proof text' from Isaiah 60.17 (corresponding neither to the Greek nor Hebrew) to find a prophecy relating to this (1 Clem. 42). Ignatius of Antioch, on the other hand, writing probably only a little later, affirmed a *threefold* ministry of bishops, presbyters and deacons, asserting that nothing must be done independently of the bishop.[18] By the time of Hegesippus (c. 166) a 'monarchical' style of episcopate seems to have been practised at Rome, though even now bishops (*episkopoi*) are not totally distinguished from presbyters, as Irenaeus bears witness. Eventually the threefold 'order' (*ordo*) of bishops, presbyters and deacons became the norm for the Church. At the same time there developed a doctrine of 'apostolic succession' in which the apostles were seen as transmitting authority to successors, and a theology of the episcopate in which the bishop is the guardian of true doctrine and natural president of the Lord's Supper, delegating authority, where necessary, to other clergy.[19] Male deacons, now often personal assistants to bishops, exercised liturgical and financial responsibilities, and rules were laid down about such minor matters as seating arrangements and the order in which clergy received Holy Communion.[20] These developments constitute a substantial departure from the flexible and open patterns of ministry in the New Testament, in which a disciple baptizes; prophets, teachers and elders lay on hands; and not even presidency at the Lord's Table is regulated.

Side by side with this formalizing of ministry occurred doctrinal developments in the understanding of the Lord's Supper (by this time often called the Eucharist), which, in spite of New Testament teaching on the uniqueness of Christ's sacrifice (see above p. 74), became increasingly interpreted as a sacrificial offering for sin.[21] A major factor in this development was the current typological and allegorical method of interpreting the Old Testament, by which Jewish institutions were seen as foreshadowing Christian counterparts. The desire to have some counterpart to rites of the pagan mystery religions (which formed a serious rival to the faith) may also have been a factor. The sacrificial interpretation of the Lord's Supper was bound to affect the status of its officiant. Quite early on we can observe an analogy being drawn between Christian ministers and Jewish priests. By c. AD 200 we see the ancient terms for sacrificial priest (Latin *sacerdos* and Greek *hiereus*) applied to Christian presbyters and bishops, even though this terminology has no precedent in New Testament usage. Increasingly Christian presbyters become understood as acting, like Jewish or pagan priests, as mediators between God and the ordinary people, and as offering sacrifice on their behalf.[22]

These changes, combined with the desire of the Church to be respectable and orderly, drastically affected women's opportunities for ministry. The fact that Jewish priests were all male, the continuation (already mentioned) of Jewish taboos on 'uncleanness', and the conviction that ministry represents authority which can be exercised only by men, all combined to exclude women from priestly ministry. The fact that the Twelve were all men was also adduced as an argument for excluding women. Thus the so-called *Apostolic Church Order* (a fourth century document purporting to describe a council of the Apostles) grounds its exclusion of women from celebrating the Eucharist on the historically questionable belief that no women shared in the bread and wine at the Last Supper (see above p.

76). But even if this were true, it would not prove that no woman could ever preside at later Christian celebrations of this event.

In imposing their limitations on women's ministry, the Fathers were influenced by two other factors: first, there were the restrictions believed to come from Paul (esp. 1 Cor. 14.34f. and 1 Tim. 2.11–15), which were applied to the contemporary situation regardless of their original context. Neither Jesus' acceptance of women as disciples and as bearers of the message of salvation, nor Paul's fundamental affirmation that in Christ there is neither male nor female, nor the witness of the New Testament to Christian freedom from the Law and the reception by women of the Holy Spirit, seem to have influenced the Fathers as much as the apparent rules for future ministry laid down in these passages. Paul's assumption (1 Cor. 11.2–16) that women may 'prophesy' to the edification of the congregation was likewise ignored or explained away, while the injunctions to silence were interpreted with such crude literalism that some Fathers actually enjoined women merely to mouth the words of psalms during worship, rather than sing or read them aloud.[23]

The second major factor was the need to react to the doctrinal and ethical threat of Gnostic and other heretical groups. In Montanist, Priscillian, and other 'charismatic' congregations women did minister, even apparently as presbyters and bishops. The evidence comes mostly from hostile sources, such as Irenaeus and Tertullian. The latter castigated the heretic leader Marcion, denouncing the audacity of women followers who exorcized, healed, and baptized, and asserting that it is not permitted for a women to 'teach, baptize, offer [sc. the Eucharist], or claim for herself a share in any male function – least of all the sacerdotal office'.[24] The fact that some heretical groups allowed female leadership made any female leadership – even among the orthodox – suspect. Fresh evidence is coming to light from inscriptions and papyri for Christian women described as *presbytis/presbytera* or *didaskalos*. It would be unscholarly to assume that such women must by definition have belonged to heretical groups.[25]

The Roman Catholic theologian H. van der Meer is among those who have asked whether the Fathers' rejection of women priests should not be seen as a historically-conditioned phenomenon, particularly in view of the way it is so frequently made in connection with the refutation of heretical views. He cites the example of Epiphanius (fourth century Bishop of Salamis), one of the patristic authorities most frequently quoted by opponents of women's ordination because of his bold claim that 'never from the foundation of the world has a woman served as priest'. But this claim occurs in a polemical passage attacking the Collyridian heresy in which women worshipped Mary as divine, and offered her, as priests, little loaves (*kollyrides*). It is in attacking this clearly unorthodox practice that he makes his well-known statement, 'Women are an untrustworthy race, prone to error, and of mediocre intelligence. Through them the Devil knows how to spew forth... ridiculous teachings'.[26] It is patently unfair to take such sentiments, uttered in response to a particular situation, and apply them to women in general, arguing that doctrinally orthodox women can never be ordained.

In their teaching on women's ministry the Fathers were deeply influenced by the secular Greek view that the proper place for women is in the home: thus Chrysostom taught that God chose men to be concerned with public affairs (*ta politika pragmata*) such as the market, law-courts and army, and women to deal with private matters (*ta idiōtika*), such as weaving and household management, for (he says) 'a woman cannot (*sic*) throw a javelin... nor express an opinion in a senate'.[27] Hence many Fathers made a sharp distinction between public and private ministry, seeing only the latter as appropriate for women. This led to some peculiar biblical exegesis, whereby women who preach, teach, or exercise leadership were seen as always doing this *privately*, not publicly. But how can one make this distinction when the early Church met in members' houses? Embarrassing texts were explained away by specious arguments or dogmatic assertions. Thus Origen claimed that though all four daughters of Philip prophesied (Acts 21.9), they never spoke in church.[28] One wonders how he could be so confident, especially as Paul, when discussing prophecy, clearly implies that it is for the benefit of the congregation (1 Cor. 11). It is ironical that the Fathers recognized some women as having equal honour with apostles – Origen described the Samaritan woman as 'an apostle' to the inhabitants of her city, and Theophylact even wrote of her receiving 'priestly consecration' from her faith; Hippolytus and Augustine (followed by Bernard of Clairvaux) saw Mary Magdalene as acting as an apostle in spreading the news of the resurrection.[29] Chrysostom and other early Fathers even recognized Junia in Romans 16.7 as a female apostle (see above p. 58 with n.8). Yet in spite of these biblical precedents the Fathers as a whole still assumed that women could not be ordained presbyters, because their ministry had to be 'private'.

One form of official ministry was, however, open to women in the Greek and Syrian Churches and that was the diaconate. The origins of this office are obscure, as is its relationship to the orders of 'widows' and 'virgins', which also seem to have their roots already in the New Testament. Female deacons appear to have been respectable widows or single older women (some canons limited this ministry to those over 40, some to those over 60), and they were expected to remain celibate. In the earliest texts they are called *diakonoi* (the same name as is used for male deacons); later they are sometimes known by the feminine formation *diakonissa*.[30] In some parts of the Eastern Church they were ordained in the sanctuary, with the invocation of the Holy Spirit and the laying on of hands; and were vested with the stole and presented with the chalice. Authors as diverse as Clement of Alexandria, Origen, Epiphanius and Basil all seem to regard these women as clergy; the Syriac *Didascalia* (ch. 9) urges Christians to honour female deacons 'in the place of the Holy Spirit' (cf. the Latin version ch. 25 and *Ap. Const.* II. 26). We know little about the work of these female ministers of the Greek and Syrian Churches apart from the fact that they ministered to the sick in their homes, where propriety forbade the entry of men, and – for reasons of modesty – assisted with baptisms, which involved the total immersion of candidates in a state of undress, bodily anointing, and rerobing.[31] But they could not actually baptize: with characteristic lack of historical perspective, Epiphanius denied women this privilege on the grounds that Jesus was not baptized by his mother! Thus it seems that for some four centuries parts of the Catholic Church recognized that women could be ordained – as deacons. Eventually the ministry of women deacons, like that of dedicated virgins and widows, was absorbed into that of nuns. It was an exception to the general pattern in which sacral leadership was regarded as a male prerogative, and seems to have been largely dictated by the need for women to serve in situations where the presence of men would offend prevailing notions of propriety.

We conclude that in this early formative period, exclusion of women from religious leadership was directly related to their low social status and the negative attitudes of some male leaders. It was also a matter of custom and the rulings of local synods or individual bishops rather than of universal church *law*. The traditional Creeds make no reference to either male or female ordination, and none of the seven Oecumenical Councils, still held in high regard by many Christians today, explicitly pronounced against women's priestly ordination. They were summoned to deal with quite different problems, and this was an issue that did not arise.[32] Yet it cannot be denied that the patristic teaching on women was to have far-reaching effects as custom became codified into law in the medieval Church. One cannot stress too strongly that the Fathers' views on women's ministry were coloured by their ascetic and negative attitudes to sexuality, the philosophical presuppositions of ancient secular thinkers, and the political, legal and social set-up of their age, whereby women were treated as permanent minors. Even their biblical exegesis was profoundly influenced by their cultural and ecclesiastical situation.

NOTES

1   Clark (1983), p. 15; cf. Heine (1987), chs. 1–2.
2   Ambrosiaster, *Quaest. Vet. et Nov. Test.*, 45.2f.; see further Gryson (1976), pp. 92–7.
3   *Cult. Fem.* 1.1. For a defence of Tertullian see Carnelley (1989).
4   Elsewhere he interprets man as standing for 'reason' and woman as 'sensuality': see van der Meer (1973), p. 62.
5   Augustine, *Trin.* 12.7; see further Børresen (1981), esp. pp. 26f.; Dempsey-Douglass (1985), pp. 73–5.
6   Ambrose, *Exp. Ev. Sec. Luc.* 10. 161. For the contrast between *nēpios* and *anēr* cf. 1 Cor. 13.11; for the 'mature' or 'perfect' human being, cf. Col. 1.28; for further examples of *anēr* used generically see Jas. 1.8, 12, 23; 3.2 (also *teleios anēr*); also LXX of Judg. 9.49; Ps. 112.1; Isa. 2.9 (noting the Hebrew and Latin versions, in most of which *ʾish* and *vir* similarly appear in an inclusive sense. On *mulier/mollities* see Swidler (1981), p. 76.
7   See Dempsey-Douglass (1985), p. 75; Børresen (1981), pp. 85–7.

8   Tr. Lambdin in Robinson (1977), p. 130; see further Vogt (1985), on
     Clement of Alexandria.
9   *Solil.* 1.10, 17, tr. Børresen (1981), p. 8; see also *Civ. Dei* 14.21–6;
     Gen. ad Litt. 9.
10   *In Zach.* 3.13 (on menstruation); *Ep.* 22.17 (on women fasting); *In Iov.*
     1.7 (on continence); see further Armstrong (1986), pp. 129, 150f., 263.
11   Warner (1976), pp. 74f.; cf. Loades (1987), pp. 44–54 (on 'holy
     anorexia'). Virgins, of course, already avoided the 'curse' of childbirth.
12   *Reg. Episc.* (tr. Armstrong (1986), p. 129f.
13   Clark (1983), p. 47; on Clement cf. also Witherington (1988), pp. 186f.
14   See Warner (1976), esp. chs. 3–7, 12–13, 16, showing how the cult of
     Mary (esp. the doctrines of her perpetual virginity, immaculate
     conception and coronation) was used to further the subordination of
     women.
15   See van der Meer (1973), pp. 91–8. Morris (1973), pp. 105–12, gives
     details of the taboo in other societies, noting that as late as 1684
     menstruating women were still being required to remain at the church
     door. See further Douglas (1966); Neusner (1973).
16   Royal women – such as Helen (mother of Constantine), Pulcheria and
     Theodora – wielded both ecclesiastical and political power, but did
     nothing to improve the low status of ordinary women.
17   Roman society was rigidly divided into classes (*ordines*) of patricians,
     equites ('knights'), freedmen, and slaves.
18   Ignatius, *Smyrn.* 8; *Philad.* 7. The bishop is here a local leader in
     charge of a congregation small enough for him to know by name.
19   The Twelve left no direct successors (see above Ch. 6). In Acts 14.23
     Paul and Barnabas appoint *presbyteroi* on their first missionary
     journey, and in 2 Tim. 1.6 Paul lays hands on Timothy (though note
     that in 1 Tim. 4.14 this is done by 'the presbytery'). But these
     examples, even taken with the injunctions to Timothy (1 Tim. 6.20)
     and Titus (Titus 1.5) to 'take care of what has been entrusted' and to
     appoint elders in every town, are a far cry from 'apostolic succession'
     as it came to be understood.
20   On deacons see Barnett (1979), chs. 4–5, and the C. of E. report,
     Deacons in the Ministry of the Church (1988), pp. 7–14.
21   Hanson (1979), pp. 46–66; relevant documents in Sheerin (1986).
22   Hanson (1979), pp. 38–45; cf. Schillebeeckx (1981), pp. 48–52, and
     (1985), pt. III.
23   e.g. Cyril of Jerusalem, *Procatech.* 14. Centuries later Calvin met with
     opposition to the idea of women joining in congregational singing!
24   Tertullian, *Virg. Vel.* 9; cf. *Praesc. Haer.* 41; cf. Pagels (1979), p. 60.
25   See, for example, Horsley (1981–87), vol. I, p. 121; vol. III, p. 138;
     vol. IV, pp. 239–44.
26   *Haer.* 3.2.79; cf. van der Meer (1973), pp. 7, 46–50, and Daniélou
     (1974), 24–6.
27   *Qual. Duc. Sint Ux.* 3.4.
28   See Gryson (1976), 28f., citing Origen on 1 Cor. 14.34f. Van der Meer
     (1973), pp. 16, 60, shows that Jerome, Theodore of Mopsuestia,

Primasius and Ambrose all make an untenable distinction between women's public and private ministry.

29 For references see Schelkle (1979), p. 150.

30 See Lampe (1961), *s.vv.* The change of form is a regular linguistic development; in ancient usage there is no particular link between the form of the name and the view that these women are or are not in 'Holy Orders'.

31 On the functions of women deacons, their role in baptisms, and their ordination rites see Daniélou (1961), pp. 20–4; Gryson (1976); Theodorou (1977); and Martimort (1982).

32 Ware (1978), p. 69 and Clark (1980), cite Photius' *Nomocanon* 1.37, which states, 'A woman does not become a *presbytera*', and mentions Canons from Nicea, Laodicea, Chalcedon, and the 'Sixth Council'. But when the texts of these obscurely-worded documents are examined – see Percival (1900), pp. 40–2, 129–31, 279, 372 – it will be found that (1) Nicea (c. 19) is concerned with the rebaptism and reordination of heretic Paulianist clergy returning to Orthodoxy: it says nothing about women *presbyterai* or priests, but merely that Paulianist deaconesses are to be numbered among the laity since they have not received the laying on of hands. (2) Laodicea – not an Oecumenical Council but a little-known local Synod – (c. 14) forbids the appointment of widows as to some senior non-liturgical function: cf. Afanasiev (1983); (3) Chalcedon (c. 15) merely prescribes that women should not be ordained deaconesses below the age of 40 and once ordained must not marry; (4) the 'Sixth Council' (? an error for Trullo or Quinisext, c. 14) prescribes minimum ages for presbyters, deacons, and deaconesses. Thus the *Nomocanon* ascribed to Photius does nothing to support the idea that the Oecumenical Councils of the 'undivided' Church expressly forbade women's priestly ordination.

7

Women and the Ministry from the Medieval Period to the Reformation

THE MEDIEVAL PERIOD

Culturally the medieval period begins with Rome's fall to the barbarians in 476 and ends with the western rediscovery of classical literature in the Renaissance of the fourteenth and fifteenth centuries. Ecclesiastically it opens with intensified rivalry between the Roman papacy – now growing in temporal power as well as spiritual influence and jurisdiction – and the see of Constantinople, the religious and political capital of the Byzantine Empire; it closes, after a long power-struggle between popes and certain national rulers, with the Reformation and the establishment of the first Protestant Churches of Europe in the sixteenth century. Thus the medieval period in the West runs parallel to the later Patristic and Byzantine Ages of the East (which continued without a major break until the fall of Constantinople to the Turks in 1453). Socially, culturally and politically it was a time of diversity and change, which makes it difficult to generalize about the position of women and their role in the Church. But it was a crucial period for the crystallization of theological arguments and views about women, some of which persisted right through the Reformation to modern times and still influence the debate on women's ministry today. At the risk of oversimplification, we must then attempt a general summary of the developments over this long period.

General attitudes to women and their religious roles

Economic, educational, legal and religious factors all contributed to maintaining a subordinate status for women. The peasant economy required their manual labour; low life expectancy through frequent war, plague and famine meant that socially their prime function was seen to be the bearing and rearing of children. The medieval universities were run by men (mostly clergy) for men. Ordinary women had very little education, even of the most elementary kind, and virtually no opportunities for practising professional careers. They were subject to numerous legal disabilities, being regarded for political, legal and taxation purposes as mere appendages to their husbands.[1]

Exceptions to this general pattern were women of noble or royal families, some of whom were highly educated and even reigned in their own right (when male heirs were lacking).[2] So too were nuns, for whom the 'religious' life of the convent offered freedom from the perpetual round of child-bearing and subordination to a husband.[3] Not all such women were shut off from the wider world. Beguines, for example, lived in open communities without vows; canonesses participated in cathedral and other services. Abbesses, who were drawn mostly from noble families, had substantial secular as well as religious powers. Hilda of Whitby (seventh century) was among those who controlled a double community of men and women. Some continental abbesses were free from the jurisdiction of bishops and exercised 'quasi-episcopal' authority.[4] Their elaborate 'ordination' rites included vesting with pallium and mitre; at Las Huelgas in Spain they received vows of obedience from men. Eventually their powers were curbed by the Council of Trent (1545–63), which also restricted the freedom of nuns to participate in activities outside the confines of their convents.

Although few women religious had great book-learning, some had profound mystic experiences. We may mention especially Hildegard, 'the sibyl of the Rhine', Bridget of Sweden, founder of the Brigittines, and the anchoress Julian of Norwich, whose *Revelations of Divine Love* became a Christian classic. Catherine of Siena (? 1347–80), who had been very diffident of appearing in public, became an outstanding spiritual leader and even 'reconciled' sinners. Her *Dialogo* and other spiritual writings were dictated to monks and translated into Latin; less than a century after her death she was declared a saint. But Joan of Arc, whose 'voices' led her into military as well as political action, was burnt as a witch (in 1431).[5] Many other women suffered cruelly for suspected contact with demonic powers; the official persecution of women as witches (which reached its height in the later fifteenth century) continued till the eighteenth century. 'Heretical' groups were also violently persecuted, including the Cathars, among whom women preached and administered sacraments.[6] But within the Catholic fold, the model laid down by the Fathers, of silence in church and subjection to male teaching and authority, remained the norm for most women. Their submission was reinforced by the strongly hierarchical and authoritarian character of the Church's ministry and by philosophical theories of 'natural law' and 'the scale of nature', which saw women as permanently subordinate to men. Fear of female sexuality and repeated attempts to impose clerical celibacy also contributed to the low estimation of women.

The formalization of women's exclusion from ordained ministry

In the twelfth century Gratian compiled his famous *Decretum*, which was to become the basis of later Canon Law. In this vast compendium of patristic pronouncements, conciliar texts and papal decrees, he declared boldly: 'Women can attain neither to the priesthood nor even the diaconate' (ch. 15, q.3). He further maintained the tradition, already widespread in parts of the Latin Church (cf. above p. 95), that not even nuns could touch sacred vessels and vestments, cense the altar, teach or baptize. Although Gratian was only a monk (from Italy) with no special jurisdiction in the Church, his 'Decree' rapidly displaced earlier law collections. Popes Pius IV and V issued official texts, and canonists like Paucapalea, Rufinus and Huguccio repeated and developed Gratian's views. Successive popes issued 'Decretals' (decrees claiming universal recognition) embodying the Decree's teachings and reducing the powers and privileges of abbesses. Theologians sought to justify its decisions on women with additional arguments; and the ban on women's ordination still remains part of Roman Catholic Canon Law.

It is important therefore that we examine briefly the grounds on which Gratian came to his conclusions. He nowhere adduces a full theological argument, but rests his case on quotations from the Fathers, including the idea that 'it is the natural law among mankind that females should obey males and children parents, for there is no justice in the higher obeying the lower' (ch. 12, citing Augustine). As biblical support he adduces the familiar patristic understanding of Genesis, that only Adam was created fully in God's image, as God's 'vicar' on earth; that man is the 'head' of woman; and woman must be veiled in the presence of a bishop (whom he sees as standing in the place of Christ) to show that she is subject and that sin began through her. This last ruling reflects a typically medieval doctrine of the episcopate, and the curious notion (found also in Lombard and Aquinas) that 'the angels' of 1 Cor. 11.10 are bishops. In her book *The Exclusion of Women from the Priesthood* (1976) Ida Raming has subjected Gratian's Decree to a closely-argued scholarly study, showing up both the weakness of its handling of the biblical material and its dependence on Roman civil law. One reason why Gratian's decision on women was so readily accepted was that he cited as a prime authority the Pseudo-Isidorian decretal of Pope Soter, which saw the handling by women of sacred vessels as a 'pestis' (plague), to be stamped out. This decretal has been shown to be a forgery,[7] but that has not stopped the judgments based on it being cited repeatedly.

Gratian's ban on women's ordained ministry was further reinforced by the medieval 'doctors' of the Church, who, not surprisingly, felt the need for fuller theological justification for what had become church Law. Most influential was Thomas Aquinas (c. 1225–74), whose massive, multi-volume (but unfinished) *Summa Theologiae* systematically expounded the Christian faith in the light of medieval philosophy and eventually became an authoritative text-book. Both here and in his other theological writings Aquinas stated unequivocally his belief that women are inherently inferior to men. For example, he dogmatically asserted: 'The power of rational discernment is by nature stronger in man [than woman]'; 'the male is more perfect in reason and stronger in virtue'; 'man is by nature superior to woman'; and 'woman is subject to man because of her weakness of nature, both in spiritual vigour and in bodily strength'.[8]

A key passage for Aquinas' views on women's ordination is his *quaestio* (a standard scholastic form of debate) on the subject of potential impediments to ordination, in which he discusses in turn whether women, young boys, slaves, murderers, illegitimate men, and those with bodily defects (e.g. missing limbs) may be ordained. He concludes that all these groups except boys are prohibited for a variety of reasons. His discussion on women's ordination requires close examination, as his teaching is still cited in the modern debate on women's ministry (cf. the 1976 Vatican Declaration and the literature arising from it).[9] Aquinas first sets out three arguments in favour, namely the existence in the Bible of female prophets, the exercise of authority by women like Deborah, who judged Israel, and the non-sexual nature of the soul, on which the 'power' (*potestas*) of Orders rests. Then he cites two arguments against, namely the ruling in 1 Tim. 2.12 that women should not teach or exercise authority over a man, and the requirement for ordinands to be tonsured (i.e. have their heads partially shaved), which would be inappropriate for women. He concludes that since 'eminence of rank' cannot be signified by women because of their subject status, they cannot receive the sacrament of ordination (*cum igitur in sexu femineo non possit significari aliqua eminentia gradus, quia mulier statum subjectionis habet, ideo non potest ordinis sacramentum suscipere*).[10]

His arguments may appear strange to those who do not share his cultural or theological presuppositions. It seems odd, to put it mildly, that he should accept as valid the Orders of young boys below the age of reason and yet reject even the possibility of women's ordination, all the more since he defends child-ordination on the grounds that no action (*nullus actus*) is necessary on the part of the ordinand, who is simply the recipient of God's grace. If God's grace can work for boys, why not for women? His position is made all the more illogical by his explanation that women could be prophets, because prophecy was a gift of God (*donum dei*), not a sacrament. But surely sacraments are also gifts of God? The weakness of his other arguments is equally apparent. He ignores the tension between Deborah's temporal and spiritual authority and the Pauline injunction that women should not govern men, and does not help his case by his explanation of the extraordinary powers of contemporary abbesses as due to the danger (*periculum*) of men living near women.[11] He also fails to meet the argument about the non-sexuality of the soul, which on his understanding of sacramental 'character' ought to mean that women could receive Orders, just as they receive baptism and confirmation. (In this very passage he admits that women can be found whose souls are superior to men's.) His argument from tonsure is so patently tied to a culture-related custom that it hardly needs refuting; he himself admits that tonsure is not strictly necessary for ordination (*non de necessitate sacramenti*), and in a different context defends the custom of nuns having their hair cut off when they make their profession, on the grounds that they are being 'raised' to the worth of men.

It is evident that the real reason for Aquinas' negative conclusion on women is his belief that women are fundamentally inferior to men, and that is why, even if they went through all the rites of ordination, they could not signify 'superiority of rank'. If his view either of ordination as signifying 'superiority' or of women as 'subordinate' (or inferior) is challenged, so too must be his conclusion. We shall return to both these points in later chapters, but it may be worth saying a little more on the reasons for Aquinas' conviction that women are, in some sense, inferior to men. There is scarcely any doubt that in this belief he was influenced not just by the low social and educational position of women of his age, but also by the fashionable, and erroneous, Aristotelian biology then current. This can be seen very clearly in another *quaestio*, in which he discusses whether or not woman ought to have been originally created. After putting the arguments for and against woman's creation, Aquinas concludes that (1) it was necessary for woman to be made, to 'help' men in begetting children (he consistently maintains that women's role in procreation is passive and subordinate); (2) that, although woman is not just a male *manqué* with reference to the human species as a whole, yet she is like something defective with regard to her individual nature (*ad naturam particularem femina est aliquid deficiens et occasionatum*), being conceived as the result 'either of the debility of the active power, or of some unsuitability of the material, or of some change effected by external influences, like the south wind, for example, which is damp, as we are told by Aristotle'; and (3) that women are by nature (*naturaliter*) subject to men, their subjection being beneficial to them.[12]

Aquinas was an outstanding scholar and one of the Church's greatest theologians; but his arguments about women are vitiated by his ignorance of the facts of reproduction, his low estimate of women's intelligence and rationality, the literalness of his biblical interpretations (elsewhere he argues that women cannot have authority since Eve was made from Adam's rib, not his head), and his understanding of 'natural order' which he took to include the subordination of women. In all this he was a child of his time. To be fair, we should add that he did not believe natural order to be immutable;[13] one wonders whether he would argue in the same way if he were alive today.

Other eminent scholastics also rejected the possibility of women's ordination. Most interestingly, Bonaventure (c. 1217–74) repudiated the idea that women are an abnormality of the species; but, like Aquinas, he still affirmed male authority over women on the grounds of Adam's creation before Eve's, and men's superiority in reason and leadership qualities, which he believed they possessed 'by nature'. He discusses the question of women's ordination quite fully in his *Commentary on the Sentences of Lombard*, noting, in favour of their ordination, that women are called both to the 'religious' life and to martyrdom – vocations which might well be thought as high as the priesthood; that abbesses have the power 'to bind and loose'; and the view that woman is as much in the image of God as a man. But he still comes down in favour of it as 'the saner or more prudent opinion' that women cannot be ordained because of the non-congruity of 'orders' with femaleness. In a fresh argument he suggests that 'the person ordained must signify Christ as mediator, and the mediator can be signified only in the male sex'; and that all Orders prepare ultimately for the episcopate, and that women cannot be bishops, since the bishop is the husband of the Church.[14] We note the literalism with which he interprets the biblical image of the believing community as a woman, and the assumption that mediators must be male because the incarnate Christ was male (on this, see below pp. 167f.).

Duns Scotus (c. 1265–1308) raised a new argument in favour of women's ordination, namely Paul's affirmation in Galatians

3.28. Nevertheless, he too decided against it on the familiar grounds that they are not permitted to handle the holy vessels (cf. Gratian's decree), and they cannot receive the tonsure because of Paul's dictum (1 Cor. 11.6) that it was disgraceful for a woman to shave her head. He countered the egalitarian interpretation of Gal. 3.28, with the argument that nature does not permit a woman to hold a position of superiority owing to the 'weakness of women's intellect and the mutability of their will'. He concluded that 'the material is not suitable [sc. for ordination]' (*non est materia capax*). Durandus of Saint-Pourçain (1275–1334) similarly excluded women from ordination on the grounds that 'a position of predominance over males is not fitting for women, but rather a state of subjection, on account of the weakness of their body and the imperfection of their mind'.[15] It is fascinating to speculate how far these learned doctors were influenced in their views of women's mental and bodily weakness by their general lack of education and frequent early death in childbirth. In western society today women are often as well-educated as men, they are legally equal to them, and their life expectancy is longer than men's.

The teachings of the Doctors have been very influential in the Roman Catholic Church and among some Anglicans. It is evident from the foregoing discussion that they are closely tied to the cultural and philosophical presuppositions of their age. Their discussions raise once again the validity of arguments 'from nature', and of the view that women are inherently inferior to men. Even those who accept the authority of the Fathers and Doctors by reason of their Church allegiance must face the question: if the primary reason for their rejection of women's ordination was their belief in woman's subject state, is their rejection still valid in a society where women are no longer subordinate?

THE REFORMATION

What we call 'the Reformation' was part of a complex movement which began in the fourteenth century with challenges to Roman authority and doctrine and culminated in the establishment of the 'Reformed' or Protestant denominations.

A primary cause was concern about abuses in the Church and the secular power of the papacy, monasteries, and clerical hierarchy. Though sometimes marred by physical violence and other excesses, the Reformation was motivated by a genuine desire to return to the faith of the Bible, and to make its teachings accessible to ordinary men and women. In particular, the Reformers rejected medieval beliefs and practices concerning the sacerdotal 'powers' of the clergy, affirming that every Christian shares in the royal priesthood of all believers.

With such an emphasis on the participation of the whole people of God in church life, one might expect the Reformers to have opened up new religious roles for women. But in fact their achievements in this area were limited. Martin Luther broke fresh ground in calling upon the civil authorities to provide education for girls (even his modest proposal of one hour's elementary schooling a day for working-class girls was revolutionary).[16] He helped women – including his own future wife – who had been compelled to become nuns against their will, to leave their convents (girls were often professed at 14 or 15, and sometimes entered nunneries as young as five). He protested against the monstrous provision of Saxon law whereby a woman was entitled to receive only a chair and a distaff on her husband's death.[17] Along with other Reformers he also affirmed the value of marriage in the face of medieval ascetic attitudes which saw it very much as second best.

Nevertheless, Luther supported the medieval view that women are inferior to men, arguing from a literalistic and one-sided interpretation of Eve's part in the 'Fall'. Like Aquinas, he believed that women are by nature weaker than men physically, emotionally and morally, that they entice men into sin, and that they are excluded by God's law from civil and religious government.[18] Although he claimed that 'whoever comes out of the water of baptism can boast that he is already consecrated priest, bishop, and pope', he seems to have confined this affirmation to male believers, limiting ordained ministry to men and arguing that the Holy Spirit has exempted women, children, and incompetent people from preaching and pastoring.[19] He strongly supported the subordination of women to men in marriage; and even his stress on motherhood as the essential vocation for women effectively reaffirmed the view that a woman's place is in the home. After describing woman as 'like a nail driven into the wall', he wrote: 'Just as the snail carries its house with it, so the wife should stay at home, and look after the affairs of the household, as one who has been deprived of the ability of administering the affairs that are outside'.[20] Xenophon and Chrysostom would have approved!

However, not all Reformation women were content with domestic roles. In the first upsurge of enthusiasm on the Continent some actively intervened in religious matters: Marie Dentière, the daughter of a shopkeeper, preached publicly and wrote a defence of women; Argula von Grumbach publicly protested on behalf of a university teacher who had been wronged; Katherine Zell, the wife of a Reformed minister in Strasbourg, defended clerical marriage.[21] Several reformers, including Martin Bucer (in 1532) and Jean Morély (in.1562) suggested that there should be a ministry of male and female deacons, though their proposals did not meet with success. They were moved by the ministerial roles in the New Testament of Phoebe and the 'widows' (1 Tim. 5.9f.), whom Morély took to be deaconesses under the supervision of men – he even went so far as to suggest that the stipulation that enrolled widows must be at least 60 years old was not designed for all time.[22]

In her recent study of John Calvin's attitude to women Jane Dempsey-Douglass has argued that he too believed that women could exercise ministry as deacons, though he was tentative about this and limited their work to care for the poor.[23] She makes much of the fact that Calvin included the Pauline injunctions to women to keep silent among things 'indifferent' (*adiaphora*), that is human rules designed to promote good order, but not universally binding. Thus Calvin interpreted Paul's statement that man (not woman) is the image and glory of God as referring to the realm of human governance rather than to any essential difference between the sexes. In extraordinary circumstances, Calvin believed, God could so endow women with the Spirit that they might lead men.[24]

Such insights could have opened up new religious roles for women. But in practice the Reformed churches accepted that public ministry should be limited to men. Calvinist ministers, elders, and deacons remained male until recent times. Like Luther, Calvin believed that the submission of women to men was part of natural order; women rulers were an example of God's working in a mysterious way to chastise men and teach them humility.

Most Reformers simply assumed that ordination and church government were a male prerogative. It is not always realized how deeply influenced they were by the patristic and scholastic tradition of Biblical interpretation, and the old idea that natural order involved the subordination of women. Such views were strengthened by the concept (particularly popular in Tudor and Elizabethan England) of the 'great chain of being', in which women were placed beneath men in a metaphysical hierarchy.[25] Not surprisingly, the right of queens to exercise government was highly controversial: Thomas Elyot (1540) defended the capacity of women to rule successfully, but John Knox vehemently attacked female rulers as usurping men's authority and acting contrary to nature. In *The First Blast of the Trumpet against the Monstrous Regiment of Women* (1558) he described the female sex as 'weake, fraile, impacient, feble, and fool-ishe;...unconstant, variable, cruell, and lacking the spirit of counsel and regiment'.[26] It is ironical that there should have been so many women ruling in Europe at this time.

Thus the Reformation achieved less than one might expect towards the liberation of women. It cherished the ideal of motherhood as opposed to virginity, but simultaneously reinforced the view that women are created for domestic roles. It supported the education of girls, and affirmed the right of all Christians to study the Bible and approach God directly in prayer, but discriminated against women in public worship, perpetuating the idea that ordination and church government belong to men. Although some small Protestant groups affirmed the right of women to preach and serve in the diaconate, the mainstream Protestant Churches continued, in this respect at least, in the tradition of the medieval Church.

NOTES

1   See Shahar (1983), esp. ch. 2.
2   Outstanding among royal women were Margaret of Scotland who carried out religious and social reform, Blanche of Castile who rode into battle, and Margaret of Denmark, Norway, and Sweden, who successfully governed three kingdoms.

3   cf. McNamara (1983); Shahar (1983), p. 38f.
4   See Raming (1976), ch. 4; van der Meer (1973), pp. 115–20; Morris (1973).
5   Joan was later rehabilitated and eventually canonized (in 1929). Catherine of Siena and Teresa of Avila (1515–82) were declared the first women 'doctors' of the RC Church in 1970. In her writings Teresa defers frequently to the authority of male clergy.
6   The Cathars were an ascetic sect, deriving their name from the *cathari*, 'pure ones' or 'perfects', among whom were women; cf. Shahar (1983), pp. 254–66.
7   See van der Meer (1973), pp. 91f.; Raming (1976), pp. 9–12.
8   See Børresen (1981), pp. 171–3; cf. also *Summa, Suppl.* III, q. 81, art. 3 (Marietti ed., vol. V, p. 664), where, however, Aquinas rejects the view (held by some on the basis of Eph. 4.13) that at the resurrection women will become perfect by assuming male bodies.
9   On the Vatican Declaration see below pp. 129, 167. Aquinas is cited in §5 to support the view that sacramental signs represent what they signify by 'natural resemblance', and that a woman cannot represent Christ in this way.
10 *Comm. in Sent.* IV, d. 25, q. 2, art. 1, repeated in *Summa, Suppl.* III. q. 39, art. 1 (Marietti ed., vol. V, p. 423, from which the quotation is taken).
11 He does not discuss 'double communities'. Aquinas also fails to appreciate the significance of ordained women deacons. For further criticisms see Kiesling (1977), p. 255; Tavard (1977), pp. 100f.; Børresen (1981), pp. 192–6.
12 *Summa* 1a, p. 92 (tr. Hill). Aristotle's view that woman is a male *manqué* is cited again in q. 99, art. 2. See further Hampson (1985), pp. 341f.
13 On Aquinas' view of natural law see O'Connor (1967).
14 *Comm. in Lib. Sent.* IV, d. 25, art. 2, q. 1 (Quarracchi ed., vol. IV, pp. 649–51). See further De Benedictis (1972), pp. 138f.; Tavard (1977), pp. 101f.
15 On Duns Scotus and Durandus see Tavard (1978), pp. 102–4.
16 Convent education was limited to upper class women and girls. Erasmus had hoped that even the 'lowliest woman' might read the Gospels and Paul, but widespread illiteracy made this impossible.
17 Haile (1980), p. 271.
18 On Luther's view of women see Behrens (1973); Haile (1980), pp. 259–80.
19 *Works* (ed. Lehmann and Pelikan) vol. XLI, pp. 154f. (tr. Gritsch).
20 *Works* (ed. Lehmann and Pelikan) vol. I, pp. 202f. (tr. Pelikan).
21 See Behrens (1973), pp. 47–50; fuller details in Bainton (1971); (1973).
22 Dempsey-Douglass (1985), pp. 90f.
23 Dempsey-Douglass (1985), esp. pp. 42–9; 90–2.
24 See esp. Dempsey-Douglass (1985), pp. 16f., 29–65.
25 See Scanzoni (1982), pp. 75–9, discussing the parallel between the

'great chain of being' and some modern 'evangelical' views of woman's relation to man.

26 Laing (1854), p. 374. As well as Bible passages (e.g. Gen. 3 and 1 Cor. 11), Knox quotes 'nature', 'good Order', Aristotle, Ambrose, Augustine and Tertullian to support his view that women are made 'to serve and obey men'.

8

Women and the Ministry in Modern Times

THE CHANGING CLIMATE

The last four centuries have seen massive changes in the status and roles of women. In Western society, in the Soviet bloc, and increasingly even in the 'third world', their legal, social, and economic position is greatly different from what it was in earlier ages. Except in countries where Islamic law is enforced and in primal communities where traditional *mores* still operate, women are generally recognized as equal to men: they are free to own property, engage in commercial transactions, and work outside the home. In democratic societies they vote, stand for political office, and participate in the judicial process. In the religious sphere women are beginning to exercise leadership and to make their voices heard in ways unparalleled before. In this chapter we survey the causes of these radical changes, describe the Church's reactions to them, and identify questions which they raise for the theology of women's ministry.

Changes in philosophical and scientific outlook

The first major cause of change is the scientific and questioning spirit which has prevailed in Western civilization since the Enlightenment of the seventeenth and eighteenth centuries. Modern scientists and thinkers rely on experiment, empirical observation, and reason as sources for knowledge rather than historical authorities (such as Aristotle) or divine revelation in Scripture and 'natural law'. Although Christian thinkers still look to the Bible and Church as sources of authority on religious matters, secular scientists and philosophers pursue all forms of knowledge in a spirit of autonomy, seeking to identify even moral values independently of any concept of divine will. The ancient idea that women are inherently inferior to men is commonly rejected, and hence any notion that the female sex as a whole should be subordinate to the male sex seems to lack reason. If women are morally, intellectually, physically and psychologically capable of doing almost all the things that men do (as well as certain things that men cannot do), there seems no rational justification for refusing to regard the two sexes as equals and giving them equal opportunities to pursue personal happiness and contribute to the common good. The growth of the concept of human rights has been an important factor here.

Political, legal, and social changes

Closely related to the changing philosophical climate has been the widespread replacement (sometimes by revolution, some-times by gradual change) of monarchical and aristocratic forms of government, with their social stratification and class dis-tinction, by democratic and socialist governments. The 1689 English Bill of Rights, and the American and French Revo-lutions of the eighteenth century, with their accompanying intellectual ferment, social upheaval, and concern for the rights of the citizen, affected women as well as men, and had repercussions far beyond their countries of origin. The idea that women should be admitted to full citizenship was canvassed as early 1790 by the French philosopher Condorcet, but failed to gain wide acceptance even in France.[1] In Britain such ideas received little sympathy because of their association with the revolutionary spirit, which had led to so much violence. Lone voices like Mary Wollstonecraft pleaded for women's rights, but it was not until John Stuart Mill's *Subjection of Women* in 1869 that they began to be taken seriously. The Russian Revolution of 1917 and the spread of Marxism drastically affected women's status in Communist countries, where women are now officially recognized as equal with men, even if in practice they often have to fulfil traditional domestic responsibilities in addition to outside work. Today, in societies of widely different political colours, it is generally accepted that nobody should be excluded from active participation in society simply because of race, colour, social class or sex. A crucial factor in the recognition of human and civil rights was the abolition (in the nineteenth century) of slavery as an institution. The widespread recognition of the desirability of racial and sexual equality followed logically upon this, and is now enshrined in both national and international legislation.[2]

Changes in the educational, medical, and economic position of women

Another major factor has been the opening up of education to women. As long as most women remained uneducated, there might seem to be some grounds for male leadership. But now in most Western societies girls have similar opportunities to boys for elementary, secondary, higher, and professional education. Of course, not all sexual discrimination has been ended: some families and some teachers still give preferential treatment to boys; opportunities in certain professions are still much more limited for women than for men.[3] But enormous efforts are being made in countries as far apart as Japan and Britain to give male and female equal opportunities in industry, commerce and education. Battles over access to the medical and legal professions have been fought and won; women are now moving into many other areas once thought to be masculine preserves, such as mathematics, engineering, the construction industries, and airline piloting. The ordinary 'person in the street' may be forgiven for wondering what there is about Christianity which makes it necessary, for example, for British Churches to be exempted from their country's Equal Opportunities legislation.

Another important element has been medical advances and improved health. The old Aristotelian biology, with its apparent reinforcement of female inferiority, was already being challenged in the sixteenth century by those familiar with Galen. Modern medical discoveries have put an end once-and-for-all to the view that women are biologically inferior to men simply because of the manner in which they are conceived. Human sexuality has been shown to be a complex phenomenon, the moral and theological implications of which are still being worked out. Current knowledge and skills mean that there is no longer any medical need for women to die young from childbirth (though some may still do so for economic or social reasons). Parents have the means of responsible family planning through reliable birth-control methods, even though some may choose not to use them. The modern woman has the potentiality for far greater control over her body than in any previous generation, and is free from the necessity to bear children merely as a result of submitting to sexual desire. Some sociologists have seen this as a major factor in women's advance towards equality. Certainly when combined with economic prosperity and the mechanization of many household tasks, it means that even mothers now have the time, the incentive and, increasingly, the opportunity to concern themselves with more than domestic issues. There are also more opportunities for single women to live a life of independence than in former generations.

The effect on social attitudes of women's comparative economic independence should not be underestimated. As long as most women were married (usually to men older than themselves), and most married women were dependent economically on their husbands, their social subordination was understandable. In recent years the woman's financial contribution to the household has become increasingly important in both democratic and communist countries. It has been estimated that in Britain today fewer than one sixth of all households contain a married couple with dependent children where the mother is a full-time housewife.[4] It is a fact of life that people are valued by their economic contribution, and the potential of educated women to earn salaries comparable with their husbands' is bound to affect male attitudes to them.

The Women's Movement

The modern feminist movement has its roots in the 'old feminism' of those who worked for women's legal and political rights in America and Europe in the nineteenth and early twentieth centuries, culminating in women's suffrage and their recognition legally as separate persons from their husbands. Since the 1960s there has been a fresh upsurge of feminist thought, which has focused more on attitudes and perceptions

than on legal rights. Modern feminists affirm the essential value
of women as people, not just as wives and mothers. They oppose
'exclusive' language (for example, the use of 'man', 'men' and
the masculine pronoun to refer to women) and the assumption
that the male is the norm of the species. Modern feminists
deliberately seek to raise public consciousness about women's
lives, emotions, and ways of thought, arguing that women have
too long been silent and allowed social values to be coloured by
masculine views. Some see men as standing for violence,
authority and power, and believe that the world would be a
better place for more female leadership; others recognise that
such views are in themselves 'sexist', and that neither sex has a
monopoly of violence and aggression (even if historically these
have been found more commonly in men).

Elaine Storkey has divided modern secular feminism into
three broad types: *Liberal feminism*, which continues earlier
campaigns for the improvement of women's legal and political
rights, their access to education, and opportunities for fulfilment
in the home and the professions (a leading proponent of this
viewpoint is Betty Friedan, whose best-selling book *The
Feminine Mystique* (1963) drew attention to the many ways in
which women have been manipulated into regarding housekeeping and the domestic scene as the true fulfilment of their
potential); *Marxist feminism*, which sees women's rights as part
of a broader struggle to eliminate the capitalist system and
private wealth, race and class differences, and sometimes even
the family (Marxist feminists frequently see the institution of
marriage as a means of subjecting women); and *Radical
Feminism*, which sees patriarchy (i.e. rule by men) as the prime
cause of women's oppression – an influential work here was
Germaine Greer's *The Female Eunuch* (1970), which spoke of
the hatred some men actually feel towards women. In recent
years radical feminism has been associated with agitation for
abortion on demand and the acceptance of lesbianism. A small
number of extremists even advocate witchcraft and bizarre
'goddess-centred' rituals.[5] These forms of secular feminism
may be distinguished from *Christian feminism*, which draws on
elements from secular thought but remains within the framework of the Christian faith.[6] It is worth stressing that modern

feminism covers a wide spread of views, and that accepting the
fundamental equality of the sexes does not entail embracing all
other tenets of feminists.

THE CHURCH'S RESPONSE TO CHANGE

The period up to World War I

The Church's reaction to these changes has been mixed. From
the seventeenth to the nineteenth centuries theologians and
church leaders either sought to repudiate discoveries made
through new scientific methods (as happened most notoriously
with Galileo, and later Darwin) or else attempted to reconcile
them with previous Christian teaching. This led to the
challenging of many traditional Christian doctrines by the
'deists' (and their vigorous defence by others). In particular the
concept of a universal and unchanging 'Natural Law' received
a severe shaking, especially the idea that it could be identified
with 'Divine Law'. The philosopher Montesquieu anticipated
modern social anthropologists in arguing that many customs
believed to arise from 'natural law' are in fact due to
environmental factors: he argued that there is nothing in the
nature of women to relegate them permanently to a position
subordinate to men.[7] Today, although the concept of natural law
still has its defendants, few can be found who would support
women's subjection as part of it.

The new scientific spirit of enquiry also affected biblical
interpretation. Beginning in Germany scholars started examin-
ing the Bible critically, applying new techniques of textual,
literary and historical criticism, with a resultant challenge to
traditional teaching on Creation, the nature of biblical authority,
and doctrines of the Church and ministry. Patristic and other
early church documents were also closely scrutinized, and
many which purported to be of 'apostolic' origin or to enshrine
apostolic teaching were shown to be products of a later age. Not
all theologians and church leaders have been willing to accept
the results of such study: side by side with new radicalism,
traditionalist and conservative scholars continue to defend old
views. The Roman Catholic Church has been slow to accept the
fruits of biblical criticism; the Orthodox Churches are only just

beginning to be touched by it. In the Anglican Communion, the concept of apostolic succession and the sacerdotal interpretation of the ordained ministry were strengthened as a result of the Oxford Movement (which began in 1833) though more recently there has been a reaction against the mechanical interpretation of these doctrines. As regards the ministry of women there is now a real division between those Christians who are open to change, and conservatives who feel bound by what the Church has believed in the past. This division cuts across denominations, but broadly speaking the Protestant and Reformed Churches have been more open to change than hierarchically-governed Churches, whose structures of authority are enforced by Canon Law.

Within the broad pattern there are always exceptions to the general rule. In our last chapter we observed that the immediate effects of the Reformation did less than one might have expected to improve the lot of women. But with their teaching on the accessibility of Scripture and the availability of the Holy Spirit to all, the Reformers did pave the way for new developments. The smaller denominations, and especially the various 'Holiness groups' with their emphasis on personal Bible study and witness, were often more willing than the mainstream national Churches to depart from traditional understandings. Moravian and Mennonite groups practised a deaconess ministry. Quaker women on both sides of the Atlantic preached publicly (suffering humiliation and persecution for so doing). Puritan women were active in social work. In Britain the eighteenth century Evangelical Revival led to fresh opportunities for women's preaching at open-air and informal meetings, though not in church buildings. Mary Bosanquet (1739–1815) was among those who became itinerant preachers. But although John Wesley welcomed women among his lay helpers and preachers, when he ordained his first ministers to serve in North America, they were men. It took till the 1970s for the Methodist Church of Great Britain to open its ordained ministry to women.

In the United States Christian women from a variety of denominations were among those who actively campaigned for the abolition of the slave trade, shocking their contemporaries by writing pamphlets, editing newspapers, and addressing public meetings. Some, like Lucy Stone (1818–93), linked their arguments for the emancipation of slaves with pleas for improvements in the legal position of women. They were quick to appreciate the equalitarian implications of Scripture passages like Genesis 1.26 and Galatians 3.28. Sarah Grimké, in a letter of 1837 to the President of the Boston Female Anti-Slavery Society, pointed out that the 'grand principles' laid down by Jesus in the Sermon on the Mount were given without any reference to 'sex or condition'.[8] Around the same time the first US colleges for women's higher education were founded, and some women even learned Greek and Hebrew to study for themselves passages of the Bible which had been used to reinforce female subjection. Lucretia Mott, an educated woman and a Quaker minister, argued that Paul's recommendations on women's silence in church were not applicable for all time, declaring her belief: 'It is not Christianity but priestcraft that has subjected woman as we find her'.[9] In 1895–8 Elizabeth Cady Stanton produced *The Woman's Bible*, in which she put forward feminist interpretations of Genesis and other passages believed to prescribe female subjection. She had earlier campaigned for women's suffrage, and attacked the inequalities of the legal position, whereby, as in Britain, married women had no separate legal existence from their husbands (the Married Woman's Property Act of 1860 did much to improve the lot of American women, and in 1869 the state of Wyoming made history by granting women the right to vote). But in all this we are dealing with the reaction of individual church members, rather than churches as organizations, which changed little in their attitudes – except for the Congregationalists who opened their ordained ministry to women (in North America) in 1853.

In Europe things moved more slowly with regard to both women's ministry and their political and legal rights. In 1836 Theodor Fliedner founded the *Diakonissenanstalt* (a Protestant deaconess community) at Kaiserswerth, thus initiating a movement which spread through Europe, reaching England (1861–2) and eventually Scotland.[10] These early deaconesses cared for the sick and needy. In the Anglican Churches their canonical status was unclear: although ordained with prayer and the laying on of hands, they were mostly regarded as lay sisters and not in 'Holy Orders'. Their work was in areas traditionally regarded as suitable for women, and since it did not include a liturgical or preaching ministry, was acceptable to 'High' and 'Low' Church alike.

However, even in Britain there were women who preached, if not yet with the blessing of the Established Church. On Whitsunday 1860 Catherine Booth made history when, after her husband had finished preaching, she timidly said, 'I want to say a word'. She mounted the pulpit, and fearlessly spoke of how the Holy Spirit had called her to share the Gospel. Her husband announced, 'My wife will preach this evening', and thus began the long tradition of women's preaching in the Salvation Army. It is hard for us to appreciate what a sensation such women evangelists must have caused among earnest Christians believing that it is a woman's place to keep silent and remain in the home. Yet William Booth saw the full implications of his wife's step. In his *Regulations for Salvation Army Officers* he recognized that women have an equal right with men to publish salvation; that they may hold positions of authority and must not be held back merely because of their sex; and that they should be treated as equals with men in intellectual and social relationships.[11]

From World War I to the present day

The First World War brought about major social change: women gained access to forms of employment previously denied them, and in 1928, after a long struggle, British women finally achieved the right to vote (with some restrictions). In this Britain was well behind other countries such as New Zealand, Denmark, and the United States. About the same time the Protestant Churches began to ordain women ministers: as in America, the Congregationalists set the lead, appointing their first woman minister in 1919. There followed the ordination of the first female ministers in Lutheran and Reformed Churches on the Continent of Europe. The Second World War and its aftermath created further social change, as educational and professional opportunities improved for women. Denmark ordained its first women clergy in 1948; Norway followed, and then Sweden in 1960. The ordination of women priests in Sweden was seen by some as a particularly significant step, since the Swedish Church, though Lutheran, is episcopally ordered.

But the change was achieved under political pressure and in the face of opposition within the Church; legislation included a controversial 'conscience' clause, which continues to cause problems. The experiences of the Swedish Church illustrate the difficulties that can arise if there is insufficient consensus for change.[12]

The Church of Scotland ordained its first women ministers in 1969; the same year the Church of England admitted women to its Lay Readership (a non-ordained preaching and pastoral ministry), just one hundred years after men had been admitted to that office. Since the early 1970s a number of non-episcopal Churches have opened their ordained ministries to women. In Reform Judaism women are now ordained as rabbis, illustrating what radical changes of attitude are possible even within a religious faith which in the past has strongly affirmed women's subordination.[13]

The position is very different in Christian Churches which preserve the traditional threefold ministry and historic episcopate. In Orthodox Churches there has been virtually no change, except a little movement over deaconesses.[14] The Old Catholic Churches of Europe have approved an ordained diaconate for women, but doubts remain over whether women should be permitted pastoral charge. In the Anglican Communion some Provinces now ordain women as priests and/or deacons but others do not, and controversy continues. As early as the 1920s forward-looking thinkers such as Charles Raven had eloquently put the case for women's ordination, but nothing happened until World War II, when early in 1944 Bishop R. O. Hall of Hong Kong and South China priested a Chinese deacon(ess) named Florence Tim Oi Li.[15] This was an emergency situation, when no male priests were available, and his action provoked a major outcry. It was not until the 1960s that women's ordination in the Anglican Churches really became a live issue: in the American Episcopal Church (ECUSA) there were 'illegal' ordinations, following the initial defeat (in 1972) of a motion to open the ordained ministry to women; but official acceptance soon followed. New Zealand and Canada were among the first Anglican Churches to ordain women, and by the 1980s large numbers of female priests and deacons had begun their ministries in these countries and the

USA. In February 1989 the first Anglican woman bishop was consecrated in Massachusetts. Other Provinces of the Anglican Communion, including Australia, Brazil, Burma, the Indian Ocean, Ireland, Japan, Kenya, Hong Kong, Uganda, and Wales, have approved women's priestly ordination *in principle*, but some have not put it into practice.[16] (Several of these Provinces have ordained women deacons, but stopped short of making them priests.) There have been difficulties over the recognition of canonically ordained women priests visiting Provinces which have not yet accepted their ministry, and consequent strain on relations within the Anglican Communion. In the USA and Canada, some church members who could not in conscience accept women priests joined breakaway 'Continuing' Churches, but numbers were very small.

Back in 1975 the General Synod of the Church of England approved the motion: 'There are no fundamental theological objections to the ordination of women to the priesthood', but moves towards implementing women's priesthood have made slow progress because of conscientious and vocal opposition by some members. Since 1986, however, women have been ordained deacon in the Church of England, the much smaller Scottish Episcopal Church, and the Church in Wales (which led the Anglican Churches of Britain in this matter). Legislation is being prepared in the Church of England for the eventuality that women will be accepted as priests, and concern has been expressed about 'safeguards' for those who cannot in conscience accept the change. Less has been said about the consciences of those who firmly believe that God is calling women as priests, and who cannot yet experience their ministry, even from women canonically ordained abroad. The debate over the rightness of women's ordination seems set to continue in Britain for some time to come.

Women's ministry, especially the possible consecration of women as bishops, was a major item of agenda at the 1988 Lambeth Conference, attended by (male) bishops from every part of the Anglican Communion. The Lambeth bishops essentially agreed to differ on the issue, and to respect the autonomy of the individual Provinces without necessarily endorsing their practice. Pessimists had predicted that the Anglican Communion might break up as a result of differences on this issue; but a strong desire to maintain unity was evident on all sides, and many bishops actually felt strengthened in their common fellowship as the result of the Conference. Nevertheless, tensions remain – and are not likely to diminish as the various Provinces make their decisions over whether or not to consecrate women bishops, and how to relate to those ordained by them in other parts of the Anglican Communion. The Lambeth delegates fully recognized the 'serious hurt' liable to occur on both sides, and asked the Archbishop of Canterbury to appoint a Commission on 'Communion and Women in the Episcopate' to examine relationships between the Provinces, and to monitor and encourage consultation. (This Commission, under the chairmanship of Archbishop Eames, has now reported.)

In the Roman Catholic Church there has been a considerable change of climate following the reforms and renewal inaugurated by the Second Vatican Council of 1962–5. These have involved the introduction of new liturgies in the vernacular, including some in sexually 'inclusive' language with reference to worshippers; the recognition of the 'apostolate of the laity', i.e. the share of the unordained in the work of mission; and the authorization of nuns and other lay-people to assist with the administration of Holy Communion. Women may now become 'extraordinary ministers of the sacraments', taking communion to the sick in their homes and administering the consecrated elements publicly in church. The Second Vatican Council affirmed that 'with respect to the fundamental rights of the person, every type of discrimination, whether social or cultural, whether based on sex, race, colour, social condition, language, or religion, is to be overcome and eradicated as contrary to God's intent'.[17] But the Roman Catholic Church continues to bar women from every form of ordination, including the diaconate. Even women 'servers' at Communion remain controversial in view of the long-standing canon law barring women from the sanctuary. Nor are all members happy about recent changes: some long for a return to the old ways; others are impatient with the slowness of change.

Controversy has centred on Roman Catholic teaching on sexual morality (including birth control, abortion and divorce), clerical celibacy, the political involvement of clergy, and the authority of the hierarchy, including the Pope. In South

America, where the shortage of priests is especially acute, there have emerged lay-centred 'base-communities', experimenting in new forms of worship and producing a genuine lay theology concerned with social and political issues. Roman Catholics are prominent among Liberation Theologians, who are emphasizing the Bible's concern for the oppressed, the underprivileged, and the poor, and who are using insights from Marxist thought. Such thinkers are concerned for women as one of the oppressed sections of humanity. Several of the Roman Catholic theologians recently censured by the Vatican for their doctrinal views have openly argued for a less authoritarian understanding of ministry and for the ordination of women.[18]

It is hard to estimate the full extent of support for women's ordination among Roman Catholics. Official policy is still adamantly against it, women's ineligibility for Holy Orders having been reaffirmed in the 1976 Vatican Declaration.[19] But many individual theologians are arguing courteously and moderately for it, or are producing writings which imply acceptance of it. Groups are being formed to promote women's ministry, and there has been considerable ferment in female religious Orders, with nuns actively demonstrating; several leading feminist theologians also come from the Roman Catholic tradition. At the same time traditional doctrines are being reaffirmed by some scholars, and by official bodies such as the Sacred Congregation for the Doctrine of the Faith. In 1988 the teaching that Christ intended to exclude women from priesthood was reiterated by Pope John Paul II in his Apostolic Letter *Mulieris Dignitatem*.[20]

At this point it may be worth saying something more about feminist theology, which cuts across denominational barriers. This has emerged since the 1960s largely in response to the secular Women's Movement (discussed above), which was itself part of the worldwide struggle for civil liberties and human rights. Thus feminism itself has been described as 'one of the basic movements for human liberty'.[21] Feminist theologians have been concerned to re-examine the biblical and ecclesiastical traditions which have been used to affirm the subordination of women, in order to assess what in them is God's will for the Church and the world, and how much is simply the result of cultural conditioning. Some feminists have been so moved by the patriarchal views of the Bible and the apparent misogyny of some traditional teaching that they have left the institutional Church.[22] But others have found much that is affirmative of women in the Bible, and have contributed fresh understandings of traditional texts, such as the Genesis creation stories, the Gospel record of Jesus' attitude to women, or Paul's teaching.[23] Such thinkers have also been concerned to express their theology in practical ways, promoting women's participation at all levels in the Church's life, and caring for oppressed groups. In particular, they have developed 'non-sexist' liturgies, in which not only are worshippers referred to inclusively, but God is addressed in 'inclusive' language. Some recently published prayers, for example, invoke the Holy Trinity as 'Giver of life, Bearer of pain, and Maker of love'.[24] All this provides the background against which the Church's traditional theology of ministry is being stretched and challenged in ways undreamt of a few generations ago.

WOMEN'S MINISTRY AND CONTEMPORARY CHALLENGES TO THE CHURCHES

It will be obvious from the above survey that the Churches today are facing profound challenges which cannot be ignored.

First, there is their continued reaction to the Enlightenment and modern scientific approaches to biblical criticism, and doctrinal and ethical issues. Can old views about 'natural law' or the subordination of women be sustained in the modern world? Can our doctrines of God, Creation, 'Man', Sexuality, and Priesthood be rethought and reformulated, so as to make them intelligible to contemporary thinkers without destroying the traditional faith?[25]

Secondly, how in practical terms are the Churches to react to the process of democratization and social change? Can they continue with hierarchical and authoritative models of ministry in the face of the modern climate – not to mention New Testament teaching about the Church as a community? How can the Churches teach the acceptability of men and women before God, and continue to discriminate against women in their own ministry and organization? How is 'apostolate of the laity' and the idea of 'every member ministry' to be put into practice?

Thirdly, how are the Churches to respond to the challenge of the feminist movement? Can we adapt our liturgies and forms of worship to include women without destroying something valuable? Is it right to address God as 'Mother' or refer to God as 'she'? Is motherhood incompatible with ministry? How can the Church make best use of the gifts and experiences of women? What difference does the admission of women clergy make to the life of the Church? Do the Bible and Tradition require an all-male priesthood, and if not, is it right for women to continue to be excluded, as they still are in some denominations?

Even if we cannot answer all these questions in a book of this scope, we shall need to bear them in mind in the coming chapters.

NOTES

1   For the role of women in revolutionary and post-revolutionary France see Spencer (1984), esp. pts. I, II, V.

2   For example, the United Nations 1952 Convention on the Political Rights of Women, and the British Equal Pay Act of 1972 and Sex Discrimination Acts of the 1970s. The World Council of Churches, formed in 1948, has also been instrumental in supporting equality for women: see Bibliography.

3   See Kroll (1975), ch. 1; Oakley (1981), pp. 135–62; Storkey (1985), pp. 22–34, who notes that by the late 1970s in the UK only 11% of university teaching staff were women (and a mere 2% of Professors).

4   Storkey (1985), p. 13.

5   See, for example, Starhawk, 'Witchcraft and Women's Culture', in Christ and Plaskow (1979), pp. 259–68, and C. Christ, 'Why Women need the Goddess', ibid., pp. 273–86.

6   Storkey (1985), chs. 7–9, 14. The literature on all forms of feminism is immense: for some representative treatments see Mitchell (1971); Dowell and Hurcombe (1981); Maitland (1983); Oakley (1985); Loades (1987).

7   See P. Kra's essay, 'Montesquieu and Women' in Spencer (1984), pp. 272–84.

8   Letter dated 17 July 1837, cited in Schneir (1972), p. 40.

9   Extempore speech at the 1854 Women's Rights Convention in Philadelphia (cited in Schneir (1972), p. 100).

10 The first Church of Scotland deaconesses were appointed in 1888, and the first Scottish Episcopalian ones in 1917. On the deaconess movement see Heeney (1988), pp. 68–74.

11 Details in Larsson (1974), pp. 13–18.

12 See Gärtner and Strandberg in Moore (1978), pp. 123–33.

13 On women in modern Judaism see (Rabbi Sally) Priesand (1975); see further Jacobs (1984), emphasizing the ability of Judaism to adapt to social change.

14 Since 1957 the Greek Orthodox Church has had deaconesses, but they are appointed, not ordained (i.e. they are lay ministers). Isolated examples have occurred of nuns being formally ordained to the diaconate or subdiaconate, e.g. by Nektarios (Kephalas) in 1911 and by Archbishop Chrysostomos of Athens a few years later; but these are controversial, rare exceptions to the general pattern. Some Orthodox theologians do not even accept that the women deacons of the Byzantine Church were in Holy Orders: see further Tarasar and Kirillova (1977); Ware (1978), pp. 86f.; Fitzgerald (1983).

15 See Li and Harrison (1985). On Raven, H. Henson, W. R. Inge, and other early champions of women's ordination see Heeney (1988), esp. pp. 134–8; also Hastings (1985), esp. pp. 44, 294.

16 The first women to be made bishop were the Revd Barbara Harris in the US in 1989 and the Revd Dr Penelope Jamieson in New Zealand in 1990. For details of the position in other Anglican Provinces see the C. of E. reports cited in the Bibliography, esp. the Background Paper by C. Howard (1984).

17 *Gaudium et Spes* §29, Abbott and Gallagher (1966), pp. 227f.

18 e.g. Küng, Schillebeeckx and Boff, cited in ch. 5, n. 22. On the 'Liberation theology debate' see further Gibellini (1987).

19 The 1976 Declaration came from the Congregation for the Doctrine of the Faith rather than *motu proprio* from Pope Paul VI himself. It has not hindered further debate: see esp. L. and A. Swidler (1977); Wijngaards (1977). In 1979 the Catholic Biblical Association of America recorded its view that 'the New Testament evidence...points towards the admission of women to priestly ministry' (see *CBQ 41*, p. 613).

20 This document, while recognizing the spiritual gifts of women and their prominent role in the Gospels, provides no fresh arguments against their ordination. See esp. §26.

21 Schneir (1972), p. xi.

22 A notable figure is Mary Daly, Associate Professor of Theology at Boston College, Mass. In 1971, when invited to preach in the Harvard Memorial Chapel (its first woman speaker), she denounced the 'sexist' structure of institutional Christianity and called upon her congregation to leave the chapel in a symbolic exodus: see Maitland (1983), p. 141, and Daly (1975), (1986), etc.

23 See esp. the works of Fiorenza, Jewett, Moloney, Moltmann-Wendel, Ruether, and Trible, in Bibliography.

24 See Cotter (1986), p. 52.; also above Introduction, n. 7.

25 For a range of views see Mascall (1977b); Metz and Schillebeeckx (1981); Newbigin (1983); and the recent Reports of the Doctrine Commission and other C. of E. bodies in the Bibliography.

9

God as Father and Mother

A major reason why some Christians today find it hard to accept a public and sacramental ministry of women is the belief in a fundamentally masculine character of God. The logic seems to be that if God is in some sense male, sacramentally and cultically 'he' should be represented by exclusively male officiants. The introduction of women priests is therefore seen as implying a change in our understanding of the nature of God and hence of the essence of Christianity.[1] The primary task of this chapter is to explore whether there are any grounds for believing that God has sexuality, and what is the significance of the masculine imagery so frequently used of God. In the following two chapters we shall consider the implications for ministry of the creation of both men and women in the divine 'image' and arguments concerning the sacramental 'representation' of God by clergy, especially at the Eucharist.

MALE AND FEMALE IMAGES OF GOD IN THE BIBLICAL TRADITION

All language which attempts to describe divinity is analogical, and that includes even the language of the Judeo-Christian tradition. The people of Israel regularly referred to God in anthropomorphic terms. Yahweh (God) is described as 'walking in the garden in the cool of the day' (Gen. 3.8). References are made to parts of God's body – face, arm, hand, and even 'back parts' (e.g. Exod. 33.23). God is depicted as having human emotions – being angry, 'repenting' or having second thoughts.

And God is frequently pictured *as a male*. Yahweh is a 'man of war' (Exod. 15.3), the Lord of hosts (i.e. armies), the king of kings, shepherd, husband, father (though this last image is much less frequent in the Old Testament than one might expect). The various names for God are masculine in gender. In Hebrew grammatical gender has no direct relation to sexuality; yet there can be no doubt that the Old Testament's persistent use of masculine nouns, pronouns, and verbal forms has reinforced the picture of God as a male.[2]

In the New Testament also God is described in masculine terms. The most usual Greek word for God (*theos*) is regularly treated as masculine (in classical Greek it is of common gender). Jesus of Nazareth, whom Christians affirm as God incarnate, was historically a man, described by New Testament writers as the 'Son of God'. Masculine titles, used of Yahweh in the Old Testament, are applied to Jesus – he is 'Lord' (*kyrios*), king, shepherd, judge. It is well-established that Jesus prayed to God as Father, and taught his followers to do likewise (Matt. 6.9, 11.25; Mark 14.36, etc.).[3] Paul and other New Testament writers follow the same pattern. The tradition of masculine imagery continues in later Christian thought, especially in the Trinitarian understanding of God as 'Father, Son, and Holy Spirit', where the Spirit also is usually pictured as male.

Superficially, then, the Bible seems to teach throughout that God should be thought of as male. But is this the case? Closer examination reveals that it sometimes uses feminine imagery. In Isaiah God is compared to a woman comforting her son (66.13), and God's love is described as greater than that of a woman for the child she nursed (49.15). Deuteronomy describes God as the one who engendered Israel and painfully gave him birth (32.18; cf. Ps. 90.2; both verbs are regularly used for the mother's part in childbirth, the latter exclusively so). In a powerful metaphor Isa. 42.13f. describes God as 'groaning like a woman in labour, panting and gasping for air'. Ps. 22.9 applies the image of midwife to God: 'It was you who drew me from the womb and soothed me on my mother's breast' (cf. Ps. 71.6; Job 10.18f.; Isa. 46.3). In Hebrew the words for 'compassion' (*rah*^a*mim*) 'to love' (*raham*), and the adjective 'merciful' (*rahum*) are closely related to the word for 'womb' (*rehem*); from this some scholars have concluded that many of the references to God's 'com-

passion' should be seen as 'motherly' images.[4] In what may be
a maternal image for divine love Hosea (11.3) speaks of God
teaching Israel, like a small child, to walk, picking him up, and
feeding him. In the book of Baruch (4.8) God is described as
'nursing' Israel (the image is of breast-feeding).

All these passages relate to human mothers, but sometimes
God is compared to a mother bird: Isa. 31.5 speaks of Yahweh
protecting Jerusalem like female birds hovering [over their
nests]. The image of a caring she-bird is also suggested by the
well-known references in the Psalms (17.8; 37.7, etc.) to seeking
protection 'in the shadow of God's wings'. In the Gospels Jesus
applies the same image to himself in a lament over Jerusalem:
'O Jerusalem, Jerusalem, you that kill the prophets... how often
have I longed to gather your children together as a hen gathers
her chicks under her wings' (Matt. 23.37; Luke 13.34). This
moving simile had a profound effect on later Christian thinking
about Jesus, sometimes leading to direct comparisons between
him and a human mother. Most striking of all is the meditation
of Anselm, Archbishop of Canterbury (eleventh century):

> And you, Jesus, are you not also a mother?
>   Are you not the mother who, like a hen,
>   gathers her chickens under her wings?
> Truly, Lord, you are a mother;
>   for both they who are in labour
> and they who are brought forth
>   are accepted by you.

Keeping up the bird metaphor, he then addresses his own soul:

> And you, my soul, dead in yourself,
>   run under the wings of Jesus your mother,
>   and lament your griefs under his feathers.
> Ask that your wounds may be healed
>   and that, comforted, you may live again.[5]

Another leading Christian who took up the maternal image
was Clement of Alexandria (late second century). He used
'Mother' to describe God's sympathy and love, and 'Father' to
describe God's ineffable nature (one notes the ancient stereotyping of the sexes). In a profound statement on the incarnation,
he wrote: 'By his loving the Father became feminine.'[6] Clement
also uses motherly imagery of Jesus as the Logos (Word), calling

him 'Father and Mother, Teacher and Nourisher', who nurses his people with 'the milk of the Father' (where 'milk' stands for love).[7]

In his *Hymns* Synesius, Bishop of Ptolemais in Libya (fifth century), invoked God with both masculine and feminine imagery:

> You are Father, you are Mother,
> You are male, you are female,
> You are voice, you are silence'.[8]

Gregory Palamas (fourteenth century) spoke of Christ nursing us 'from his own breast, as a mother, filled with tenderness, does with her babies'.[9] Julian of Norwich (also fourteenth century) is famous for her feminine images for God. She describes Jesus as 'the true Mother of our nature, for he made us...our Mother too by grace, because he took our created nature upon himself', adding that 'all the lovely deeds and tender services that beloved motherhood implies' are appropriate to him. She also declares that God the Father is 'as truly our Mother as he is our Father.'[10] God, or Jesus, as mother is found also in Bernard of Clairvaux, Aelred of Rievaulx, and many other Christian mystics.

In the Old Testament the Hebrew word for spirit (*ruaḥ*) is feminine, as is also the Aramaic and Syriac, and this encouraged the early Syrian Church's picture of the Holy Spirit as a woman. Sometimes this was linked with bird imagery in the Old Testament, especially Gen. 1.2 where the Spirit of God 'broods' or 'hovers' over the waters in Creation. The verb used (from the root *rḥp*) was particularly associated with the actions of a mother bird. Some scholars have linked this with the descent upon Jesus at his baptism of the Holy Spirit in the form of a dove (Mark 1.10).[11] The Spirit was also pictured as female in the *Odes of Solomon* (possibly hymns of the Syrian Church) and in writings of the foremost Syrian Church Fathers, Aphrahat and Ephrem, who use the noun *ruḥḥapa* ('brooding') specifically of the Spirit's action in baptism, in the Eucharist (at the epiclesis) and in ordination.[12]

Feminine imagery for the Holy Spirit is also found in the Greek *Homilies* of Macarius (probably written in Syria), which pick up the Isaianic image of God as a mother comforting her child: 'The Spirit is our Mother, because the Paraclete, the

Comforter, will comfort us as a mother her child (Isa. 66.13) and because the believers are "reborn" as children of the mysterious mother, the Spirit (John 3.3, 5)'.[13] It also occurs in various Gnostic writings and in Kabbalistic tradition, and reappears in some representations of the Holy Trinity in medieval art.[14] Yet the predominant Christian image of the Spirit through the centuries has been male. Here again we may see the influence of grammatical gender: in Latin *spiritus* is a masculine noun; and although the regular Greek word for Spirit is neuter, John set a pattern for Western Christianity by using a masculine pronoun to refer to the 'Paraclete' as the Spirit of Truth.[15]

Returning to the Old Testament, some scholars have argued that at some periods and in some places Yahweh was pictured as having a female consort, like the chief Canaanite gods. The evidence for this, which is partly literary and partly archaeological, is difficult to assess, especially as the Old Testament contains strong denunciations of Canaanite and other goddesses; but the suggestion illustrates the dangers of dogmatism in claiming an exclusively male nature of God in Hebrew thought. Certainly divine Wisdom (Hebrew *ḥokmah*; Greek *sophia* – both feminine nouns) is regularly pictured as a woman, who invites seekers to enjoy her hospitality of food and drink, and spiritual teaching; this goddess-like figure personifies cosmic order, and is closely associated with God in the work of creation (see esp. Prov. 8–9; Ecclus. 24.1–22). In the Book of Wisdom (esp. ch. 7) she is praised in the highest possible terms. Some scholars believe that in Wisdom we have preserved memories of an early Hebrew goddess.[16] In later Jewish thought Wisdom is closely associated with the precious *Torah* (Law), the 'daughter' of God, who existed before the creation of the world and gives life to it. Thus the feminine figure of Wisdom is regarded as a 'hypostasis' or manifestation of God.[17]

In the New Testament Jesus Christ himself is implicitly, and sometimes even explicitly, identified with Wisdom (1 Cor. 1.22–4, 30; cf. 8.6; Matt. 11.19, par.; Luke 7.35; Col. 1.15–20). It is generally agreed that the depiction of Christ as the Logos in the Johannine Prologue is heavily dependent on the Wisdom tradition.[18] This semi-poetic or hymnic identification of Jesus with divine Wisdom influenced the development of traditional

Christian doctrine of the incarnation and the Nicene declaration that through Christ 'all things were made'. It plays an important part in recent feminist prayers. In a moving article Elizabeth Johnson has written that 'Jesus as Sophia incarnate includes all in the call to be friends of God, and can be represented by any human being called in Sophia's Spirit, women as well as men.' Speaking of 'Wisdom Christology' as 'an untapped resource of the Christian tradition', she suggests that Jesus as Sophia can be thought, even in his human maleness, 'to be revelatory of the graciousness of God imaged as female'.[19]

THE THEOLOGICAL SIGNIFICANCE OF THE IMAGES

The theological implications of all these images, whether masculine or feminine, need to be very carefully assessed. The Bible itself warns us that God is not a human being (Num. 23.19; 1 Sam. 15.29). In an important study G. B. Caird has pointed out the dangers of taking metaphorical language too literally.[20] There is no necessary relationship between the sexuality of the image and that of the person compared to it: Jeremiah compares male Israelites to a 'wild she-donkey...snuffling the breeze in desire' (Jer. 2.24) without implying that they are female! Non-anthropomorphic terms, such as lion (Hos. 5.14; Rev. 5.12), fire (Heb. 12.29), sun (Mal. 4.2 RSV = 3.20 NJB), light (1 John 1.5), or lamb (John 1.29; Rev. 5.12) generally have a lower degree of comparison than human ones. If God is described as a rock (Pss. 28.1; 62.2, etc.), this means God is strong and reliable, not that God is hard and igneous. Hebrew is very rich in picture-language, and does not readily distinguish the figurative from the literal; sometimes it uses widely different metaphors in rapid succession (in Isa. 42.14, cited above, the image of God as a woman in childbirth is immediately preceded by one of God as a warrior advancing in battle). The point of comparison may be very low indeed, as when Hosea describes God as like a moth or dry rot (5.12 RSV; 'ringworm' and 'gangrene', NJB).

Thus the feminine images for God have to be kept in proportion, and understood for what they are – picture-language designed to convey spiritual meaning. But so too are the masculine images. As Caird and others have shown, biblical images of God serve to illuminate understanding and affect emotions: they speak to us of relationships and reveal aspects of divine character. And 'if God is not to be depersonalized, then terms which are characteristically applied to male or female persons must also be applied to "him"'.[21] To interpret these images for our own age, we need to 'unpack' their meaning, bearing in mind the social conditions and thought-forms which created them; sometimes we may need to re-express them in tems applicable to our own culture. In Hebrew thought 'father' conveys primarily the ideas of authority and responsibility (e.g. Deut. 32.6; Jer. 31.9; Mal. 1.6; 2.10), sometimes also loving discipline and protection (esp. Prov. 3.11f.; Pss. 68.5; 103.13). 'Mother', as we have already seen, signifies life-giving, nurture, tender care and comfort (cf. also Gen. 3.20 – Eve as the 'mother of all living' – and the examples of loving mothers in 1 Sam. 2.19; 1 Kings 3.27; 17.23; 2 Kings 4.20). Although honour and obedience were enjoined to both parents (Exod. 20.12; Mark 7.10; Luke 2.51, etc.), it would have been inappropriate in biblical culture for 'mother' alone to stand for an authority figure. But this is not necessarily so in our society. Conversely in the ancient world maternal images denoted *par excellence* intimate loving care, like that of a mother for her baby. Today, some fathers care for young children in ways which would have shocked earlier generations. So for us the paternal image may also convey tenderness.

Now some scholars have suggested that the masculine images of the Bible are of a different order from the feminine ones. John Saward, in arguing against the ordination of women, condemns 'a failure to appreciate the differing status of "father-talk" and "mother-talk" as applied to God', describing father-talk as fundamental, mother-talk as metaphorical. He also insists that by fatherhood biological paternity is intended, the 'active' male role being an effective symbol for God the Creator; women, being 'passive' in the sexual act, cannot symbolize this active role.[22]

But how can one make this distinction between 'fundamental' and 'metaphorical' images? It cannot be made merely on the basis of comparative frequency in the Bible, for it is only natural that in a patriarchally-ordered society male images will predominate. Nor can it be solely because Jesus addressed God as 'Father', and is described in the New Testament as 'the Son'. For Jesus' sonship is of no mere biological kind. The biblical title 'son of God' symbolizes kingship and, almost certainly, also Messiahship. It implies a quality of character like that of God, and obedience to God's will. In intertestamental Judaism and early Christianity pious men *and* women were called 'sons of God' (cf. Matt. 5.9; Rom. 8.14–17). Of course, Christians believe that Jesus was God's 'son' in a unique way. But even the birth narratives do not imply biological paternity in the sense that in Greek mythology Zeus became the father of Herakles by sexual intercourse with Alkmene (on the implications of Jesus' incarnation as a male see further Chapter 11, pp. 167f.).

Moreover, Saward's argument from 'active' and 'passive' sexual roles is sadly faulted: it is simply a resuscitation of the erroneous biology of Aristotle and Aquinas. The production of a child entails the combination of chromosomes from both parents; to describe the woman's part as 'passive' because the masculine 'seed' is 'received' by the feminine 'vessel' is playing with words. Conception results from the uniting of the female and male gamete; it is not analogous to the placing of a seed in a furrow. Furthermore, women not only take an active part psychosexually in lovemaking (as Saward himself recognizes); they also perform the onerous and demanding roles of carrying and nurturing the child in the womb, giving birth (painfully and sometimes at risk to their own lives), and feeding the new baby from their own bodies. To describe all this process as 'passive', compared with the male's 'activity' and 'creativity' is well-nigh incredible.

It cannot be too strongly stressed that the biblical image of God as Father is not a biological one. It is concerned about qualities of character and relationships, not physical begetting (the whole discussion has been hampered by crude interpretations of the virgin birth of Christ). And once it is recognized that the female role in ordinary human procreation is just as active and 'creative' as the male, any need to envisage God's parental love in exclusively male terms vanishes. The essentially non-sexual nature of the biblical metaphors can be appreciated from both the illustrations cited earlier in this chapter and other examples of the Church's free mixing of male and female images (e.g. when the Council of Toledo described Christ as born from the womb (*uterus*) of the Father).[23] Thus it may rightly be claimed, 'in neither the Old nor the New Testament is the concept of divine fatherhood "sexual" or "sexist".'[24] Traditional Christianity affirms that God is suprasexual, as is well expressed in some of the Church's historic formularies.[25] But because we need human language to describe God, and because Christians believe God is personal rather than impersonal, it is appropriate to use both male and female images. To say this is not for one minute to suggest that we should all start praying to 'our Mother in heaven'. Many, if not most, Christians will prefer to follow Jesus' example and continue to pray to God as 'Father', especially since there is no instance in the Bible of God being directly addressed as 'mother', and 'Father' in the teaching of Jesus is such a tender, loving image (see, for example, Matt. 6.26, 32; 7.11; Luke 15.11–32, though note also Matt. 6.15; 18.35). But the fact remains that God, in so far as God is knowable, has qualities which we associate with both male and female. The examples of the Church Fathers and other leading Christian thinkers show that there are occasions when feminine imagery for God may be appropriate.

MALE-FEMALE IMAGERY AND THE ORDAINED MINISTRY

It remains to consider the relationship of sexual imagery to the ministry. In the ancient world there was no direct relationship between the sex attributed to a deity and his or her ministrants, and it is simply untrue that female priests belong exclusively to earth-goddesses.[26] No Old Testament text ever links the maleness of Israel's priesthood with the 'masculine' qualities of Yahweh.[27] In any case the Christian ordained ministry is not directly modelled on the Jewish priesthood, even though in some traditions it has been deeply influenced by it. Thus the recognition that women may serve God as priests (or ministers) no more implies a female deity than the existence, for so many centuries, of male clergy implies that God is actually male. God, as we have seen, is suprasexual, but shares characteristics in common with both the male and female parts of humanity. If the ordained ministry in any sense represents God, as well as humanity, there is good reason for it to include both male and female members.

NOTES

1 cf. Oddie (1984); Hayter (1987), pp. 7–11, citing C. S. Lewis and E. L. Mascall.

2 Trible (1978), p. 23, n. 5; cf. Hayter (1987), p. 9, citing R. Patai.

3 Even the more sceptical New Testament scholars agree that Jesus had a strong sense of 'filial consciousness': see esp. Jeremias (1978), on his use of *abba*, 'father', together with Barr (1988), pp. 173–9.

4 See esp. Trible (1978), ch. 2. Trible has been criticized for reading 'motherly' connotations too readily into the Old Testament use of this word-group. It is true that words quickly lose their etymological meanings, but they can also be used with deliberate consciousness of them. See further Miller (1986); Smith (1988), p. 179.

5 Anselm, *Prayers* 10: 398–403, 465–9 (tr. Ward). The extracts come from a meditation on the apostle Paul as mother (cf. 1 Thess. 2.7; Gal. 4.19). On Jesus as 'mother' in other medieval writers and in Middle English prayers see Ward (1973), p. 67; Loades (1987), pp. 92f.

6 Clem. Al., *Quis Div. Salv.* 37.

7 *Paedagogus* 1. 42. In a series of somewhat mixed metaphors Clement also speaks of Christ as a cluster of grapes, milk, flesh and blood.

8 Synesius, *Hymns* 5 (2) 63f. (ed. Lacombrade).

9 See Lewis (1984), p. 50.

10 Julian, *Revelations of Divine Love Chs. 58f.* (ed. Wolters).

11 The Greek is *peristera*, a feminine noun. But great caution needs to be exercised in assessing the significance of gender in such imagery, as the ancients often referred to some birds and animals in the fem., and some in the masc., without implying biological sex. The dove was, however, a regular symbol for the 'feminine' qualities of gentleness, affection, and marital faithfulness, being esp. associated with female deities of love: see Thompson (1936), pp. 238–47. A fuller study of dove-symbolism in rabbinic, Near Eastern, and Greek thought might well throw light on the deeper meaning of Mark 1.10.

12 See Murray (1975), pp. 142–4.

13 See Moltmann-Wendel and Moltmann (1983), ch. 6, esp. p. 103. Macarius also refers to the Holy Spirit as 'a good and kind mother'.

14 See Pagels (1976), and (1979), esp. pp. 51–3, with Heine (1987), pp. 106–23 (on Gnostic concepts); Murray (1975), p. 320 with Moltmann-Wendel and Moltmann (1983), p. 102 (on the Holy Spirit as female in art).

15 Grammatically the pronoun *ekeinos* in John 14.26, 15.26, 16.8, 13, 14 refers to the 'paraclete', Greek *paraklētos*, meaning 'advocate' or

'defence attorney', or hence 'champion' or 'helper', rather than to the Spirit as such (*pneuma* is neuter).

16 See L. Swidler in L. and A. Swidler (1977), pp. 167–75; Lang (1986); and Hayter (1987), pp. 12–18 (evaluating the work of Patai and Ringren).

17 On Wisdom and Torah see Johnson (1985), esp. pp. 265f.

18 See Schnackenburg (1980–82), vol. I, pp. 229–81, 481–93; Dunn (1980), chs. 6–7.

19 Johnson (1985), p. 294. Wisdom already plays an important role in Russian religious and philosophical tradition: see Visser 't Hooft (1982), p. 130.

20 Caird (1980), esp. chs. 7–8.

21 So Hayter (1987), p. 39.

22 Saward (1978), pp. 12f.

23 See Hayter (1987), p. 35.

24 Hayter (1987), p. 37; cf. Hamerton-Kelly (1979), esp. p. 102; Moltmann, 'The Motherly Father' in Metz and Schillebeeckx (1981), pp. 51–6.

25 e.g. Article 1 of the Thirty-Nine Articles (of the C. of E.): 'There is but one living and true God, everlasting, without body, parts, or passions'; cf. Westminster Confession of Faith, ch. 2.

26 So Russell and Dewey (1978), p. 95. In the ancient world female priests regularly served in the cult of male deities, such as Dionysos, Calaurian Poseidon, and Thasian Herakles, as well as of a wide range of goddesses, including Athene, Demeter and Vesta: see Farnell (1904).

27 The reasons for Israel's all-male priesthood have been much debated: the notion of cultic 'uncleanness' was probably a major factor – so J. and G. Muddiman (1984), pp. 4f; cf. Hayter (1987), pp. 60–79. Other possible causes are the need to distinguish Yahweh's worship from Canaanite cults with female ministrants (including cult-prostitutes), the subordinate position of women in the Jewish world, and the idea that in religious, as in other, matters they can be appropriately 'represented' by men.

10

Male and Female: Equal before God?

Opponents of women's ordination frequently argue that to ordain women is to deny God-given differences in the two sexes. We saw in Chapters 6 and 7 how many older writers, including Church Fathers and medieval thinkers, did not hesitate to suppose that the differences between men and women involved a male superiority in terms of intellect, creativity and leadership, in contrast to female 'weakness', dependency, sensuality and proneness to sin: in short, it was widely assumed that women are actually *inferior* to men. By contrast, modern writers who stress the differences between women and men usually recognize their fundamental *equality*, but still affirm that women's nature designs them for tasks other than priesthood.

The argument can readily be illustrated from writers of three different ecclesial traditions. Stephen B. Clark, a Roman Catholic, in his influential and substantial *Man and Woman in Christ*, vigorously maintains that the differences between men and women are not due to socialization or cultural conditions, but are part of God's plan for the ordering of the world; he believes that the Creation narratives, Ephesians 5 and other texts show that 'the whole of the woman's life (everything she does) has to be subordinate to her husband'; this applies not only to marriage, but also to the Christian community, where women's leadership must always be under the direction of men.[1] Graham Leonard, Bishop of London, and leading Anglican opponent of women's priesthood, in a popular article cites Clark's work approvingly, affirming that 'the difference between the sexes is part of the Divine Plan for creation'.[2] Bishop Kallistos Ware, a distinguished Orthodox theologian, similarly claims that the differences between the sexes are an aspect of humanity's natural state before the Fall, writing: 'It is one of the chief glories of human nature that men and women, although equal, are not interchangeable. ... There exists between them a certain order or hierarchy, with man as the "head" and woman as the partner or "helper".' Because of this hierarchical order, as well as for other reasons to which we shall return in Chapter 11, Ware argues that women cannot serve as priests.[3]

Such writers rely mainly on two types of material: biblical and patristic passages which enjoin, or seem to enjoin, female subordination; and observations from human behaviour and the supposed characteristics of male and female, supported by findings and opinions of some psychologists and social scientists. We take these in turn.

ARGUMENTS FOR THE SUBORDINATION OF WOMEN FROM THE BIBLE AND TRADITION

The heart of the argument comes from the Creation narratives of Genesis 1–3 together with their use in the New Testament. From these some have deduced, first, that women are not made in the image of God to the same degree as men; and, second, that the Bible teaches a 'Creation Ordinance' involving the permanent subordination of women to men. But close examination shows that neither of the two accounts of Creation in Genesis 1–2 offers any strong support for these views. Misunderstandings have arisen from the use in these narratives of the Hebrew term ʾadam, which may be used generically for mankind, for man in the sense of male, and even as a proper name Adam (so, probably, first in Gen. 3.17 and 21).

In the first account of Creation in Gen.1 ʾadam is used for mankind or humanity in general, including both male and female simultaneously: this meaning is clearly illustrated in the key verses (1.26f.):

God said, 'Let us make man in our own image, in the likeness of ourselves, and let *them* be masters of the fish of the sea, the birds of heaven, the cattle, the wild animals, and all the creatures that creep along the ground.' God created man in the image of himself, in the image of God he created him, male and female he created *them*.

We note that ꜣ*adam* here explicitly includes female as well as male, and the plural 'them' (in Hebrew a pronominal suffix) shows that the author saw both man and woman as created in God's image and as having 'dominion' (i.e. caring stewardship) over the animal world. There is no hint of anything but equality between the sexes. The profound significance for the ministry of women of this affirmation, that woman – like man – is made in the *imago dei* and has a share in God's purpose for the world, should not be underestimated.

The second account of Creation in Genesis 2 might, at first sight, seem to give more support to the idea of female subordination. It has been noted that in this account (i) the female is made after the male; (ii) she is taken from the man's rib; (iii) she is designated as his 'helper'; and (iv) she is named by the man. From this it has been deduced that women are secondary to men in God's plan for Creation and must be permanently subordinate to them. But every element in the story which has been used to support these views may be challenged.

(i) There is no emphasis whatever on the masculinity of the human being first fashioned by God from 'the dust of the ground' (Gen. 2.7). We are so used to artistic representations of Adam as a male (e.g. Michelangelo's in the Sistine Chapel), that we overlook the possibility that ꜣ*adam* may here be used with its most common meaning of 'human being' (cf. the translation 'Mensch' in some German versions). Genesis 2 regularly uses this word with the definite article, *ha-ꜣadam*, 'the man/human being', rather than as a proper name, Adam (see 2.7f., 15f., 19–23, 25). Thus the command not to eat the forbidden fruit (2.16) may be seen as applying to the woman as well as to the man, even though she has not yet been 'created' as a separate being (cf. her share in the punishment for disobedience); likewise the 'naming' of the animals may belong to humanity, rather than just its male part. An androgynous, or sexually undifferentiated, interpretation of ꜣ*adam* has been forcibly argued by Phyllis Trible, and accepted by many recent writers and exegetes. But problems arise in vv.23–25, when woman is formed from man's rib: can one really talk about 'the human being' and his wife?[4] For this and other reasons, some scholars prefer to follow the traditional view that, even when ꜣ*adam* is used with the definite article, it is intended to describe a male person, created before the female part of humanity. But even if they are right, one must remember that chronological priority does not necessarily imply superiority: in Genesis 1 the animals were made before mankind, but this does not make them superior to human beings.

(ii) No special significance should be attached to taking of the woman from man's *rib*, rather than his head as the seat of intelligence (cf. above p. 110 on Aquinas). There is nothing particularly dishonourable about the 'rib' as such, any more than there is about 'the man' being made from the dust or soil. 'Adam's' poetic description of the woman as 'bone of my bone and flesh of my flesh' (Gen. 2.23) is a vivid expression of the essential unity or 'family solidarity' of male and female.[5] Moreover, we must not forget that we are here dealing with an ancient aetiological myth (tale of origin), involving a double pun on two different Hebrew words for man – (1) *ʾadam*, 'human being', alongside *ʾadamah*, 'earth', and (2) *ʾish*, 'husband', 'male', alongside *ʾishshah*, 'wife', 'woman' (both nouns first occurring in 2.23). The apparent derivation of *ʾish* from *ʾishshah* no more indicates subordination than the feminine form 'poetess' means that all women poets must be subordinate to male poets.[6]

(iii) In Gen. 2.18 the Hebrew word for 'helper' (*ʿezer*) brings with it no connotation of subordination – rather the reverse – since it is regularly used for a superior 'assisting' a subordinate (cf. above p. 30). The phrase *kᵉnegdo*, traditionally rendered 'meet' or 'suitable' for him, more probably means 'as his counterpart', or 'corresponding to him', and may even be designed to temper any hint of the *superiority* of woman over man (so Trible and Hayter)!

(iv) The so-called 'naming' of the woman in Genesis 2.23 (which does not even include the proper name Eve) implies not domination, but rather recognition: it is a cry of discovery, that here is *ʾishshah*, 'woman'![7]

Against all these arguments we have to set the fact that many commentators in the past, including some New Testament writers, *have* interpreted Genesis 2 as indicating male superiority (usually because they take *ʾadam* in an exclusively male sense). Paul seems to have done so when he argued that woman reflects man's glory and that he is her *kephalē*, i.e. 'head' or 'source' (1 Cor. 11.3–10; cf. 1 Tim. 2.13; see above pp. 65f.). Biblical tradition as a whole presupposes the seniority of the elder over the younger – though God sometimes reverses this.[8] But before we draw any conclusions from these points, we need to look at the 'Fall' narrative of Genesis 3. It is here above all that those who argue for the inferiority or the subordination of women to men rest their case. In Genesis 3 the woman sins first and then persuades her husband to sin, and it is expressly said that as a result she will have pain in child-bearing, her desire will be to her husband, and he will 'rule' over her.

This argument that Eve was the first sinner and therefore women as a whole are weaker or more sinful than men has been reiterated from Tertullian to Luther and John Knox, and still appears in modern discussions of women's ministry. The view is even apparently supported in the New Testament: 1 Timothy 2.9–15 urges that women should be silent in church and not exercise authority, on the grounds that 'Adam was not deceived, but the woman was deceived and became the transgressor'. It has its roots in older Jewish exegesis, including Ben Sirach's striking assertion: 'Sin began with a woman, and thanks to her we must all die' (Ecclus. 25.24). But are these interpretations in keeping with the Genesis author's original intention?

Modern scholarship shows that Genesis 3 was composed not as a sophisticated allegory, but as an aetiological story with a religious message. Its author has a sense of humour, as is witnessed by the brilliant scene in which Eve and Adam in turn each seek to 'pass the buck' for the act of disobedience. In a society where women normally obeyed their husbands it adds a touch of irony to have the woman take the initiative, as Eve does, but morally Adam is as much to blame as his wife – indeed more so, if it is believed authority rested with him. Many peoples have stories in which women bring evil into the world (cf. the Greek myth of Pandora's box).

But Genesis 3 is surprisingly free from misogyny. In the 'curse' on woman (v.16) it encapsulates the day-to-day experience of women in ancient societies – subordinate to their husbands and experiencing pain in childbirth. John Gibson observes this in his percipient commentary, adding:

What we must not do, however, is to take out of it [this verse] any notion that woman's unhappy state is a particular cross she has to bear because she is particularly sinful. Our Victorian forefathers were fond of citing this verse as a reason for resisting the use of anaesthetic at childbirth and as a justification for not giving women the vote. We must reject out of hand such an obscene recourse to Scripture.

He continues:

This is a story, not a treatise on morals. It is sketching lightly some and only some of the effects of human sin, and it is at this point concentrating on the female half of the fallen race. But it could easily have gone on to say that all disease and suffering, all slavery and exploitation, whether felt by or dealt out to male or female, have their origin in the same undivided guilt of humanity. This would have been just as true, but we would never have dreamt of concluding from it that hospitals or doctors or the overthrow of tyranny or the making of just laws were contrary to God's will.[9]

By the same logic one should not conclude that the subordination of women to men is God's will for all time. At the most it can be seen as the result of the 'Fall'; certainly not part of any original 'Creation order'.

As for the New Testament, both passages in question (1 Tim. 2.13f. and 1 Cor. 11.3–10) are re-interpreting the Genesis narrative for paraenetic purposes, and going well beyond the intentions of the original author(s). It may be questioned how far it is right for us to re-echo their arguments. Even such a conservative scholar as R. N. Longenecker argues that Christians should not reproduce New Testament exegesis which evidences itself to be 'merely cultural' or 'ad hominem in nature'.[10] Both 1 Cor. 11.3–10 and 1 Tim. 2.13f. seem to be just this: they are exploiting traditional Jewish exegesis to support their case for what they see as good order in the Church. They are clearly arguing ad hominem, and whatever their authorship, they must surely be interpreted in the light of Paul's more universal teaching on sin, redemption, and the new creation in Christ (cf. 2 Cor. 5.17; Eph. 4.24; Col. 3.10; and above pp. 55f. on Gal. 3.28, where Paul seems to be specifically setting aside the old Jewish sexual inequalities).

Quite apart from ignoring the New Testament evidence, in

their handling of the Genesis texts theologians such as Clark, Ware and Leonard seem to be living in a pre-critical age. We must constantly remember that Genesis 1–3 is not a factual account of historical events but early myth, serving a theological purpose. We misuse it if we distort it to make it serve some totally different purpose from that for which it was intended.

It remains to say something about the patristic and medieval use of the Creation narratives. However high a view is taken of the authority of the Church Fathers and Doctors, there can be few Christians who would wish to accept it if it could be shown to be contrary either to the Bible or to reason. Their subordinationist exegesis of Genesis 1–3 rests on very insecure foundations, especially the idea that women are made less in the image of God than men, which is quite contrary to any reasonable understanding of Genesis 1.26f. The Fathers felt the need to support their biblical interpretations with reference to 'nature', i.e. arguments from reason. This leads us to the second part of our chapter.

OBSERVATION FROM HUMAN BEHAVIOUR AND THE ARGUMENT FROM 'NATURE'

Discussion here hinges on the differences between the sexes, which it has been suggested show that women are designed 'by nature' to be subordinate (or inferior) to men and should therefore not be ordained. For this argument to be effective it must be shown that (1) these differences are not caused by environment and social upbringing, but are inherent to women as such (differences that are merely the result of cultural conditions cannot logically be used to support the *permanent* exclusion of women from ordained ministry, but only their temporary exclusion as long as these conditions prevail); and (2) such differences as are securely identifiable are in fact relevant to ministry. The differences fall into two broad categories: (i) biological and physical; and (ii) intellectual, psychological and social.

Biological and physical differences

Those who regard biological maleness as essential for priesthood tend to maximize the physical differences between men and women. Thus E. L. Mascall (former Professor of Historical Theology at King's College, London) writes: 'Men and women are not just two species of the *genus homo*...Humanity is, so to speak, essentially binary; it exists only in the two modes of masculinity and femininity'.[11] Similarly Graham Leonard speaks of the 'profound and deep' (*sic*) differences between the sexes and of the 'duality' which runs through creation.[12] Since the biological difference between male and female is apparently so essential, we must begin by defining it. At first sight it seems obvious: women have female sex organs; they produce female egg-cells; they menstruate and they have babies. Men on the other hand have male genitalia, and produce sperm as potential fathers. Secondary sexual characteristics include the shape and weight of male and female bodies, their degree of muscular development and of hairiness, and voice-pitch. None of these characteristics, except perhaps the last, would seem to have any special relevance to ordained ministry.

Moreover, none of the primary characteristics is *invariably* true of all women or all men. Not all women bear children, nor do all menstruate; not all men can produce sperm or become fathers. Both male and female sexual organs may be altered by surgical operation or accident. Is a male with defective genitalia to be considered ineligible for priesthood, as happened in ancient Judaism? As for secondary characteristics, not all men are taller, heavier, hairier, or more muscular than all women; not all women are physically weaker than men. If a man's body-build has something to do with qualifications for priesthood, then some athletic women might well qualify. Few women's voices can be so weak that they cannot be heard in church with or without the aid of amplification; some men have weak voices. The ability to sing a bass or tenor line in choral music is surely a job-requirement for specific types of cathedral post rather than a *sine qua non* for every type of ordained ministry.

At a more general level, we also need to consider the phenomenon of transsexualism: some men and women, while displaying the physical characteristics of one sex, may have an overwhelming feeling that they belong to the opposite one. Modern surgery and hormone treatment may so alter a person's sexuality that he or she may take on the character of the opposite sex: if maleness is necessary for ministry, would females who have undergone such changes be eligible?

But of course the physical differences in the sexes go deeper than all this. Experts today agree that the real difference between men and women does not lie in observable outward characteristics, but in their chromosomes: a female baby results from the linking of two X chromosomes, a male from XY.[13] Yet even here there are ambiguities: every year numbers of people are born with chromosome abnormalities, resulting in failure to conform to the regular pattern of male-female sexual characteristics. The effect of all this is that rather than emphasizing, with Dr Mascall and others, the polarity or binary nature of the sexes, many experts today prefer to speak of a 'spectrum of sex' and 'M–F scales'. The fact remains that, whether in its masculine or feminine form, the human race stands as a single species, clearly differentiated from other species.

Intellectual, psychological and social differences

But those who argue against women's ordination on sexual grounds usually adduce further arguments from apparently masculine and feminine qualities of personality, skills, and way of life, which they believe arise from their different sexual make-up. Here we enter into the notorious 'battle of the sexes'.

Over the centuries it has been continually asserted that men display qualities of leadership, creativity, initiative and courage; women those of dependence, supportiveness, and care for others. Men have been associated with the power of intellectual reasoning; women are seen as more emotional and intuitive. Such views are found even in the writings of modern theologians like Karl Barth, who on the one hand argues that it is better to avoid 'generalized pronouncements' about male-female differences, and then proceeds to categorize the male as the 'inspirer, leader, and initiator' in his common being and action with woman, and to speak of his need to avoid 'self-glorification' because he is 'superior in relation to woman'.[14] The arguments have been elaborated at length in relation to women's ministry by Stephen Clark, who draws on material from the social sciences to argue that women are designed for different spheres of activity from men, since in them 'heart, intellect and temperament are much more interwoven', whereas 'in man there is a specific capacity to emancipate himself with his intellect from the affective sphere'; that 'the male mind discriminates, analyzes, separates, and refines', while the...'feminine mind knows relatedness, has an intuitive perception of feeling'.[15] In other words, shorn of jargon, Clark reaffirms the old view that women are emotional, men rational.

But what are the scientific facts? Can men be shown to have greater objectivity than women and a greater capacity to reason? And if they have does it make them more suitable for priesthood?

The facts are that there is no general agreement among researchers about the personality traits which feature so largely in popular discussions of the psychology of the sexes. With regard to intellectual capacities, attempts to show that women's brains are proportionally smaller than men's have failed.[16] Psychological tests have produced varying results: it has been claimed that, in general, men have better co-ordination of gross bodily movement and more physical speed than women, but that women have better manual dexterity. In some tests boys have been found to excel girls in visual-spatial orientation, and certain mathematical skills, while females often outdo males in speed and accuracy of perception and in memory, verbal fluency and other linguistic skills.[17] But two points must be made here. (1) None of these tests prove that these particular skills and qualities belong inherently (i.e. 'by nature') to men and women. Upbringing and social conditioning affect drastically the capacity of a male or female for certain tasks. For example, the idea that males are naturally more 'scientific' than females is belied when statistics are compared from differing social backgrounds: proportionally far more women study engineering in the Soviet Union than in Europe or the United States; there are proportionally more women scientists in Japan than the West.[18] Obviously cultural expectation has much to do with these trends. Where there is so much cultural variation, great caution needs to be exercised before drawing general conclusions about the relative intellectual capacities of male and female. (2) Even if it were true that men and women in general have the capacities outlined above, it is doubtful what relevance this would have to the ordained ministry, where good memory and verbal skills might well be thought more useful than visual-spatial ability and arithmetical reasoning.

Turning now to the more affective qualities of personality, it is well established that males are, in general, more aggressive than females (this applies to animals as well as to the human species).[19] Some social psychologists have also argued that men are more achievement-oriented than women, who are more easily discouraged by failure, but also more social and amenable than men (these findings have been disputed). It is likely that a major cause of male aggressiveness is hormone make-up: already in the womb, as a result of their different chromosomes, male foetuses produce the hormone androgen; and in puberty further hormones are released, resulting in the growth of what we regard as typically masculine physique and behaviour. But a *biological* causal connection between aggressive behaviour and male hormone levels remains hard to prove[20] (women, as well as men, can be aggressive, especially verbally). One should add that the relative abilities of male and female vary according to age and maturity, as well as from individual to individual. Moreover, most tests have been carried out in Western societies, so that their conclusions may not be universally true. And within the general patterns already discussed there are enormous variations. As V. Klein has acutely observed, 'Masculinity and femininity are not mutually exclusive alternatives, but are combinations of traits, unevenly distributed among individuals of either sex'.[21] Even if it could be conclusively proved that aggressiveness and domination are characteristically male qualities, one would have to ask whether these qualities are more to be desired in a Christian minister than gentleness and care for others.

Motherhood, female sexuality, and ministry

One loophole remains for those who adduce biological or social arguments from the differences in the sexes to oppose women's ordination: if motherhood or feminine sexuality could in themselves be shown to be incompatible with Christian ministry, then they might have a case. Many traditionalists simply assume that the true 'vocation' of a woman is to become a mother, with the implication that she cannot simultaneously be a priest. Thus, Jean-Jacques von Allmen, a well-known Calvinist theologian, has argued that ministry 'is a grace which has not been purposed for them [women], because it would divert them from their being and their vocation [as mothers]'.[22] Similarly John Saward, an Anglican scholar, has warned of the 'dehumanization of life', which he believes will follow if men and women are regarded as interchangeable and women are ordained.[23] Women thinkers sometimes take the same view. Susannah Herzel asks: 'If I had to choose, would I rather be a woman or a priest?', as if these were mutually exclusive alternatives, arguing: 'If we just place woman in a role which is essentially masculine [i.e. the priesthood], woman will sooh forget how to be woman. She will become incurably frigid, a sort of Lot's wife'.[24] Margaret Hood, a leader of the Association for the Apostolic Ministry, suggests that 'women in their natural vocation' (sc. motherhood) do not need to be ordained as priests.[25]

Such arguments overlook certain essential points. (1) Not all women become mothers: to argue that motherhood is *the* natural vocation of all women is to condemn a substantial section of womankind to 'unnatural' activities. (2) There is no evidence whatever that becoming a minister or priest defeminizes a woman – similar arguments were once adduced against giving women the vote. (3) It is perfectly possible in today's world to be both a mother and an ordained minister. In days past, before modern medicine and family planning, motherhood may have been a full-time occupation for some women, but this is no longer the case, especially in the Western world when even married women have many years of potential for fruitful service after their children have grown up. The old argument of Chrysostom and other ancient writers that public activities are masculine, and domestic ones feminine, no longer holds water in the light of women's access to the professions, and their proven ability to cope with them, sometimes even when their children are young.[26] As so often, time-bound social customs have been confused with universal truths or laws of nature.

The only logical reason for excluding women from ministry

on the basis of their maternal roles would be if feminine sexuality were somehow less acceptable to God than male sexuality. Maybe at times some members of the Church have believed this (cf. above Chs. 6–7); but it is both contrary to modern understanding of sexuality and a perversion of biblical teaching, which rather stresses the value before God of sexual love within marriage and of the procreation of children. The idea, once evoked by the Church Union in response to the 1935 Archbishops' Commission on the Ministry of Women that 'the ministrations of women will tend to lower the spiritual tone of Christian worship' because they will incite erotic emotions in the men by their physical attractiveness, now seems laughable in the light of women's regular public roles in positions of leadership and the experience of Churches which already ordain women.[27] Such sentiments are worthy of the ancient *Testament of Reuben* (see above p. 29).

Finally we must mention the so-called 'purity laws' regarding menstruation and childbirth. These may have been a factor in the exclusion of women from the Jewish priesthood, but were never invoked in the New Testament in connection with ministry, not even by those who wished to restrict women's leadership roles. They must be regarded as superseded for Christians along with dietary laws and circumcision. Taboos and fears about menstruating women lie deep in the minds of some people; but, for those who affirm that both male and female are made in God's image and both are redeemed in Jesus Christ, there can be no rational objection to women performing sacral duties while experiencing the natural feminine functions of menstruation or pregnancy, any more than there can be to married men serving as ministers or priests while being fathers.[28]

CONCLUSIONS

Neither the biblical accounts of Creation nor the observable differences in the sexes prove that women are inherently inferior to men and must therefore be subordinate to them. Yet to argue that women must be subordinate, not because they are inferior, but because they are merely 'different', lacks logic, unless it can be shown that these differences are of such a sort as to make subordination desirable. None of the writers whose views we have examined shows this to be the case. It follows therefore that the traditional argument that women must be excluded from ordination because they are 'under authority' and cannot symbolize 'eminence' (cf. Aquinas) must be rejected. We must also reject modern re-expressions of the argument which affirm sexual 'equality' while simultaneously excluding women on the grounds of the 'profound' psychological differences between the sexes, (which have been greatly exaggerated).

But perhaps there remains something about the nature of *ministry* or *priesthood*, which makes it impossible for women to partake of it. It is to this question that we must now turn.

NOTES

1 Clark (1980), esp. pp. 83, 181–4, 605f. Clark rejects female priesthood, but believes women may serve as deaconesses (under men).
2 Leonard (1984), pp. 43f.
3 Ware (1978), p. 84.
4 See Trible (1978); (1979); Hayter (1987), chs. 5–6; cf. Morley (1984); Jewett (1975); Ellingworth (1978); Ellington (1979).
5 cf. Gen. 29.14. Judg. 9.2, etc., where the same phrase is used of family relationships, and the idiomatic use of *ꜥeṣem* (lit. 'bone') for the very essence of something.
6 It is, in fact, doubtful whether *ʾishshah* has any etymological connection with *ʾish*. See Hayter (1987), pp. 96–110, with criticisms of the handling of these passages by Aquinas and Barth.
7 On the 'naming formula' here and in Gen. 3.20 (where the proper name Eve first appears), see Ramsey (1988), correcting Trible.
8 Striking examples are God's choice of Jacob rather than Esau, and of David in preference to his older brothers.
9 Gibson (1981), vol. I, p. 137.
10 Longenecker (1975), p. 219.
11 Mascall (1978), p. 21.
12 Leonard (1984), pp. 43, 47; cf. Amiel (1988).
13 See Hutt (1972), esp. chs. 1, 5; Kessler and McKenna (1978), ch. 3; Oakley (1985), ch. 1.
14 Compare Barth (1958–61), pt. 2, p. 287 and pt. 4, p. 170.
15 Clark (1980), p. 381 (citing von Hildebrand), and p. 383 (citing Bardwick).
16 See Griffiths and Saraga (1979), esp. p. 20, showing there is no conclusive evidence either that the female frontal region is smaller than the male, or that this part of the brain is responsible for intelligence.
17 The complex evidence is discussed in detail in a standard work,

Maccoby and Jacklin (1974), chs. 2–7; further references in their
substantial Annotated Bibliography, pp. 395–627.

18 See further Griffiths and Saraga (1979); McMillan (1982), criticizing
Rousseau, Hegel, Freud, and Simmel for their views of women's
'intuitive' reason.

19 Hutt (1972), ch. 8; Maccoby and Jacklin (1974), p. 352; see further
Lips and Colwill (1978), esp. ch. 9; also Clark (1980), pp. 371–448.

20 See further Wijngaards (1977), pp. 24–32 and the literature cited
there.

21 Klein (1974) p. 908.

22 Von Allmen, in Mascall (1977a), p. 18; cf. Pope Paul VI, as quoted by
Daly (1986), p. 3.

23 Saward (1978), p. 18.

24 Herzel (1978), esp. pp. 107, 120.

25 Hood (1986), and elsewhere.

26 Some types of ministry may be hard to combine with the care of very
young children, but this should not prevent all women from being
ordained, esp. when non-stipendiary options are available.

27 *Women and the Ministry* (1936), pp. 24f., on which see Furlong (1984),
p. 2. Some men may be attracted to a woman in the pulpit; but neither
are women members of a congregation immune to male attractiveness:
cf. Raven (1928), pp. 78–84. On motherhood and ministry see further
Hebblethwaite (1984).

28 It is beyond our present scope to discuss the reasons for the current
Roman Catholic practice of normally permitting only single men (or
widowers) to be ordained priest. On this see esp. Schillebeeckx (1981),
pp. 85–99.

11

Women, Authority, and Priesthood

At the end of our previous chapter we asked the question whether there is anything in the nature of ministry or priesthood as such which might preclude the presence of women. For the purposes of our discussion it will be necessary to make a distinction between the general ministry of the people of God as a whole, in which women have always participated and to which few people object, and the specialized ministry of leaders officially authorized to fulfil certain functions, especially those who are ordained as *clergy*, among whom women have only recently been accepted, and then only in some denominations. Because the chief controversies concern *ordained* ministry for women, we will focus mainly on this, while recognizing that lay and ordained ministry should perhaps better be viewed as a totality.

THE FUNCTIONS OF THE ORDAINED MINISTRY

Ordained ministers or clergy may be defined by their function or by their ontology, i.e. by what they do or by what they are. Since there is far more agreement between Christians about ministerial functions than ontology, we may begin here.

Most Christians would agree that clergy are called to preach, to teach and to evangelize; to lead the Church in worship and to exercise its discipline; to care for the sick, the weak, the poor, and to build up the community of all those entrusted to their care. They would also agree that it is a special function of the clergy to administer the sacraments (though they might differ as to the nature and number of these). In order to fulfil these roles clergy are expected to have knowledge of the Scriptures, of church doctrine and history, and of the principles and practice of pastoral care. Such knowledge is normally acquired through specialized training, usually of some length. Clergy are also expected to have a sense of vocation (i.e. divine calling) to their ministry, and to be people of prayer, living a life of faith, discipline, and love towards God and their fellow men and women. In making this last statement we cross the borderline between function and ontology, because the two can never be completely separated.[1]

There is no serious doubt that women are as capable as men of fulfilling all the functions just outlined, granted that they have the necessary spiritual, personal and intellectual qualities – a proviso that applies to men just as much as women. As we have already shown (Ch. 10), there is nothing in women's intellectual capacities to render them less effective than men in reasoning and expounding subjects cogently; indeed some experimental tests have suggested that women in general have greater verbal fluency than men and an aptitude for languages – gifts likely to aid preaching and exposition. On the practical level, contrary to what has sometimes been alleged, there is nothing about female voices as such to make them unsuited to public address; it is the present writer's experience that women leading worship often speak with greater clarity and feeling than their male counterparts.

For centuries women taught children in the home and in elementary schools; more recently, since the opening of university education to them, they have shown that they are capable of coping with intellectually demanding courses, and have proved highly effective teachers at secondary level, and in colleges, universities, seminaries, and other forms of higher and further education. All over the world, growing numbers of women are acquiring theological expertise. In 1988 the prestigious international Society for New Testament Studies had as its president a woman Professor of New Testament from Cambridge (England). In many countries women are actively involved in training candidates for ordination: there seems to be something illogical about permitting them to train others for what they are ineligible for themselves (as happens in parts of the Anglican Communion). The apparent New Testament ban on women teaching (1 Tim. 2.12) is commonly disregarded, and surely with good reason: it was geared to a particular social situation when women were denied public roles and lacked access to proper education. It need hardly be added that there is no evidence that women as such are more prone than men to 'heretical' doctrine, and that for many years they have been active in mission work at home and overseas, often braving difficult conditions with as much fortitude and patience as their male colleagues.

It is also abundantly clear that women are capable of undertaking pastoral care; indeed this ability would seem to follow naturally from those maternal qualities of care and compassion which some opponents of women's ordination praise so highly. Women serve as social workers, deaconesses, and specialist chaplains, caring effectively and sympathetically for the young and the elderly, the sick and the whole. There is no evidence that women are more deeply shocked by tragedy than men, or less able to cope with society's problems: while at certain times in their lives (e.g. during the later stages of pregnancy) women may need protection, it is a misplaced chivalry to think that they must be always be shielded from the unpleasant. In nursing, in war, and in times of disaster they can cope with pain and distress, as is strikingly illustrated by the labours of Mother Teresa in Calcutta and by the recent heroism of a British woman doctor and nurse in Beirut.[2] In denominations where women are ordained as ministers there is no evidence that they experience any greater strain in undertaking pastoral duties than men.

As for administration and discipline, the role of modern women in business, commerce, law and politics shows that, given the right opportunities, they are effective decision-makers and administrators. For a long time they have exercised 'discipline' in the traditional feminine roles of mother, abbess (Mother Superior), headmistress, and hospital matron. Recent experience suggests that they are quite capable of doing so in the Church.

Turning now to the Sacraments, there does not seem to be anything relating to their celebration which might make this difficult for women; indeed there are reasons why women might be thought particularly appropriate persons for this function. They are perfectly competent at baptizing, presiding at the Lord's Supper, and performing the other rites accepted as sacramental by many Christians – i.e. confirmation, penance, ordination, unction and matrimony (in Roman Catholic theology the man and woman marrying are in any case seen as the 'ministers' of the sacrament). It could readily be argued that women's experience with children, and in the care of others, makes them especially well suited to handling infants in baptism, preparing children and other young people for confirmation, and counselling those in trouble. Married women in particular may be better equipped to advise young people embarking on marriage than celibate male clergy; and women's traditional experience in nursing, the care of the dying, and laying out of the dead, might suggest their suitability for such sensitive tasks as anointing the sick and dying, conducting funerals and counselling the bereaved. In many denominations women are already fulfilling these tasks.

It has sometimes been suggested that although women are physically and intellectually capable of performing all the functions of clergy, they should not do so for psychological reasons. For example, it is alleged that men may have problems in relating to women in authority over them, perhaps because of suffering in childhood from over-dominant mothers. In an article opposing women's ordination, Gilbert Russell and Margaret Dewey paint a gruesome picture of the traumas that they believe will follow if women adopt the 'masculine' function of priestly Church leadership.[3] But if some men find it hard to relate to female leaders, it may be precisely because they have been conditioned from early childhood to expect women to be 'passive' and men to be active and dominant. Some men have real problems in coping with the expectations of aggressive leadership thrust upon them. Once one realizes that the stereotyping of one sex as active and the other as passive is a distortion of our psychological make-up, then female leadership presents no more difficulties than male. Overbearing fathers can cause as many problems as dominant mothers.[4]

Nor is there any reason to suppose that women who offer themselves for ministry are likely to become 'unfeminine'. We have already shown that the caring, nurturing, and other pastoral functions of the clergy are precisely the kind of activities which, outside the Church, are regularly associated with women, and which those who stereotype the sexes see as peculiarly feminine. It is a gross injustice to the heartfelt aspirations of women who feel called to the ministry to insinuate, as do Russell and Dewey, that their deepest desire is to become men,[5] or to suggest that if women are ordained it will lead to a total breakdown of sexual distinctions. Women priests and ministers are as capable of retaining their feminine identity as are women doctors, lawyers, or engineers. Bishop Leonard's comparison[6] of the effects of ordaining women to a cancerous growth caused by a multiplicity of identical cells is both offensive and unfair.

It remains to mention the spiritual qualities associated with priesthood and other ordained ministries. The biblical call to be 'holy' applies to all Christian people (see esp. 1 Pet. 1.16, addressed to both men and women). Both Old Testament and New teach that women as well as men have access in prayer to God, and receive spiritual revelation; both Testaments demonstrate the existence in biblical times of female prophets and spiritual leaders, such as Miriam, Deborah, and Priscilla; intercessory prayer was one of the chief functions of the New Testament 'widows' (1 Tim. 5.5). Throughout the history of the Church there have been female mystics and spiritual leaders, to whom both men and women have gone for counsel, and some of whom have been canonized as saints. To suggest that women are incapable of prayer would be absurd. Finally, with regard to 'vocation', as more women receive opportunities for theological education and they perceive 'role models' in ordained women from other denominations, or even other sections of their own communion, so the numbers of women experiencing a deep sense of calling to ordination and priesthood grows: their feelings of exclusion and rejection can be seen in groups like MOW (Movement for the Ordination of Women) in the Church of England and the St Joan's International Alliance in the Roman Catholic Church; their sense of fulfilment – and their continuing frustrations in a male-dominated Church – are illustrated in the moving accounts of their experiences by such pioneers, in Anglicanism, as Florence Tim Oi Li and Elizabeth Canham.[7]

Thus the evidence of both experience and reason shows that

women can fulfil the essential *functions* of ministry and priesthood. The record of women clergy in those denominations which have opened their ordained ministries to them bears eloquent testimony to this fact.

ONTOLOGICAL AND SYMBOLIC CONSIDERATIONS

But ministry is not just about function. Most Christians would recognize that clergy also occupy a representative and symbolic role in the Church and in society. Some would go further than this and argue that through ordination clergy receive an indelible 'character' which marks them out as different in some essential way from the rest of the people of God. Many who take these views consider it impossible that a woman, no matter how saintly, may be ordained, simply by reason of her sex. The ontological and symbolic arguments fall into two main groups, concerned respectively with (a) male 'headship' and female lack of 'authority'; and (b) representative and 'iconic' considerations.

Male 'headship' and women's lack of 'authority'

Concern about the 'principle' of male 'headship' has been expressed both by biblically-orientated Protestants and by 'Catholic' Christians. The concern is explicitly based on the desire to be faithful to Bible teaching, and sometimes also to Church Tradition.

It needs to be said straight away that *there is no universal biblical principle of male 'headship' over women*. As was seen in our earlier discussion (Ch. 2), the Old Testament knows both subordinationist and equalitarian attitudes to women; the New Testament also contains texts affirming the equality of men and women before God, as well as ones apparently advocating male authority or 'headship' (cf. Chs 3–5). Where the Bible displays a diversity of teaching, those who take its authority as primary must examine the literary contexts and the social circumstances in which the texts were composed, with a view to determining which are culturally conditioned and which might be seen as embodying universal principles; it may also be helpful to consider which texts come closest to the heart of the Christian Gospel and Jesus' teaching as we know it (cf. above pp. 35–8).

Study of the Bible's cultural background shows that it took shape in a society in which female subordination was taken for granted. Yet it affirms the principle that in Christ women and men are equally accepted, redeemed, and gifted by the Spirit. Most of the texts which have been used to support male authority over women are in fact geared to specific situations, e.g. the conduct of worship in a disorderly charismatic community (1 Cor. 11) or teaching in a situation threatened by heresy (1 Tim. 2). It would be a mistake to see these as prescriptions valid for all time. Other texts (e.g. Eph. 5 and 1 Pet. 3) are dealing with relationships within *marriage* and cannot simply be applied as a matter of principle to all human relationships; like the biblical injunctions to masters and slaves they must be understood in their social context (cf. above Ch. 4, on the 'Household Codes'). Some of the key texts which feature in the arguments (notably Gen. 2–3 and 1 Cor. 11.2–16) are open to a number of interpretations. We have suggested that they should be seen as describing rather than prescribing the lot of women in their contemporary societies, and must be understood in the light of broader principles, also enunciated in biblical texts, notably the creation of both male and female in God's image (Gen. 1.26f.; 5.1f.; cf. Gal. 3.28), and their mutual interdependence (Gen. 2.21–4; Mark 10.6f.; 1 Cor. 11.11). The Old Testament texts also need to be interpreted in the light of Paul's teaching about the new creation in Christ, fulfilling and superseding the old Jewish Law (e.g. 2 Cor. 5.17; Gal. 6.15), and of Jesus' own very positive attitude to women and lack of any specific teaching on their subjection.[8]

As for the Fathers and medieval Doctors, we have seen in earlier chapters, how their teachings were based on literalistic biblical exegesis, sometimes even involving linguistic misunderstandings.[9] They were deeply rooted in the cultural presuppositions of their day, including negative attitudes to female sexuality and women's general lack of legal authority in the secular sphere, which was assumed to be part of 'natural law'. Today we live in a different secular world, in which women regularly exercise authority as magistrates, judges, and

MPs; in Britain we have had a woman prime minister, and have a woman sovereign (crowned by the Church of England's highest representative and prayed for regularly as one set in authority over us). Yet some theologians still speak of women being 'in subjection'. Biblical fundamentalists are often criticized for failing to exercise reason in their handling of texts; but at times one feels that some opponents of women's ordination handle the patristic evidence in a quite uncritical manner, regardless of the social and theological contexts in which the original documents were written.

Representative and 'iconic' considerations

An argument which has frequently been adduced against the ordination of women is that they cannot *represent* Christ. To many Christians this seems an extraordinary proposition. In the Gospels Jesus sets a child before the disciples as an example to them with the words: 'Anyone who welcomes a little child such as this in my name, welcomes me; and anyone who welcomes me, welcomes not me, but the one who sent me' (Mark 9.37; cf. Matt. 18.5; Luke 9.48) – in other words he sees children, in all their weakness and dependence, as representing him. In Matthew's prophetic picture of the Last Judgment (often called the 'parable of the sheep and the goats') the King or glorified Son of Man identifies himself with the sick, the hungry, the imprisoned, and the stranger, saying: 'In so far as you did this [i.e. showed kindness] to one of the least of these brothers of mine, you did it to me' (Matt. 25.40). If children, the poor, and the outcast can represent Christ, then surely so too can women. Moreover, if believers – either as individuals or as a corporate whole – dwell 'in Christ', as taught by John and Paul, how can it be that only part of that believing community in union with him may represent him?

But those who deny that women can represent Christ use the word in a special sense to refer to those who 'represent' Christ sacramentally in the Eucharist. Thus Bishop Ware quotes the ninth-century monk, Theodore the Studite: 'Standing between God and men the priest in the priestly invocations is an imitation of Christ...an icon [Greek: *eikōn*] of Christ'.[10] Such an understanding of the priest's role can be found in traditional writings of both East and West. In the thirteenth century it was expressed by Bonaventure (cf. above p. 110), when he wrote: 'The person ordained must signify Christ as mediator, and the mediator can only be signified in the male sex.' It was reaffirmed in the 1976 Roman Catholic Declaration, *Inter Insigniores* (para. 5): 'The priest...acts...*in persona Christi*, taking the role of Christ, to the point of being his very image, when he pronounces the words of consecration.' It is in this technical sense that it is denied women can represent Christ, the argument running as follows: *sacerdos alter Christus* – 'the priest is a second Christ'; Christ was incarnate as a man; therefore the priest must be male.

Now not all Christians will agree with this understanding of the eucharistic celebrant: it might indeed well be argued that it is the consecrated elements which 'represent' Christ rather than the officiating minister. Nevertheless, since the 'iconic' argument has loomed large in recent discussions of women's ordination, including the most recent Church of England Bishops' Report (1988), it is important to speak to those who find it significant.

The fallacy with the argument is threefold: first, as Ware himself admits, an icon does not have to look like what it represents in a realistic way. Priests may – in some sense – be *representatives* of Christ, but they are not *representations* of him. There is no more reason to argue that because Jesus was male, priests must be male too, than there is to argue that because Jesus was a celibate, bearded Galilean, all priests must also be celibate, bearded Galileans.[11] The Eucharist is not a dramatic re-enactment of the Last Supper in which all those taking part need to look as much as possible like the original participants. More fundamentally, if Genesis 1 can describe both male and female as created in the image (Greek: *eikōn*) of God, then for those who think in these terms surely women can 'represent' God or Christ iconographically (cf. above Ch. 10).

Secondly, and very importantly, the point about the incarnation is not that God became a *male*, but that God became *human*. The New Testament makes this quite plain: John's Prologue – the clearest New Testament expression of the doctrine – states: 'The Word became flesh' (*ho logos sarx egeneto*), not 'the word became male' (John 1.14). Paul, in a key christological passage, speaks of Jesus 'being made in *human likeness*'... 'being in every way like a *human being*' (Phil. 2.7 NIV and v.8 NJB).[12] In his great affirmation of the doctrine of redemption in Romans, Paul writes that just as through one representative human being (*anthrōpos*) sin came into the world, so through one person (*anthrōpos*) – Christ – grace has abounded (Rom 5.12–21). The parallelism between Adam and Christ is hammered home repeatedly in this passage, as it is again in 1 Corinthians. But in neither passage is any mention made of Christ's maleness, only of his humanity. To say, as Saward does, that the priest's 'traditional maleness is an efficacious sign of the new Adam',[13] is to misunderstand the meaning of 'Adam' in these key New Testament texts, where it stands for all humanity. To take it in an exclusively masculine sense is to deny the redemption of women. It may be primarily a matter of historical contingency that Jesus was a male; for God in becoming human in a particular historical context chose to accept certain limitations caused by that context. In the Jewish world of the first century AD only a man could have done the sort of things that Jesus did, and this – *pace* Mascall and others – is surely why he was born as God's 'son' and not God's 'daughter', not because God wanted all future priests and ministers to be male. Theologically the significant point is that in his life and death, resurrection and ascension Jesus Christ represents all humanity. The Epistle to the Hebrews (2.14–18) likewise speaks of Christ as sharing our *human nature* that he might by his death set us free. Christ's loving and atoning work – which is what we celebrate in the Eucharist – was accomplished by a perfect human being on behalf of all human beings, both male and female.[14] So, then, if the priest at the Eucharist is to represent Christ our risen Redeemer, it is surely appropriate that he should be represented by women as well as men. It is also worth remembering that the Eucharist is a meal, the Lord's *Supper* (a lovely biblical term now falling into disuse among Anglicans); what could be more appropriate symbolically than that the one who presides at the Lord's table should be a figure associated with feeding, loving care and the gift of life? (cf. Chap. 9 *passim*, on the biblical symbolism of woman).

The third fallacy with the line of argument we are exploring lies in its doctrine of eucharistic grace. In traditional Catholic teaching the celebrant acts only through the grace of God; the efficacy of the sacrament in no way depends on the officiant's worthiness. As Chrysostom put it: 'It is not the man who is responsible for the offerings becoming Christ's body and blood; it is Christ himself'.[15] Bishop J. A. Baker, rightly comments:

> 'An iconic theory of the eucharistic presidency, confining that role to someone of the same gender as the incarnate Lord, runs the risk of suggesting that Christ is present and active in the eucharistic minister in a unique mode and degree, an idea for which there is no basis in the general doctrine of grace or in specific authoritative teaching'.[16]

The priest only represents Christ in a limited and imperfect way; he does not *become* Christ. All Christians are called to be like Christ and share his Spirit. The one who presides at the Lord's Supper also represents the worshipping community – a Church made up of women as well as men. The Eucharist is the whole Church's celebration, not that of the officiant on the people's behalf.[17]

There remains one important aspect of symbolism not yet discussed. In some Roman Catholic, Anglican and Orthodox thinking much is made of the idea that Christ is the *bridegroom* and the Church his *bride*: only a male can represent Christ in this capacity.[18] Now the image of Christ as bridegroom is rooted in biblical teaching: the Synoptists record Jesus as using the metaphor with reference to himself (Mark 2.19f. par.). In John's Gospel, the Baptist describes Jesus as the bridegroom and himself as the 'bridegroom's friend' (John 3.29). Ephesians refers to the profound mystery of Christ's relation to the Church, likening it to that of a man to his wife (Eph. 5.22–33). Revelation, in describing the new heaven and the new earth, speaks of the new Jerusalem coming down from heaven, 'prepared as a bride dressed for her husband' (Rev. 21.2).

However, it needs to be stressed that in all these passages 'bride' and 'bridegroom' are *metaphors*. It was common practice in the ancient world to refer to cities and peoples as female. In the Old Testament Jerusalem and Zion are regularly referred to as if they were women (e.g. Isa. 54; Zech. 9.9; cf. Paul's use of Sarah and Hagar in Gal. 4: 24–6). The prophets speak of God as Israel's husband (e.g. Hos. 2.16), and adultery was often used as a metaphor for religious unfaithfulness. Such images are utterly natural in patriarchal societies which think of God in largely masculine terms (and adultery as a woman's offence). The later Jewish and Christian interpretations of the Song of Songs as an allegory of God's love for Israel, or of Christ's love for the Church, are another example of this way of thought.

But one must be wary of mistaking metaphors for reality. We saw in Chapter 9 how God is spoken of in feminine as well as masculine terms, and how the Bible also uses other images for God, Jesus and the Spirit. We need to go beyond the picture-language to see what theological truths it is seeking to convey. In the ancient world masculine imagery usually denoted authority; it *may* have also suggested initiative and creativity (though this is by no means clear in the biblical writings). But, as was shown in our previous chapter, there is in fact nothing intrinsically masculine about these activities; women too can exercise authority, take initiative, be creative. Some scholars have made far too much of the creative aspects of *begetting*,[19] without appreciating that the woman's part in love-making and the 'feminine' activities of nurturing and giving birth are also highly creative, as was expressed long ago by the early Syrian Church when it pictured the Holy Spirit as a woman. Greek uses the same verb, *gennaō*, of both begetting and giving birth; it can sometimes be hard to tell which meaning is intended (cf. John 1.13; 1 Pet. 1.3; 23); sometimes even in the New Testament a feminine image appears to be implied for God (e.g. John 3.3–5 with its reference to the mother's womb).

However, in handling biblical metaphors, we need to be wary of pressing them beyond the point of comparison. In Mark 2.19 Jesus is replying to criticisms about his disciples not fasting with an analogy from experience: one does not fast at a wedding; the reference to himself as bridegroom is indirect and may even be due to the allegorizing tendencies of the early Church. In John 3.29 the point is the Baptist's humble and subsidiary role compared with Christ's; the maleness of Christ as the bridegroom is no more significant here than in 2 Cor. 11.2, when Paul uses the image of himself as a marriage-arranger (or parent) presenting his converts like a bride to a husband. There is big leap from the metaphor of Christ as the husband of the Church here, in Ephesians 5, and Revelation 21, to the view that Christian priests must also represent this 'male' role. It cannot be too strongly stressed that that idea is totally unbiblical. It seems to have originated in the patristic period with reference to *bishops*, and was first used as an argument against women's episcopal consecration in the Middle Ages by Bonaventure.[20] Images and metaphors must be kept in proportion: the problems involved in applying the masculine image of a bridegroom to a woman priest are no greater than those of applying the feminine image of the Church as a woman to its male members. And in any case if there is a sense in which priests represent Christ as the 'bridegroom' and 'divine begetter', there is also a sense in which they represent the Church as 'bride' – and God as the loving spiritual 'mother' who gives us birth, nurtures and comforts us.[21]

Bishop Leonard has made much of the argument that 'as a human being, whether I am male or female, I must be feminine to God to receive him'.[22] By 'feminine' he means receptive and dependent (following his stereotyping of sexual roles). But receptivity to God's will is every bit as important for clergy as it is for laity. To see priests as male initiators and 'begetters' and laity as passive and obedient 'females' is to distort both the sexual roles of man and wife and the relationship of clergy and people. A more biblical image is of all Christians as the *children* of God, dependent on their one heavenly Father.

It remains to say a few words about priestly 'character' in relation to women's ministry. Not all Christians share the idea of ordination as an irreversible sacramental ordinance, but for those who do the traditional teachings of the Church are important. According to the Council of Trent: 'In three sacraments, namely, baptism, confirmation and Order, there is...imprinted on the soul a character, that is, a certain spiritual and indelible mark, by reason of which they cannot be repeated.'[23] Those who accept this doctrine (including many Anglo-Catholics as well as Roman Catholics) often maintain that women are by their nature incapable of receiving priestly 'character', as was argued most notably by Thomas Aquinas. We have already demonstrated the inadequacy of his arguments against women's ordination from their state of 'subjection', their lack of 'pre-eminence', their 'weakness' of nature, and unsuitability for tonsure (above pp. 108–10). Leonard Hodgson, formerly Regius Professor of Divinity at Oxford, has shown that Aquinas is equally unconvincing on the question of Orders and the soul:[24] Aquinas believed that all human beings are a union of soul (*anima*) and flesh (*caro*). Men and women differed in their flesh, but not their soul. If therefore 'Orders' are imprinted on the soul, that is the spiritual part of a Christian – and male and female souls do not differ in essence – there is no reason why women should not receive priestly 'character', just as – in Catholic theology – they receive sacramental 'character' through baptism and confirmation.

But one must question how helpful this mechanical and almost magical idea of sacramental character is. 'Character' in the technical sense is by origin a metaphor, being derived from a Greek word meaning 'stamp' or 'impression' (as on a coin). The doctrine, which depends on a rather cut-and-dried view of body and soul, was designed to explain both the unrepeatability of certain ordinances in Catholic theology and the sacred power (*potestas*) of the priest, as then understood. Some today still hold to these views.[25] But many Protestant and Reformed Christians (including quite a few Anglicans) reject the doctrine altogether and see no ontological difference between priests and laity.[26] Others, while still accepting Orders as an irreversible sacrament, interpret character much more broadly to refer to priestly formation, devotion, and sacrificial love – qualities given by God's grace, which begin to develop before ordination and continue to develop afterwards.[27] There can be no doubt that many ordained women in both episcopally-ordered and other denominations exhibit saintly, 'priestly' characters, just as do many of their male colleagues. Sanctity of character and priestlike qualities are also often found in lay Christians. As R. C. Moberly noted in his classic work, *Ministerial Priesthood*: 'There are not only priestly functions, or priestly prerogatives: there is also a priestly spirit and a priestly heart... This priestly spirit... is *not* the exclusive possession of the ordained ministry' (his italics).[28]

CONCLUSIONS

In the first section of this chapter we argued that women are capable of performing the traditional *functions* of ordained ministers. We saw, moreover, that the qualities of caring, nurture, sympathy and wholehearted devotion, commonly associated with women, are peculiarly valuable for priests and ministers, and that women also have other gifts to contribute, including ones of intellect, rationality and facility with language. But we also noted that, for many Christians, clergy have symbolic as well as functional roles: those of the 'catholic' tradition sometimes see priests as symbols of God's initiative in creation and redemption, and of Jesus' human masculinity. We have argued that women too can be a potent symbol of creativity and initiative, and of Jesus Christ's incarnation as a *human being*. If the ordained ministry represents God, then God is neither male nor female, but shows the characteristics of both. If it represents Christ, then Christ stands for all humanity; if it represents the Church, then the people of God includes both men and women. While not denying that an all-male priesthood has served God faithfully for many centuries, it is surely possible to affirm that the presence of women in the priesthood adds a *wholeness* to that ministry which is lacking when it is reserved for the male sex. It is an irony that for so many Christians a barren, celibate male may symbolize God's creativity and paternity, whereas a fertile married woman may not. Women and men, working together in collegiality in ministry, are surely better able than an all-male priesthood to provide a paradigm or 'icon' of the nature of God and the complementarity of the sexes, made in the divine image. This is all the more important where God is understood as Trinity, that is a unity of equal 'Persons' in a loving relationship to one another.[29]

Some Protestant 'evangelicals', as well as some 'Catholic' Christians, have argued that masculinity stands for 'headship' and authority, and that therefore ministers (or priests) must be men. But this ignores both the limitations of the image, and the extraordinary paradox of the Christian faith, whereby the one who was 'in the form of God...emptied himself, taking the form of a slave, becoming as human beings are' (Phil. 2.6f.), and chose 'those who by human standards are weak to shame the strong' (1 Cor. 1.26). Jesus himself repeatedly emphasized ministry as *service* and bade his followers eschew rank and pre-eminence; it is another irony that his ordained ministry should sometimes be seen as symbolizing just this.

Some have also cited the biblical use of marital imagery to support an exclusively male priesthood. But this both exaggerates the significance of the 'bridegroom-bride' metaphors, and belittles the mutuality of the married relationship, which is not a matter of male activity, and of female passivity, far less of male command and female obedience, but of the expression of *mutual* love, care, and respect – of a partnership in which both female and male may be creative as well as receptive. This is not to deny that some biblical passages use masculinity to symbolize leadership; but the highest ideal of the Bible is of the complementarity of the sexes, and of the mutual support and love of all Christians for one another.[30]

NOTES

1   Definitions of the functions of ordained ministers can be found in most Ordinals. On the Anglican tradition see the *BMU* Report, (in Bibliography *s.v.* Church of England), esp. ch. 7. For ecumenical agreements on the nature of ordained ministry see *ARCIC 1*, pp. 29–45; *GRU*, pp. 46–65; *BEM*, pp. 20–32 (in Bibliography *s.v.* Anglican-Roman Catholic International Commission, Anglican-Reformed International Commission, and World Council of Churches respectively). On 'job-descriptions' in the Scottish Ordinals see Edwards (1986), pp. 11–14.
2   Dr Pauline Cutting and Miss Susan Wightman.
3   Russell and Dewey (1978).
4   cf. Hayter (1987), pp. 50f.
5   *op. cit.*, p. 100. They write of active campaigners for women's ordination of their own acquaintance, but with implications for other women.
6   Leonard (1984), pp. 43f.
7   Canham (1983); Li and Harrison (1985).
8   For sensitive discussions on authority, written from a conservative evangelical view, see Mollenkott (1977), Howe (1982), Craston (1986).
9   See ch. 6 on Ambrosiaster and Ambrose. Another example is Aquinas' view that Eph. 5.22 teaches that wives must be obedient to their husbands 'as to a lord'; from this he deduces that the relation of a husband to his wife is like that of a master to a servant: *Comm. on Eph.* ed. Lamb (1966), p. 216. In fact, Ephesians urges wives to obey their

husbands in the Lord (i.e. Christ). Aquinas may have been misled by the absence of a definite article in Latin.

10 Ware (1978), p. 80; cf. Aghiorgoussis (1976), p. 3; Schmemann, in Lutge (n.d.), pp. 14f.

11 This point has often been made: e.g. by Hampson (1979), p. 9; J. & G. Muddiman (1984), p. 8; Boff (1986); see also Baker (1985).

12 Some translations have 'in the likeness of men' and 'in appearance as a man'; but the Greek terms are inclusive, *anthrōpos*, not *anēr*.

13 Saward (1978), p. 11.

14 Confusion may be caused for some English speakers by traditional formularies which use 'man' for both 'male' and 'human being'. When the Apostles' Creed, speaks of Christ becoming 'man' for our salvation, it means 'a human being' (Greek: *anthrōpos*; Latin: *homo*, not *vir*). It is by no means clear that the ascended and glorified Christ should be thought of as having the male sexuality of the incarnate Jesus.

15 Quoted by Baker (1985), p. 356. We are not here concerned with the question of 'transubstantiation'.

16 *op. cit.* p. 357.

17 This point is made in several recent ecumenical documents: see, e.g., *The Ecclesial Nature of the Eucharist* (1973), esp. p. 14 (in Bibliography *s.v.* Joint Study Group and *BEM*, p. 14 (see above n. 1). cf. also Lloyd (1977), p. 9 (citing R. W. Dale), and Mackey in Dunn and Mackey (1987), p. 111. In many modern eucharistic rites (e.g. the Scottish 1982 Liturgy) the congregation join in prayers once reserved for clergy, thus expressing the whole people's sharing in celebration.

18 cf. Mascall (1977a), pp. 15f. (citing C. S. Lewis); Saward (1978), p. 8; Ware (1978), p. 84; Hopko (1983), p. 117 and many Roman Catholic writings (e.g. *Inter Insigniores*).

19 cf. Dyson (1984), p. 93, criticizing Leonard's use of 'begetting' as a 'primary theological principle'. It must be stressed that the biblical picture of God lacks any concept of physical maleness, in contrast to that of many pagan gods (e.g. Zeus), who beget numerous children, and divinities such as Dionysos, Hermes, Priapus, or the Egyptian Min, who are often represented as ithyphallic males. Thus Pope John Paul II quite rightly repudiates the idea that God's eternal 'generating' is in any sense linked to physical maleness (*Mulieris Dignitatem* §8).

20 cf. above ch. 7 at n. 14; also van der Meer (1973), p. 130.

21 cf. the womanly images in some feminist eucharistic prayers (for example, Morley (1988), pp. 36–45).

22 Leonard (1984), p. 47; cf. Amiel (1988), p. 10.

23 Quoted in Galot (1985), p. 195.

24 Hodgson (1974), p. 7f.; cf. Tertullian on the nature of the soul (*De Anima*).

25 See *Lumen Gentium*, esp. §10, and *Sacerdotium Ministeriale* (1983); but see also Sigurbjörnsson (1974); Mackey in Dunn and Mackey (1987), pp. 104–19.

26 e.g. Harvey (1975), p. 49f.; see further Green (1983), ch. 7; the *BMU*

Report (see above n. 1), p. 56 (citing Cranmer and Hooker); also *GRU*, §§ 80–84; Küng (1972), pp. 46–8 (with some strong criticisms of traditional Roman Catholic doctrine).

27 cf. Macquarrie (1986), pp. 169–78; on 'priestly' qualities, esp. sacrificial love, see further Rahner (1968); Hughes (1973); Ramsey (1985); Clark (1989).

28 Moberly (1899), ch. 7, esp. pp. 261; cf. Macquarrie (1977), p. 427.

29 See further Moltmann (1985), ch. 9.

30 The references are too numerous to list out here; note esp. Eph. 4.2 (supporting one another in love); Eph. 5.21 (mutual 'subjection'); Gal. 6.2 (sharing burdens); Rom. 12.10 (preferring others in honour); Paul's 'hymn to love' (1 Cor. 13); and, above all, Jesus' 'love command' (Mark 12.31 par.; John 15.17, etc.) and its many echoes (e.g. Rom. 13.9; 1 Pet. 1.22; Jas. 2.8; 1 John 4.7–11).

12

Women and the Threefold Ministry

Since controversy has been especially acute over the place of women in the threefold ministry of bishops, priests and deacons, we devote a separate chapter to this. It needs to be said straight away that Churches which uphold the threefold ministerial Order, including the Orthodox, Roman Catholic, Old Catholic, and Anglican Communions as well as some Lutheran Churches, differ in their theology of it, which makes it difficult to deal with them collectively. However, in recent years, there has been a growth of common understanding, even with Churches not maintaining the threefold Order, notably in the Lima Report of the World Council of Churches and in other ecumenical documents.[1] This agreement will be borne in mind as we discuss the functions of the three Orders and problems felt by some theologians about the Church's authority to introduce change.

THE EPISCOPATE

The episcopate is concerned with pastoral care and oversight, deriving its name from the New Testament term *episkopos* meaning overseer or superintendent (cf. above p. 79). It is believed by some – but by no means all – members of Churches practising it to be the essential Christian ministry, following in direct 'succession' from the apostles themselves.[2] Bishops are seen as a personal focus of the ecclesial community, symbolizing the link between the local diocese and the wider and universal Church, which exists beyond the boundaries of time and space.

Bishops baptize, confirm, absolve and exercise 'discipline', ordain, and preside at the Eucharist. They also serve as a *pastor pastorum* to other clergy. But bishops are – or should be – more than this. They are those to whom the Church looks especially for vision, and to preserve, expound and teach the faith as leaders and pioneers.[3] Even if these functions sometimes become swallowed up by administrative and liturgical duties, they remain an ideal.

It is hard to see why women cannot perform any of these episcopal functions. Some theologians have doubted their ability to do so on the grounds that the bishop is the 'head' of the eucharistic community. As long as women remained 'in subjection' this concern was quite understandable. But once one grants that the Bible contains no fundamental principle of male 'headship' over all women, that women can exercise leadership effectively in society, that 'headship' means service, and Christ is the only head of the Church and true celebrant of the Eucharist, then the difficulties vanish. Sometimes problems are also felt about the role of bishops as successors to the apostles and the fact that the Twelve chosen by Jesus were all male. We have already argued that the fallacy here lies in seeing the apostles as a precise model for future bishops and assuming that maleness is essential to their role.[4]

Another potential difficulty, particularly in the Anglican Communion, is the bishop's role as a focus for unity. It has, for example, been argued that now that the American and New Zealand Churches have each consecrated a woman bishop, the Anglican Communion will become hopelessly divided. But we must here distinguish between a theological ideal and possible practical consequences of a particular action. There is no inherent reason why a woman should be any less a focus of unity than a man; indeed, those who stress the differences between the sexes often draw attention to the special role of women as a unifying element in the family and home. How appropriate that they should also fulfil this role, insofar as any human being can, in the family of the Church! Even if the consecration of women bishops may cause disharmony and pain for some, and conceivably even a division in the Anglican episcopate, it must be recognized that pain and disharmony already exist. If an action is right, then it cannot indefinitely be postponed. On the positive side, as already hinted, women may well have special gifts and insights to offer to the episcopate arising out of their distinctive feminine experiences, especially as wives and mothers. Their skills in caring, articulation, and theological learning have already been discussed (above Ch. 10).

In essence the case for women bishops is no different from that for women pastors of any kind – or indeed for women moderators, patriarchs, cardinals or a woman pope.

THE PRESBYTERATE OR PRIESTHOOD

The priesthood or presbyterate derives its name from the *presbyteroi* or elders of the New Testament, who were not clearly distinguished from the *episkopoi* or overseers (cf. above, pp. 80–2). Bishops and presbyters act together collegially, and in the Western tradition are often seen as exercising essentially the same ministry except that bishops direct their responsibilities primarily to a diocese and presbyters to a local church.[5] Certain functions (notably ordination and confirmation) are normally reserved to bishops;[6] presbyters (priests), in common with bishops, baptize, reconcile the penitent, preside at the Eucharist, preach, teach, evangelize, care for the needy and build up the community. Sometimes they are seen as the bishop's delegates when they perform these actions.[7] Like bishops, presbyters ideally serve as a focus in their community, enabling others to bring out their talents. All these functions seem to be ones which may be fulfilled admirably by women.

If women may become bishops, *a fortiori* they may also become priests. For those who accept that there is no essential difference between the episcopate and presbyterate, the converse is also true. It is indeed hard to see any logical grounds whereby a denomination can admit women to priesthood without also recognizing the possibility that one day suitably experienced women will become bishops.

THE DIACONATE

Traditionally the diaconate is regarded as a supportive or serving ministry, deriving its name from the Greek word *diakonos* (see above pp. 79f.). Its roots go back to the New Testament, but it greatly developed as a ministry in the Patristic period, when male and female deacons exercised a supportive liturgical and social ministry, and men, at least, assisted bishops in administrative and financial affairs (cf. above pp. 101f.). In the Orthodox Churches the diaconate is still basically a liturgical ministry, the deacon having a prominent role in the Divine Liturgy communicating between priest and people. For many centuries in the Roman Catholic, Old Catholic and Anglican Communions the diaconate served chiefly as a probationary period for priesthood, but recently it has been revived in all three as a distinctive ministry. In the Anglican Communion deacons may assist at the Eucharist, perform baptisms, preach, teach, and undertake pastoral care – though not all deacons do all this. As was argued earlier, there seems no reason why women cannot fulfil every one of these functions. The fact that women deacons existed in the primitive church, combined with the emphasis of this ministry on humble service, has meant that women deacons have proved less problematic for some Anglicans than women priests or bishops.[8] But it should be noted that in the traditional Anglican Ordinal the diaconate is still an authoritative ministry.[9] In practice many women deacons fulfil almost all the functions of presbyters except those forbidden them by church law. Both the wisdom and the logic of admitting them to this ministry but not to the presbyterate and episcopate may be questioned.[10] In traditional Catholic theology ministerial 'Order' is a unity,[11] and bishops and priests remain deacons even after their ordination to these additional offices. If the diaconate is retained as a first step towards priesthood, as well as being a serving ministry in its own right (cf. n. 10), the regular 'promotion' of male, but never of female, deacons to priesthood will be seen as sexist and discriminatory.

We may then conclude that there are strong grounds for admitting women to all three Orders of ministry within the threefold tradition, viz. the episcopate, presbyterate and diaconate. It should be added that there seems no reason why women should not be ordained, on equal terms with men, to either stipendiary and non-stipendiary ministry, the latter offering special opportunities to women who need to devote a substantial part of their time to domestic and other duties. The theological implications of the self-supporting or non-stipendiary ordained ministry, whether of women or of men, still remain to be worked out. It can be seen as a valuable symbol of the fact that the secular and the sacred are inextricably linked; women clergy who combine motherhood or a profession (or both) with ordained ministry offer to God their total work; in so doing they bring insights from 'secular' and family life to the Church, and from the Church to the wider world. Celibate women, likewise, should have the same opportunities to serve the Church as celibate men.

THE CHURCH'S AUTHORITY TO MAKE CHANGE

Some of those who express unease about the ordination of women to the threefold ministry do so because they feel that the Church does not have authority to make a change of this sort. They point to the long tradition of male ministry and sometimes cite Vincent of Lérins' famous definition of the Catholic faith: *quod ubique, quod semper, quod ab omnibus creditum est* ('what has been believed everywhere, always and by everyone').[12] Sometimes they suggest that the ordination of women could only be permitted by the authority of an 'oecumenical council'. The impracticability of such a gathering has often been pointed out.[13] But a universal council is not only impracticable; it is also unnecessary.

Throughout its long history the Church has regularly made changes without first authorizing them in this way. We saw in Chapters 6–7 how it changed and developed its theology of ministry and eucharistic doctrine. It has also changed its practice over infant baptism, the necessity of confirmation, clerical celibacy, and most recently the secular employment of clergy. The Reformation brought about many changes in church government and doctrine, which the Reformers saw as a return to primitive purity; the Roman Catholic Church for its part has in quite recent years promulgated as dogma the Immaculate Conception and Assumption of the Blessed Virgin Mary without any reference to an Oecumenical Council. Even the Orthodox recognize that Tradition is not wholly static, but must be allowed to develop.

All this suggests that change in itself cannot be ruled out. In John's Gospel Jesus declares that the Spirit will guide Christians into truth (John 16.13). It cannot be supposed that the Spirit ceased to act with the formation of the New Testament canon, or the Council of Nicea, or even the Photian schism. The Church cannot remain for ever bound by the decisions of Councils of the early centuries AD, which in any case never explicitly forbade women's ordination as such (cf. Ch. 6, n. 32), but which did forbid a range of activities now treated in the Western Church as acceptable.[14]

The 'primitive catholic uniformity' admired by so many traditionalists is in reality something of a romantic myth:[15] the early Church had varieties of theology, even about such central doctrines as the Trinity. What matters is whether a change is consistent with the principles of truth as revealed to us through Scripture, reason, and the on-going life of the Church. We would argue that women's ordination represents no departure from the spirit of Scripture or Tradition. It is simply doing things a new way in accordance with the Spirit's continuing guidance and to meet the needs of the Church in present-day society.[16] Those who see it as a 'betrayal' of the gospel and a 'monstrous' innovation which will destroy the Catholic faith have lost their sense of proportion.

Women's ministry should rather be seen as a natural consequence of the Gospel message, comparable to the admission of uncircumcised Gentiles to table-fellowship, carried out despite Jesus' original command to the Twelve not to go to the Gentiles (Matt. 10.5). That momentous step was first taken by Peter when he accepted Cornelius, and he did it without first consulting even his colleagues (Acts 10). His action was ratified by a meeting of church leaders at Jerusalem, but the admission of Gentiles remained controversial for some time (cf. Acts 11.1–18; 15).[17] It is perhaps not over-imaginative to see a parallel between Peter's action and that of Bishop Hall in ordaining Florence Tim Oi Li (see above p. 126). A parallel may also be seen in the modern abolition of slavery, an institution never denounced in the Bible, accepted by the Church for centuries and even defended by some of its ablest theologians, but now universally recognized as contrary to Gen. 1.26f. and the spirit (though not the letter) of the New Testament.[18]

This is not the place to discuss the mechanics of how any particular denomination should make change. There needs to be a reasonable consensus among the faithful, if there is not to be unhappiness and division, and ecumenical courtesies should also be observed. But that does not mean one denomination holding back on what it believes to be God's will simply because another is not yet ready for it. We may compare the different rates at which the Churches have responded to the parallel concept of racial equality, especially in southern Africa. Where some within the Church fail to recognize the truth, an element of division may have to occur.

NOTES

1   *BEM* (1982); cf. *ARCIC* 1 (1982); *GRU* (1984) (see Ch. 11, n. 1).

2   See, for example *Lumen Gentium*, § 18; Hebert in Kirk (1946), esp. pp. 528–31; Zizioulas (1985), esp. pp. 196ff.; but note also the criticisms of Montefiore in Carey (1954), pp. 105–27; Hanson (1975), pp. 99–119; Barrett (1985) 79, etc.

3   cf. *BEM*, p. 26; the C. of E. Bishops' report, *The Nature of Christian Belief* (1986), 34–9; and the ACC 7 Report, *Many Gifts, One Spirit*, (1987), pp. 39f. The role of the bishop as a personal focus of unity is a patristic development; in the New Testament it is Christ himself who unites, as 'head' of the Church (see Eph. 1.22f.; Col. 1.16–18; 3.11; cf. 1 Cor. 3.4–11; Heb. 12.2).

4   See above pp. 76–9, and p. 96 with n. 19. The New Testament knows no doctrine of 'apostolic succession' in the sense of a special grace handed down mechanically from the original Apostles to male successors. For a broader concept of faithfulness to an apostolic tradition in which women play their part see Küng (1972), pp. 33–43; Green (1983), pp 60–95.

5   On the close relation of bishop and presbyter cf. Chrysostom and Jerome in Lienhard (1984) esp. pp. 109, 160; also Sigurbjörnsson (1974), pp 20f.; Zizioulas (1985), pp. 171–208.

6   Presbyters join with bishops in ordaining other presbyters. In some Churches priests may confirm, or anoint the newly baptized with oil previously blessed by a bishop.

7   cf. Ignatius, in Lienhard (1984), pp. 15, 26–32.

8 e.g. Leonard (1984), pp. 48f.

9 cf. the bishop's words, 'Take thou authority to execute the Office of a Deacon in the Church of God' (BCP Ordinal).

10 The recent opening of the ordained diaconate to women in Wales, Scotland, and England was greeted by many as a step forward for women. But as long as this is perceived as a subordinate ministry, in which women are permanently under male authority, it will cause frustration and heartache.

11 cf. Galot (1985), pp. 177–90. The Roman Catholic diaconate remains all-male; women may be 'extraordinary ministers of the sacraments', performing what in other traditions are diaconal tasks.

12 See Ware (1978), pp. 70f.

13 e.g. by Lampe (1974), p. 7.

14 The Anglican Thirty-Nine Articles state that General Councils 'may err, and sometimes have erred, even in things pertaining unto God' (Art. 21). Among other things the Councils forbade the secular employment or military service of clergy, their entering inns, attending theatres and horse-races, their not wearing clerical clothes when travelling, their teaching in cities 'not their own', the translation of bishops to other sees, and their remarriage after bereavement: see Percival (1900).

15 So Green (1983), p. 67.

16 cf. Vincent's other much-quoted dictum, *Nove, non nova* ('in a new way, not new things').

17 According to Gal. 2.11–18 for a time Peter stopped dining with Gentiles in the face of criticism from a party within the Church (he was openly rebuked for this by Paul): see Bruce (1982), pp. 128f.; cf. Marshall (1980b), pp. 242–7 (discussing historical problems raised by Acts 15, etc.).

18 See Wijngaards (1977), p. 14; but note also Eppstein (1935), ch. 15.

Conclusion

This study of women's ministry has sought to present the evidence of Bible, Tradition, reason, and experience as objectively as possible. But theology is not an exact science like mathematics. The very nature of biblical revelation and the differing approaches to it in the Christian community lead inevitably to a variety of 'theologies' of any major Christian doctrine or topical issue in the Church. Moreover, there is bound to be a personal element when we are dealing with a faith which is not only comprehended intellectually, but also felt in the heart and lived out in action.

It is important to acknowledge this personal element, which has influenced the debate on women's ordination more than is generally appreciated. For it includes, on the one hand, the intensely spiritual experiences of those who have become aware of God's nature through particular forms of worship and service, and, on the other, many less worthy emotions, which owe more to our psychological make-up and environmental pressures than to God's Spirit. Such emotions and attitudes are often profoundly influenced by 'non-theological' factors, such as our childhood, relations with parents, marital happiness or unhappiness, and positive or negative experiences in Church and society. Our difficulty in handling them is that they vary so much from one individual to another.

Some are convinced that to ordain women is to destroy the faith. For them women's ministry has become inextricably associated with 'liberal' theology, sexual permissiveness, and aggressive agitation for women's 'rights'. But belief that God is calling women to serve in ministry has no direct connection with any of these, and may be combined with theological and ethical

conservativism – or radicalism. Those who suggest that sup-
porters of women's ordination are 'betraying the Gospel' in
order to 'accommodate to the world',[1] or who speak of this
controversy as 'an absolute battle regarding the fundamentals',[2]
are confusing a whole complex of issues. The belligerent tone of
such remarks reveals how much they are prompted by emotion
rather than rational argument.

All of us, then, need to analyse honestly why we take the
views we do on this matter. Many clergy and ordinary church
members simply 'feel' that it is wrong for a woman to preach
or exercise a sacramental ministry, but are not able to formulate
why they think so. Men in this position should ask themselves
whether their attitudes have been coloured by fears about their
own adequacy, negative feelings towards women, inhibitions
about women's 'uncleanness' or embarrassment over sexuality.
Women who are uncomfortable with one of their own sex in a
position of church leadership should consider whether they may
be subconsciously assuming that women are inferior to men or
are somehow less acceptable to God. Conversely those who
passionately advocate women's ordination need to make sure
that they are not merely attempting to assert female 'superiority'
over men or bolster their own self-esteem rather than seeking
God's glory and the good of the Church.

Fortunately theology is not something to be studied by
individuals in isolation. We pursue it as part of a community,
which includes, for most theologians, the Church. Women's
ministry is an issue which cuts across denominational boundaries. But inevitably our perceptions are influenced by our
relation, however strong or weak it may be, to a particular
denomination or tradition. Dialogue with people who think
differently from ourselves is essential, and this means interaction
with those trained in different academic disciplines as well as
those of different ecclesial persuasion.

If this book stimulates a clear and well-reasoned response
from readers who do not accept women's ordination, it will have
served a useful purpose. But our hope is to go beyond this – to
help those who are undecided on this issue to make up their
minds, and to assist those who already support women's
ministry to discover a more clearly articulated rationale for their
conviction. Our purpose is also to urge the Churches to follow

their faith through to its logical consequences in action. If that faith includes the acceptance of women as *full* members of Christ, then this must be reflected in the structures and practice of the Church.

With these considerations in mind, we now set out seven guiding principles relevant to the theology of women's ministry.

The real equality of the sexes

The bedrock of any theology of women's ministry must be the essential equality before God of women and men. This is the logical implication of the Old Testament teaching that both male and female are made in God's image (Gen. 1.26f.) and of Jesus' incarnation, earthly life, death, and resurrection on behalf of all humanity – men and women alike. It is summed up by Paul in his great affirmation that 'in Christ there is neither Jew nor Greek, there is neither bond nor free, there is neither male nor female' (Gal. 3.28 RSV; cf above p. 55). The truth that God is 'no respecter of persons' (Acts 10.34 AV) applies as much to sexuality as it does to race and social status.

This belief, that women and men are equal in God's sight, stands out in distinction from those of almost all ancient peoples (cf. Ch. 1). It constitutes a fundamental principle which must take priority over Old Testament or New Testament passages (e.g. Gen. 3.16; 1 Cor. 11.3) which have been interpreted by some as implying a universal rule that women should be subordinate to men. These passages, as was argued earlier (esp. pp. 35, 62–70, 146–50, 165), were geared to particular social contexts, often serving aetiological or parenetic purposes. They should not be seen as embodying permanent truths applicable for all time.

This primary principle of Scripture must also carry more weight than arguments from Tradition, whether based on the sentiments and teachings of the Fathers, the medieval Doctors, or the Protestant Reformers. Their views on the inherent inferiority or 'weakness' of women, as we saw earlier (Chs. 6–7, esp. pp. 99–101, 105–11) resulted from cultural and economic factors in societies where most women neither received education nor exercised secular authority, and from one-sided, pre-critical biblical interpretations. If it is objected that here we are simply substituting modern socially-conditioned views for equally tenable ancient ones, we must reply that there is no scientific or rational evidence which convincingly shows that women are inferior to men, but rather much to support the idea that, though differing in their physiology and psychological make-up, they are essentially equal in gifts and ability (see Ch. 10).

Some theologians have suggested that, although men and women are equal, God has appointed a hierarchical 'Creation order', in which man is the 'head' of woman and woman occupies a 'subordinate' role (cf. above pp. 144f.). Those who take this view frequently call on 'woman' to submit voluntarily to 'man' not because he is more intelligent or more spiritual than she, but merely because he is a man. This is surely unreasonable – in the strictest sense of the term. It rests on misreadings of scriptural texts, most of which were concerned in their original contexts about relationships within marriage. If one substitutes 'women' for 'woman' and 'men' for 'man', thus suggesting that all women must submit in principle to all men, its injustice and absurdity at once become apparent.

In his recent Apostolic Letter, *Mulieris Dignitatem*, Pope John Paul II spoke eloquently of the essential equality of men and women 'since each of them – the woman as much as the man – are created in the image and likeness of God. Both of them are equally capable of receiving the outpouring of the divine truth and love in the Holy Spirit'.[3] The implications of this equality need to be recognized and acted upon.

The complementarity of the sexes

The acceptance of the principle that women and men are created equal, and that both are capable of being endowed with spiritual gifts, does not involve, as some opponents of women's ordination assume, the belief that men and women are identical. The Bible teaches the need of man for woman, and the mutual dependence of the two sexes (see above p. 165). Biologically, psychologically and socially this mutual need is expressed most obviously through marriage and sexual intimacy, and the joint upbringing of children. But for many centuries the Church, as represented by its theologians and leaders, suffered from lukewarm, or even negative, attitudes to marriage and human sexuality. The situation was made worse by out-dated biological theory, which understood human life as transmitted solely through the male 'seed', and the idea that the male part in sexual relations is 'active' and the female 'passive' (cf. above pp. 92f., 109f.). These misapprehensions fostered the view that priests must be male, as representing God's active and creative role, while women were to remain 'passive'. A stereotyped understanding of the Virgin Mary's role encouraged women to be meek and 'receptive', responding to God's (and men's) initiative.

Today the biblical figure of Mary is being interpreted more positively for all Christians (and not just women) as a model of faith, radical obedience, and active participation in God's work of liberation.[4] Thanks to modern science, we know much more about the biological processes of reproduction and appreciate that, by the grace of God, the creation of a new life requires a physical contribution from both female and male parents. Woman is no passive 'vessel' or receptacle, but plays an active and indispensable part in the process of love-making, as well as in the conception, growth, birth and nurture of a new baby (cf. above p. 140).[5] Psychologists, theologians, and many ordinary people now affirm that marriage and sexual union have intrinsic value as an expression of *mutual* love, self-giving and support. The true Christian understanding of married love is not that of a passive female 'submitting' to the active male, but as a sacrament of a mutual and intensely personal relationship of love (cf. above pp. 33f. on the Song of Songs). All this means that, while circumstances may sometimes make a particular ministry more appropriate for a married or single person, neither motherhood nor the married state should in themselves be a bar to priesthood or public ministry. Rather the presence of women – and of married men – in the ordained ministry affirms the biblical teaching that sexuality is a gift of God and that male and female sexuality are equally acceptable to God (cf. above Ch. 10. esp. pp. 154–6).

Female and male also complement one another in their personal qualities and wider relationships. The common, though not universal, pattern of the male serving as provider and the female as home-maker, has led men and women to develop different characteristics of personality. Women are frequently more tender, compassionate, and skilled at the care of the weak and the young; men are often more assertive, more interested in public affairs, and more prone to cast themselves in the role of leaders. But the fact that women and men are often different in these respects is in itself no argument for excluding women from ordination – rather quite the reverse! For Christian ministry is about loving and caring every bit as much as it is about leadership and initiative, and it is certainly not about the aggression and self-assertiveness so commonly associated by psychologists with masculinity.

But none of the qualities we have discussed are equally applicable to all men or all women. Some men are immensely tender and caring; some women sharp and aggressive. Many of the observable differences between the sexes are due to socialization rather than inborn qualities. We also have to admit that the data of behavioural psychology are subject to differing interpretations. It is theoretically conceivable that one day scientists might prove that women are intellectually inferior to men (or vice versa), or that men and women have inborn characteristics which make them radically different in important respects. But even if this were to happen, it would not upset this principle of the complementarity of the sexes, or show that women (or men) are unsuitable for ordination. For the qualities needed by a Christian minister are not strong physique, high intelligence or any particular set of psychological traits, but rather spiritual and personal gifts – which can be found in women no less than in men. Whether one stresses the differences between the sexes, or the overlap of their gifts and talents, on either view it is appropriate that both should be represented in the Church's leadership.

Christian Ministry is service rather than the exercise of domination

All too often in the debate about women's ordination, it has been assumed that ministry is concerned with rule and government. Hence it has been argued that women being 'in subjection' are not capable of exercising authority (cf. above pp. 90f., 108f., 112). In contrast, the New Testament teaches that the primary characteristic of Christian ministry is humble, self-denying service (cf. Ch. 5, esp. p. 83). The prime example is Jesus' own life and teaching: 'I am among you as one who serves' (Luke 22.27 RSV); 'The Son of Man himself came not to be served but to serve' (Mark 10.45); 'If I, then, the Lord and Master, have washed your feet, you must wash each other's feet' (John 13.14) – an example of the humblest service of all. The disciples found it hard to grasp this teaching, and so too has the Church.

In the patristic and medieval periods ordination was frequently seen as setting the clergy above the laity, and as conveying degrees of rank. Even today such concepts are perpetuated in some ordination rites, in distinctions of ecclesiastical title, dress, and areas of authority and obedience (often enforced by Canon Law), and in attitudes of clergy and laity. These things seem out of place in a community which was founded as a family. They owe their origins more to secular concepts of status and social order than to the teaching of Jesus (cf. above pp. 96, 105). Consequently any argument that women ought to be excluded from ordination because of their 'subjection' to men and their inability to 'signify pre-eminence' (so Aquinas) must fail as being alien to the heart of the Gospel; it is particularly inappropriate in an age like our own, where women are no longer treated as subject to male authority.

To say all this is not to deny that power and authority have a place in ministry. But they are a power and authority quite unlike those of the secular world (Luke 22.24–6; John 18.36). The 'power' of Jesus' followers is the Divine power of the Holy Spirit, by the grace of God working in them (Acts 1.8; Eph. 3.20). Their authority is the Divine authority of the Christ who sends, not the personal authority of those sent (cf. John 20.21). As the Archbishop of Cánterbury has recently emphasized, it is 'the authority of the servant' whom the Master has entrusted with a particular responsibility.[6] Ministers are no more than God's stewards (1 Cor. 3.5—4.1), giving a shepherd's care to those entrusted to them on behalf of the chief shepherd (1 Pet. 5.1–4). The apostle Paul bluntly recognizes his own limitations: 'There is no question of our being qualified in ourselves: we cannot claim anything as our own. The qualification we have comes from God; it is he who has qualified us to dispense his new covenant' (2 Cor. 3.5f. NEB). And he stresses that God's power comes to human beings in their weakness: 'My grace is all you need; power comes to its full strength in weakness' (2 Cor. 12.9 NEB).[7] Jesus Christ himself experienced weakness and vulnerability in his life of poverty and his death of ignominy. He promised to his faithful followers not earthly glory, but suffering and persecution – and reward 'in heaven'. It is ironical that one who lived a life of such humility should be seen by some as instituting an authoritarian, hierarchical ministry from which women are excluded by the very virtue of their supposed lowly status.

The traditional 'weakness' and 'dependence' of women, and the fact that so many of them devote their lives to the support and care of others, should be an argument *for*, not *against*, their ordination. If Pope John Paul II is right that 'woman can only find herself by giving love to others', then her place in his Church's ministry ought to be assured. In practice, he seems to understand women's loving service as finding its fulfilment only in physical motherhood, or in the 'spiritual motherhood' of nuns and dedicated virgins.[8] Or it is suggested (especially by some Anglicans) that women may fulfil the ministry of humble service as deacons, but not as priests or bishops. We must affirm that women's gifts of spirituality, intellect, verbal fluency, practical organization, nurture, loving care, and their frequent role as the focus of unity in the family, admirably suit them for ordained ministry, including all three traditional Orders of bishop, priest and deacon (see Chs. 11–12). But we also affirm that humility, loving service, and dependence on God belong to men as well as women, and to all who exercise authority in the Church, whatever its form of government. Indeed they should be characteristic of all Christians.

Priesthood and ministry belong to the whole people of God

In many religions only special classes of persons may minister. The Jewish priesthood, for example, was normally restricted to male descendants of Aaron and men of the tribe of Levi, who had to fulfil certain physical qualifications (including sexual integrity). In the New Testament this Levitical priesthood was superseded by Jesus Christ, who though not a member of this

tribe became the 'high priest of our profession' (Heb. 3.1).
Through their union with him the whole people of God
constitute a 'royal priesthood', and are called to exercise of
ministry (cf. above Ch. 5).

A sacerdotal priesthood was revived in the patristic and
medieval periods, and the celebration of sacraments, especially
of the Lord's Supper or Eucharist, became the prerogative of
clergy alone. Some Christians believe that this sacerdotal
priesthood is of the essence of Christianity and that the only
'valid' Eucharist is one celebrated by a male ordained within a
succession of bishops extending back to the male Apostles
themselves (cf. above Ch. 12 with n.2). Others rightly point to
the variety and flexibility of the New Testament pattern of
ministry in which every member had a part to play, and to a
much broader concept of 'apostolic succession' (cf. above Ch.
5). This suggests that the current restriction, in many denominations, of sacramental acts to formally ordained ministers should
be seen as a matter of internal discipline rather than of the
essence of the Gospel. In spite of all the progress that has been
made towards an ecumenical understanding of ministry, there is
still a broad division in the Churches between those who take it
in a priestly, ontological sense and those who do not. We believe
that in the course of history God has blessed and used both
sacerdotal and non-sacerdotal forms of ministry, and that the
absence from the New Testament of any clear prescriptions on
this matter shows that no method of church government can
uniquely represent a 'Divine Institution'.

For those who believe that any Christian may, in appropriate
circumstances, celebrate the sacraments it should make no
difference whether that celebrant is a woman or a man. To those
who believe that presidency of the Eucharist belongs exclusively
to ordained ministers or priests, or that they alone, by virtue of
the 'character' conferred on them at ordination (or for any other
reason), may baptize, declare sins forgiven, teach authori-
tatively, exercise 'discipline', or lay on hands in healing and
blessing, it may be suggested that there can be no difference
between male and female clergy *qua* clergy, because of the
equality of the sexes before God and their equal redemption
through Jesus Christ. Whatever our views, we must always keep
in mind the New Testament insight that all Christian people are

called to priestly service through the sacrificial offering of their lives to God and the proclamation of the Gospel (cf. Rom. 12.1, and the other passages cited above, p. 74).

Women and men may equally 'represent' humanity

If our fundamental premise is correct that women and men are equal before God, it follows that both may represent their fellow human beings liturgically and pastorally. In the Old Testament men frequently represented their wives and children in worship, sacrifice, and in the keeping of festivals; and the covenant sign of circumcision was given to males only (cf. above pp. 25–7). But in the New Testament both men and women are baptized as full members of the new covenantal community (cf. above p. 56), and have equal access to God through Jesus Christ (note esp. Rom. 5.2; 8.14f.; and Heb. 5.16, 7.25, 10.19–22). The idea, found in Augustine, Gratian, and others (see above pp. 92, 107), that women somehow relate to God differently from men, in an indirect way through their husbands, violates the central New Testament affirmation that Christ alone mediates the New Covenant (cf. 1 Tim. 2.15; Heb. 9.15).

Humanity consists of men and women: for too long men have been regarded as the primary example of *homo* (mankind); women as some kind of aberrant or special form. The differences between the sexes have been polarized and their 'binary nature' or 'duality' seen as part of some profound theological principle running through God's creation (cf. above Ch. 10, esp. p. 151). More than a generation ago Dorothy L. Sayers wrote: 'The fundamental thing is that women are more like men than anything else in the world. They are human beings. *Vir* is male and *Femina* is female: but *Homo* is male and female'.[9] All too often a man has been treated as both *homo* and *vir*; a woman as merely *femina*. Liturgy and art have reinforced this idea. Traditionally through the centuries in representations of the Creation, God has been depicted as male, and 'Adam' or mankind as male: it is with a sense of surprise that most of us view Anne Parsons' redrawing of Michelangelo's 'Creation of Man' with both God and 'man' shown as female.[10] But this is a valid, and valuable, interpretation of one aspect of theological truth.

In the past many women may have been content to let men serve as their 'representatives', but this is rapidly ceasing to be so. In the West, at least, women think independently; they do not automatically have husbands; they are not regularly 'represented' by men in their secular lives. The appearance of only men in the public face of the Church suggests that women are, in some sense, unacceptable. Women priests and church leaders could be a powerful sign to the secular world that the Church has at last accepted women as truly human.

Women and men may equally 'represent' God

Many Christians believe that the ordained ministry in some special way represents Christ to humanity. A priest, especially when celebrating the sacraments, is sometimes seen as an 'imitation' or 'icon' of Christ: *sacerdos alter Christus*, 'a priest is another Christ'. Some in the 'catholic' tradition also see priests and bishops as 'father-figures', symbolizing in a special way God, the Creator and heavenly Father. They then go on to argue that only men can represent Christ or God in ordained ministry, since Christ was incarnate as a male, and a woman cannot symbolize the Divine Begetter and initiator. In the Reformed tradition there are also those who see ordained ministers as holding a special authority or 'headship' over a congregation, which cannot be exercised by a woman (cf. above Ch. 11, esp. 164–71).

To those who understand ministry in this way we would reply that a woman can 'represent' both Christ and God just as adequately (or inadequately) as a man. For Christ in his role as Redeemer represents all humanity, and not just its male part. One does not need to be of the same sex as a person to 'represent' him (or her): a female ambassador may 'represent' a male president (and vice versa). What matters in this case is not the physical sex of Christ's ministerial 'representatives' but their authority and their qualities of character. Moreover, all talk about God as 'Begetter' and Father is metaphorical: God is Spirit, not a man (John 4.24; cf. Hos. 11.9), and the Bible and Christian tradition use motherly images of God, Christ, and the Spirit, alongside fatherly and masculine ones (cf. Ch. 9, esp. pp. 133–7). A woman, as the one who nurtures and gives birth to a child, may be just as effective a 'representative' of God as the man who 'begets' a child by giving his sperm to merge with a woman's ovum. Both male and female may symbolize 'creativity', just as both may symbolize 'receptivity'. A woman minister may also 'represent' God in the exercise of loving discipline and authority in the family of the Church, just as a good mother cares for and disciplines her children in the home. A woman in a position of ecclesial authority no more undermines a 'Creation order' than a man (cf. above pp. 144–150). And the presence of women in the ordained ministry does not turn the Christian God into a pagan fertility goddess, like Astarte, as some critics imply with their disparaging references to 'priestesses' who belong to earth-mother cults, any more than male priests turn God into a male fertility-god, like Baal or Min or Dionysos.

But the whole concept that priests, or bishops, or any other ordained ministers 'represent' God in a unique way is a dangerous one, because it can so easily devalue Jesus Christ's unique role as mediator and lead to an unnatural separation between the ordained and lay members of Christ's Body, the Church. For all Christians by their baptism are made 'members of Christ' and as such represent him. All of them are children of God, called to be like their heavenly Father. They are all exhorted to 'put on Christ' (Rom. 13.14; Gal. 3.27, both RSV), to abide in Christ, like the branches of a vine (John 15.4, 7). The summons to follow Christ, to imitate God and Christ (Eph. 5.1; 1 Thess. 1.6) and to 'share the divine nature' (2 Pet. 1.4) applies to every Christian. Those who undertake church leadership have a special responsibility to serve as examples to the 'flock' entrusted to their care – a responsibility which, if taken seriously, should fill them with humility (1 Pet. 5.5). But in essence they are no different from the rest of God's people. Through personal holiness and self-denying service to others, as well as through word and sacrament, God's people, lay and ordained, are all called to demonstrate the love of God – Creator, Redeemer and Holy Spirit[11] – to a world in desperate need. The ordained ministry is the public 'face' of the Church. If, in community with the lay people of God, it in any sense represents God's nature, then it is essential that it should include women as well as men.

All ministry is by God's grace, not by right

Perhaps the most important principle of all, on which a proper understanding of women's ministry must rest, is that no ministry is ours by merit or right, but by the grace of God. This is generally agreed by opponents and proponents of women's ordination alike. But once this principle is granted, it is hard to see how sexuality can then be invoked as a barrier to ministry. Both Old Testament and New Testament make it clear that women receive spiritual gifts and revelation as well as men (cf. Joel 2.28f., quoted in Acts 2.17f., the references to women prophets, and other passages cited in Chs. 2–5). Experience through the ages likewise testifies to women's spiritual sensitivity. Why should the Church be deprived of the benefit of their insights?

Sometimes it is proposed that we need here to make a distinction between public and private ministry (usually equated with ordained and lay ministry respectively). Women, we are told, may counsel and even instruct others privately, but not teach or exercise authority as public representatives of the Church.[12] Such a distinction is artificial (cf. above p. 99). Is it a public or private ministry to serve as an elder or church warden or vestry member; to give a religious talk in church premises or on television; to lead or take part in a house-group; to teach theology in a church college or secular university? The New Testament knew of no dichotomy between 'official' and 'private' ministry. The patristic development of a priestly and public ordained ministry, performed by men, and a private (or diaconal) ministry, permitted to women, was a stereotyping and limiting of the much more flexible pattern found in the New Testament (cf. Chs. 5–6).

The comparative rarity until recent times of women exercising public ministry is no argument against women's ordination in our age. It must be seen not as caused by any inherent difference in the abilities of the two sexes, but rather as arising from social conventions, reinforced by domestic and economic conditions, and legal restrictions in a male-dominated Church and political system. Our survey of challenges and changes (Ch. 8) showed how, once women attained freedom with respect to their bodies, their education, and their legal and social positions, then their gifts emerged. The twentieth century has witnessed a massive increase in the part played by women in political and intellectual leadership, in administration, in medicine and social care, in the creative arts, in business, and in science and technology. Inevitably women also seek to play a fuller role in the Church's life. Women's gifts are gifts of God just as much as men's are. As George Eliot's character Dinah Morris pungently puts it: 'It isn't for men to make channels for God's Spirit, as they make channels for the water-courses, and say, "Flow here, but flow not there".'[13] Those words apply as much to the grace of ordination as to preaching and other manifestations of the Spirit.

To conclude, we turn to some wider applications of this study. We asked in the Introduction whether the new freedom for women in the Church's life and their increased opportunities for ministry are really compatible with the Bible's teaching. Our answer must be an emphatic 'Yes' – because they are in keeping with basic principles found in the Bible and with its affirmation that the Holy Spirit falls on women as well as men. But women's gifts can only be made effective where opportunities exist for their exercise. The time has now come for Christian Churches to re-examine their attitudes to women and to open their ordained ministries to them where they have not already done so. There seem to be three areas where change is most needed.

First, if women are to take their place as church leaders they need proper theological education. The majority of students in seminaries and theological colleges (except perhaps in a few Western institutions) are still male. Places need to be made available for women, and women encouraged to take them up. Alongside conventional courses, women should be offered new opportunities, including education through part-time and extension studies, so that they may combine ministerial training with domestic commitments. They also need courses which will enable them to develop their own special gifts where these are not the same as men's. Some women are extraordinarily diffident of their abilities, often because of society's – or their family's or spouse's – low expectations of them, whereas men, as psychologists have often noted, are inclined to have a high opinion of their own potential. Such women will need positive encouragement to undertake training and develop their gifts. They also need 'role models' in the presence of more women theological teachers and ministers in denominations where women are already ordained, including women in senior positions. All this calls for imagination on the part of those responsible for appointments.

Secondly, women need fuller opportunities to exercise their talents in the day-to-day life of the Church, both within denominations which currently ordain women and in those which do not. In some Christian groups women are barred simply *qua* women even from addressing a Sunday congregation. Members of these traditions must seriously ask themselves whether, by denying women the opportunity of speaking publicly, they are stifling the Spirit of God (cf. 1 Thess. 5.19). Women's active participation in preaching, prophecy, and the leading of worship need not be an open door to licence and chaos, as some have feared. It would be absurd to suppose that the need for order in worship (cf. 1 Cor. 14.40) entails an all-male public ministry, or the virtual silence of women, as enjoined by some Church Fathers. In traditions where sacramental ministry is barred to women, this will need to be opened to them – not merely as 'extraordinary ministers' or as 'assisting' deacons, but in its fulness, so that women may serve as priests and pastors of congregations and be eligible, on an equality with men, for 'higher' office.

Sooner or later the strange idea must go that women are properly concerned only with domesticity and with private, 'behind-the-scenes' ministry. The Church needs its Marthas: we are all grateful to those who selflessly devote themselves to the traditional 'feminine' tasks, such as child-care, church-cleaning, flower-arranging, tea-making, fund-raising, and privately supporting those in need. But this is not the sum total of women's gifts. The Church needs also its Marys, its Phoebes, and its Priscillas – perhaps even its Deborahs – who in a twentieth-century context are likely to find themselves in the forefront of public ministry, pastoral, priestly and episcopal.

For this to take place some denominations will need to amend their Canons, their Ordinals, and their ecclesiastical law, so as to remove discrimination against women. Church leaders will need to foster discussion and interchange of ideas, so that congregations and church groups may be encouraged to accept women in new roles. Hospital and college chaplaincies, senior positions in lay training, parish education, youth work and church administration can all appropriately be filled by women. Women should be encouraged to share in church government at all levels, participating on equal terms with men in synods and councils, and contributing to decisions on doctrinal as well as pastoral issues. Fuller use of 'inclusive' language in preaching, prayer, and liturgy, as well as in official church documents could also foster among women a sense that they belong to the Church and are cherished by it.

Finally we point to the Church's need to promote respect for women in the wider world. While individual Christians and some of the smaller denominations have long been concerned with the care of minorities, the major institutional Churches are often in the rearguard in caring for women in areas where they are oppressed; at times they have even used their official teaching to hinder women's progress and to help enforce their subordination to men. But if men and women are to be recognized as equal – as is being proclaimed today even by some of the most conservative theologians – then the Church must be seen to be promoting the full dignity of women. This will involve being prepared to speak out against all forms of discrimination, exploitation, and prejudice. It will involve supporting the positive efforts of governments and individuals to promote women's education, welfare and freedom. It will mean, where necessary, the Churches setting their own house in order so that women may be perceived, not as second-class ecclesial citizens, but as children of God, called equally with men to proclaim the divine love to all humanity. And it will mean openness to the Spirit and courage to do new things to the glory of that God whose power, working in us, can do infinitely more than we can ask or imagine.

NOTES

1 Aghiorgoussis (1976), p. 2.
2 Leonard in Amiel (1988).
3 See *Mulieris Dignitatem*, §16.

4   cf. Moloney (1985), esp. pp. 40–56, 87–92; Halkes in Küng and Moltmann (1983), pp. 66–73, esp. pp. 69f. on Rosemary Ruether's interpretation of 'the subversive Magnificat'. It lies outside the scope of this book to discuss the complex relationship of the cult of the Virgin Mary to the Christian doctrine of God.

5   Regrettably the idea of the bio-physical 'passivity' of motherhood is perpetuated in *Mulieris Dignitatem*, § 19.

6   See Runcie (1988), pp. 4f.

7   'Weakness' is a recurrent theme in 2 Cor. See further Best (1988), on Paul's concept of his authority.

8   *Mulieris Dignitatem*, §§ 17–27, p. 30, esp. p. 109.

9   Sayers (1971), 37.

10 'Feminist Recreation', illustrated on the cover of Morley and Ward (1986).

11 Leonard (1984), p. 49, takes up a suggestion discussed in Ware (1978), pp. 87f., that while only a male priest may 'represent' Christ as Saviour, a woman deacon might have 'a distinctive role as icon of the Paraclete' (cf. the texts from the *Didascalia* and *Apost. Const.*, discussed above p. 100). But in traditional Christian theology 'we worship one God in Trinity, and the Trinity in Unity; neither confusing the Persons nor dividing the Substance' (Athanasian Creed). It is quite artificial to divide 'representation' of God this way; in any case the prime model for the diaconate, whether of men or women, is surely Christ, among us as 'one who serves'.

12 See, for example, Hurley (1981), pp. 240–252 – a work very influential among 'evangelical' Christians. Many older writers in the 'Catholic' tradition of the Church take a similar view.

13 *Adam Bede* (1859). George Eliot is believed to have modelled the character of Dinah Morris on her aunt, Elizabeth Evans, who was herself a Methodist woman preacher. See further Hanson (1979), p. 115, using this quotation to good effect.

Bibliography

Abbott, W. M. and Gallagher, J., eds., (1966) *The Documents of Vatican II*. Piscataway, NJ, NC Publications. (For *Lumen Gentium* and *Gaudium et Spes*.)

Afanasiev, N., (1983) 'Presbytides or Female Presidents', in Hopko (1983), pp. 61–74. (Original Russian publication 1957.)

Aghiorgoussis, M., (1976) *Women Priests?* Brookline, Ma., Holy Cross Orthodox Press.

Amiel, B., (1988) 'Fighting for the Fundamentals' (interview with Bishop Graham Leonard), in *The Times*, 12.12.88.

Anderson, H., (1976) *The Gospel of Mark*. London, Marshall, Morgan & Scott.

Anglican Consultative Council, (1987) *Many Gifts, One Spirit* (Report of ACC 7, Singapore). London.

Anglican group for the Ordination of Women to the Historic Ministry, see *s.vv* Hodgson (1974), Lampe (1974), Woollcombe & Taylor (1975).

Anglican-Reformed International Commission, (1984) *God's Reign and Our Unity* (Report of the Woking Consultations, 1981–84). London, SPCK; Edinburgh, St Andrew Press (= *GRU*).

Anglican-Roman Catholic International Commission, (1982) *The Final Report*. London, CTS/SPCK (= *ARCIC 1*).

Aquinas, Thomas, *Summa Theologica*, vol. 5 (*Supplementum Partis Tertiae*), Marietti edn Turin, 1927. See also *s.vv* Hill (1963), Lamb (1966).

Armstrong, K., (1986) *The Gospel According to Woman*. London, Elm Tree Books.

Baelz, P. and Jacob, W., eds., (1985) *Ministers of the Kingdom*. London, CIO.

Bainton, R. H., (1971) *Women of the Reformation in Germany and Italy*. Minneapolis, Augsburg Publications.

Bainton, R. H., (1973) *Women of the Reformation in France and England*. Minneapolis, Augsburg Publications.

Baker, J. A., (1985) 'Eucharistic presidency and women's ordination' in *Theology* 88, pp. 350–57.

Balch, D. L., (1981) *Let Wives be Submissive* (SBL Monograph Series 26). Chico, Ca., Scholars Press.

Balsdon, J. P. V. D., (1962) *Roman Women*. London, Bodley Head.

Barbour, R. S., (1972) *Traditio-Historical Criticism of the Gospels*. London, SPCK.

Barnett, J. M., (1979) *The Diaconate: A Full and Equal Order*. New York, Seabury Press.

Barr, J., (1988) '"Abba, Father" and the familiarity of Jesus' speech' in *Theology* 91, pp. 173–9.

Barrett, C. K., (1962) *A Commentary on the Epistle to the Romans*. Rev. edn, London, Black.

Barrett, C. K., (1971) *A Commentary on the First Epistle to the Corinthians*. Rev. edn, London, Black.

Barrett, C. K., (1978) *The Gospel according to St. John*. Rev. edn, London, SPCK.

Barrett, C. K., (1985) *Church, Ministry and Sacraments in the New Testament*. London, Epworth.

Barth, K., (1958–61) *Church Dogmatics*, vol. III. 1–4. ET, Edinburgh, T. & T. Clark.

Beare, F. W., (1981) *The Gospel according to St. Matthew*. Oxford, Blackwell.

Bedale, S., (1954) 'The meaning of *kephalē* in the Pauline Epistles' in *Journal of Theological Studies* 5, pp. 211–15.

Behrens, M. S., (1973) *Martin Luther's View of Woman* (thesis presented to North Texas State Univ.). Ann Arbor, Mi., University Microfilms.

Best, E., (1986) 'Paul's apostolic authority?' in *Journal for the Study of the New Testament* 27, pp. 3–25.

Best, E., (1988) *Paul and his Converts*. Edinburgh, T. & T. Clark.

Blackman, E. C., (1957) *Biblical Interpretation*. London, Independent Press.

Boff, L., (1986) *Ecclesiogenesis*. ET, London, Collins.

Bonaventure, *Doctoris Seraphi S. Bonaventurae Opera Omnia*, Collegium Sancti Bonaventurae, Quaracchi, Vol. 4, 1889.

Børresen, K. E., (1981) *Subordination and Equivalence: the Nature and Role of Woman in Augustine and Thomas Aquinas*. ET, Washington, DC. University Press of America.

Brooten, B. J., (1977) '"Junia...outstanding among the Apostles" (Romans 16: 7)' in L. & A. Swidler (1977), pp. 141–4.

Brooten, B. J., (1982) *Women Leaders in the Ancient Synagogue*. Chico, Ca., Scholars Press.

Brown, R. E., (1971) *The Gospel according to John* (Anchor Bible, 2 vols.). London, Chapman.

Brown, R. E., (1979a) *The Birth of the Messiah*. Garden City, NY, Image Books.

Brown, R. E., (1979b) *The Community of the Beloved Disciple*. New York, Paulist Press.

Brown, R. E., (1985) *Biblical Exegesis and Church Doctrine*. London, Chapman.

Bruce, F. F., (1952) *The Acts of the Apostles*. Rev. edn, Leicester, IVP.

Bruce, F. F., (1960) *The New Testament Documents*. Rev. edn, Leicester, IVP.

Bruce, F. F., (1982) *The Epistle to the Galatians*. Exeter, Paternoster.

Bultmann, R., (1968) *The Gospel of John*. ET, Oxford, Blackwell.

Bultmann, R., (1972) *The History of the Synoptic Tradition*. Rev. edn, ET, Oxford, Blackwell.

Caird, G. B., (1980) *The Language and Imagery of the Bible*. London, Duckworth.

Canham, E., (1983) *Pilgrimage to Priesthood*. London, SPCK.

Carey, K. M., ed., (1954) *The Historic Episcopate*. London, Dacre Press.

Carnelley, E., (1989) 'Tertullian and feminism' in *Theology* 92, pp. 31–5.

Catholic Biblical Association of America, 'Women and priestly ministry: the New Testament evidence' in *CBQ* 41 (1979) pp. 608–13.

Childs, B. S., (1984) *The New Testament as Canon*. London, SCM.

Christ, C. P. and Plaskow, J., eds., (1979) *Womanspirit Rising*. New York and London, Harper and Row.

Church Literature Association, see *s.vv.* Mascall; Saward.

Church of England:

Deacons in the Ministry of the Church (Report to the House of Bishops 1988). London, Church House Publishing.

The Nature of Christian Belief (Statement and Exposition by the House of Bishops 1986). London, Church House Publishing.

The Ordination of Women to the Priesthood (A Consultative Document presented by the Advisory Council for the Church's Ministry 1972). London, Church Information Office.

The Ordination of Women to the Priesthood: Further Report (A Background Paper by C. Howard 1984). London, CIO Publishing.

The Ordination of Women to the Priesthood (A Report by the House of Bishops 1987). London, General Synod, Church House.

The Ordination of Women to the Priesthood (A Second Report by the House of Bishops 1988). London, General Synod, Church House.

The Priesthood of the Ordained Ministry (1986). London, Board for Mission and Unity, General Synod, Church House. (= *BMU* Report.)

We Believe in God (1987). London, Doctrine Commission of the General Synod of C. of E., Church House Publishing.

See also *s.vv.* Anglican Group for the Ordination of Women; Church Literature Association; Church Union; Movement for the Ordination of Women.

Church of Scotland: Women's Guild/Panel on Doctrine, see *s.v.* Lewis.

Church Union: *Women and the Ministry: Some Considerations on the Report of the Archbishops' Commission on the Ministry of Women* (1936). London, Church Literature Association.

Clark, E. A., (1983) *Women in the Early Church* (Message of the Fathers 13). Wilmington, Del., Glazier.

Clark, G. C., (1989) 'A rumour of priests' in *Theology* 92, pp. 20–25.

Clark, S. B., (1980) *Man and Woman in Christ*. Ann Arbor, Mi., Servant Books.

Conzelmann, H., (1975) *1 Corinthians* (Hermeneia). ET, Philadelphia, Fortress.

Copleston, F. C., (1955) *Aquinas*. Harmondsworth, Penguin.

Cosby, M. R., (1984) *Sex in the Bible*. Englewood Cliffs, NJ., Prentice-Hall.

Cotter, J., (1986) *Prayer at Night*. Rev. edn, Exeter, the author.

Cranfield, C. E. B., (1975–79) *The Epistle to the Romans* (ICC, 2 vols.). Edinburgh, T. & T. Clark.

Craston, C., (1986) *Biblical Headship and the Ordination of Women*. Bramcote, Notts., Grove Books.

Creed, J. M., (1930) *The Gospel according to St. Luke*. London, Macmillan.

Cressey, M., (1983) 'The ordination of women: theological and biblical issues (1)' in *Epworth Review* 10, pp. 56–66.

Cullmann, O., (1953) *Peter: Disciple, Apostle, Martyr*. ET, London, SCM.

Dalman, G., (1902) *The Words of Jesus*. ET, Edinburgh, T. & T. Clark.

Daly, M., (1986) *Beyond God the Father*. London, Women's Press.

Danby, H., (1933) *The Mishnah*. OUP.

Daniélou, J., (1974) *The Ministry of Women in the Early Church*. ET, rev. edn, Leighton Buzzard, Faith Press.

De Benedictis, M. M., (1972) *The Social Thought of Saint Bonaventure*. Westport, Conn., Greenwood Press.

Dempsey-Douglass, E. J., (1985) *Women, Freedom, and Calvin*. Philadelphia, Westminster Press.

De Vaux, R., (1973) *Ancient Israel*. ET, London, DLT. (Original French edn, 1958–60.)

Dix, G., (1946) 'The Ministry in the Early Church' in Kirk (1946) pp. 183–303.

Dodd, C. H., (1960) *The Authority of the Bible*. Rev. edn, Glasgow, Fount (Collins). (Original edn, 1929.)

Dodd, C. H., (1963) *Historical Tradition in the Fourth Gospel*. CUP.

Douglas, M., (1966) *Purity and Danger*. London, Routledge and Kegan Paul.

Douglass see *s.v.* Dempsey-Douglass.

Dover, K. J., (1978) *Greek Homosexuality*. London, Duckworth.

Dowell, S. and Hurcombe, L., (1981) *Dispossessed Daughters of Eve: Faith and Feminism*. London, SCM.

Drewery, B. and Bauckham, R., eds., (1988) *Scripture, Tradition, and Reason*. Edinburgh, T. & T. Clark.

Dunn, J. D. G., (1977) *Unity and Diversity in the New Testament*. London, SCM.

Dunn, J. D. G., (1980) *Christology in the Making*. London, SCM.

Dunn, J. D. G. and Mackey, J. P., (1987) *New Testament Theology in Dialogue*. London, SPCK.

Dyson, A., (1984) 'Dr Leonard on the ordination of women: a response' in *Theology*, 87, pp. 87–95.

Edwards, R. B., (1986) *Christian Priesthood*. Group for the Ministry of Women in the Scottish Episcopal Church, Dundee and Glasgow.

Edwards, R. B., (1987) 'What is the theology of women's ministry?' in *Scottish Journal of Theology* 40, pp. 421–36.

Edwards, R. B., (1988) 'Woman' in *ISBE* 4, pp. 1089–97.

Ellington, J., (1979) 'Man and Adam in Genesis 1–5' in *The Bible Translator* 30, pp. 201–5.

Ellingworth, P., (1978) '"They were both naked, the *Mensch* and his/her woman"? A response to Walter Vogels' in *Église et Théologie* 9, pp. 505f.

Eppstein, J., (1935) *The Catholic Tradition of the Law of the Nations*. London, Burns, Oates & Washbourne.

Epstein, I., (1938–52) *The Babylonian Talmud*. ET, 35 vols., London, Soncino Press.

Farnell, L. R., (1904) 'Sociological hypotheses concerning the position of women in ancient religion' in *Archiv für Religionswissenschaft* 7, pp. 70–94.

Fee, G. D., (1987) *The First Epistle to the Corinthians*. Grand Rapids, Eerdmans.

Fiorenza, E. S., (1983) *In Memory of Her: A Feminist Theological Reconstruction of Christian Origins*. London, SCM.

Fiorenza, E. S. and Collins, M., (1985) *Women – Invisible in Theology and Church* (*Concilium* 182). Edinburgh, T. & T. Clark.

Fitzgerald, K. K., (1983) 'The Characteristics and Nature of the Order of the Deaconess' in Hopko (1983) pp. 75–95.

Fitzmyer, J. A., (1981) *To Advance the Gospel*. New York, Crossroad.

Fitzmyer, J. A., (1981–85) *The Gospel according to Luke* (Anchor Bible, 2 vols). Garden City, NY, Doubleday.

Friedan, B., (1963) *The Feminine Mystique*. London, Gollancz.

Furlong, M., (1984) *Feminine in the Church* London, SPCK.

Galot, J., (1985) *Theology of the Priesthood*. ET, San Francisco, Ignatius Press.

Gardner, J. F., (1986) *Women in Roman Law and Society*. London & Sydney, Croom Helm.

Gaudium et Spes see *s.v.* Abbott and Gallagher.

General Synod of the C. of E, see *s.v.* Church of England.

Gibellini, R., (1987) *The Liberation Theology Debate*. ET, London, SCM.

Gibson, J. C. L., (1981) *Genesis* vol. 1 (Daily Study Bible). Edinburgh, St Andrew Press.

Gottwald, N. K., (1962) 'Song of Songs' in *IDB* 4, pp. 420–26.

Green, M., (1983) *Freed to Serve*. London, Hodder.

Greenslade, S. L., (1963) *The Cambridge History of the Bible*, vol. 3, CUP.

Greer, G., (1970) *The Female Eunuch*. London, MacGibbon and Kee.

Griffiths, D. and Saraga, E., (1979) 'Sex differences in cognitive abilities: a sterile field of enquiry?' in Hartnett, Boden and Fuller (1979) pp. 17–45.

Group for the Ministry of Women in the Scottish Episcopal Church (now Group for Whole Ministry), see *s.vv.* Edwards; Hampson.

Grudem, W., (1985) 'Does *kephalē* ("head") mean "source" or "authority over" in Greek literature?' in *Trinity Journal* 6, pp. 38–59.

Gryson, R., (1976) *The Ministry of Women in the Early Church*. ET, Collegeville, Minn., Liturgical Press.

Haenchen, E., (1971) *The Acts of the Apostles*. ET, Oxford, Blackwell.

Haile, H. G., (1980) *Luther: A Biography*. London, Sheldon Press.

Hamerton-Kelly, R., (1979) *God the Father*. Philadelphia, Fortress.

Hampson, D., (1979) *Let Us Think About Women*. Group for the Ministry of Women in the Scottish Episcopal Church, St Andrews and Glasgow.

Hampson, D., (1985) 'The challenge of feminism to Christianity' in *Theology* 88, pp. 341–50.

Hannon, V. E., (1967) *The Question of Women and the Priesthood*. London, Chapman.

Hanson, A. T., (1975) *Church, Sacraments and Ministry*. London & Oxford, Mowbray.

Hanson, A. T., (1982) *The Pastoral Epistles*. London, Marshall, Morgan & Scott.

Hanson, R., (1979) *Christian Priesthood Examined*. Guildford & London, Lutterworth.

Hartnett, O., Boden, G., Fuller, M., (1979) *Sex-Role Stereotyping*. London, Tavistock Publications.

Harvey, A. E., (1975) *Priest or President?* London, SPCK.

Hastings, A., (1986) *A History of English Christianity, 1920–1985*. London, Collins.

Hayter, M., (1987) *The New Eve in Christ*. London, SPCK.

Hebblethwaite, M., (1984) *Motherhood and God*. London, Chapman.

Heeney, B., (1988) *The Women's Movement in the Church of England, 1850–1930*. OUP.

Heine, S., (1987) *Women and Early Christianity: Are the Feminist Scholars Right?* ET, London, SCM.

Hengel, M., (1974) *Judaism and Hellenism*. ET, London, SCM.

Hengel, M., (1981) *The Charismatic Leader and his Followers*. ET, Edinburgh, T. & T. Clark.

Hennecke, E., (1965) *New Testament Apocrypha* ed., W. Schneemelcher, vol. 2: *Writings Relating to the Apostles: Apocalypses and Related Subjects*. ET, London, Lutterworth.

Herzel, S., (1978) 'The Body is the Book' in Moore (1978) pp. 101–22.

Hestenes, R., ed., (1982) *Women and Men in Ministry*. Pasadena, Ca., Fuller Theological Seminary.

Hill, D., (1972) *The Gospel of Matthew*, London, Marshall, Morgan & Scott.

Hill, E., ed., (1963) *St Thomas Aquinas, Summa Theologiae*, vol. 13. London, Blackfriars edn, Eyre & Spottiswoode.

Hodgson, L., (1974) *Theological Objections to the Admission of Women to Holy Orders*. Anglican Group for the Ordination of Women. Rev. edn, Midhurst, Sussex.

Hood, M., (1986) 'Woman's Unique Bond with God' in the *Times*, 18.1.86.

Hooker, M. D., (1963–64) 'Authority on her head: an examination of I Cor. xi.10' in *NTS* 10, pp. 410–16.

Hopko, T., ed., (1983) *Women and the Priesthood*. Crestwood, New York, St Vladimir's Seminary.

Horsley, G. H. R., (1981–87) *New Documents Illustrating Early Christianity*. 4 vols., Sydney, Macquarie University.

Howard, C., see *s.v.* Church of England.

Howe, E. M., (1982) *Women and Church Leadership*. Grand Rapids, Zondervan.

Hughes, J. J., (1973) *Man for Others*. London, Sheed & Ward.

Hurley, J. B., (1981) *Man and Woman in Biblical Perspective*. Leicester, IVP.

Hutt, C., (1972) *Males and Females*. Harmondsworth, Penguin.

Inter Insigniores, see *s.v.* Sacred Congregation.

Jacobs, L., (1984) *A Tree of Life: Diversity, Flexibility and Creativity in Jewish Law*. OUP (for the Littman Library).

Jeffery, R., ed., (1987) *By What Authority?* London & Oxford, Mowbray.

Jeremias, J., (1966) *The Eucharistic Words of Jesus*. ET, London, SCM.

Jeremias, J., (1969) *Jerusalem in the Time of Jesus*. ET, London, SCM.

Jeremias, J., (1971) *New Testament Theology*. ET, London. SCM.

Jeremias, J., (1978) *The Prayers of Jesus*. ET, Philadelphia, Fortress.

Jewett, P. K., (1975) *Man as Male and Female*. Grand Rapids, Eerdmans.

Jewett, P. K., (1980) *The Ordination of Women*. Grand Rapids, Eerdmans.

Joint Study Group of Representatives of the RC Church in Scotland and the Scottish Episcopal Church, (1973) *The Ecclesial Nature of the Eucharist*. Edinburgh & Glasgow.

Johnson, E. A., (1985) 'Jesus, the Wisdom of God: A Biblical basis for non-androcentric Christology' in *Ephemerides Theologicae Lovaniensis* 61, pp. 261–94.

Kelly, J. N. D., (1963) *A Commentary on the Pastoral Epistles*. London, Black.

Kessler, S. J. and McKenna, W., (1978) *Gender: An Ethnomethodological Approach*. New York, Wiley.

Kiesling, C., (1977) 'Aquinas on Persons' Representation in Sacraments' in L. & A. Swidler (1977) pp. 253–7.

Kirk, K. E., ed., (1946) *The Apostolic Ministry*. London, Hodder.

Klein, V., (1974) 'Women, status of', in *Encyclopedia Britannica*. Rev. edn, vol. 19, pp. 906–16.

Knight, G. W., (1984) '*Authenteo* in reference to women in 1 Timothy 2:12' in *NTS* 30, pp. 143–57.

Knox, J., see *s.v.* Laing.

Kroeger, C. C., (1979) 'Ancient heresies and a strange Greek verb' in *Reformed Journal* 29, pp. 12–15 (reprinted in Hestenes (1982) pp. 60–63).

Kroeger, C. C., (1986a) 'The Classical Concept of the "Head" as Source' (paper delivered to the Evangelical Theological Society, Nov. 1986), now published in G. G. Hull, ed., (1987) *Equal to Serve*. Old Tappan, NJ, Revell.

Kroeger, C. C., (1986b) '1 Timothy 2:12 – a Classicist's View' in Mickelsen (1986) pp. 225–44.

Kroll, V., (1975) *Flesh of my Flesh*. London, DLT.

Kümmel, W. G., (1975) *Introduction to the New Testament*. ET, rev. edn, London, SCM.

Küng, H., (1972) *Why Priests?* ET, Glasgow, Fontana.

Küng, H. and Moltmann, J., eds, (1983) *Mary in the Churches* (*Concilium* 168). Edinburgh, T. & T. Clark.

Laing, D., ed., (1854) *The Works of John Knox*, vol. 4 (Wodrow Society ed.). Edinburgh, Johnstone & Hunter.

Lamb, M. L., ed., (1966) *Aquinas: Commentary on Saint Paul's Epistle to the Ephesians*. Albany, NY, Magi Books, Inc.

Lampe, G. W. H., (1949) *Some Aspects of the New Testament Ministry*. London, SPCK.

Lampe, G. W. H., (1961) *A Patristic Greek Lexicon*. OUP.

Lampe, G. W. H., (1974) *The Church's Tradition and the Question of the Ordination of Women to the Historic Ministry*. Rev. edn, Midhurst, Sussex, Anglican Group for the Ordination of Women.

Lang, B., (1986) *Wisdom and the Book of Proverbs*. New York, Pilgrim Press.

Larsson, F., (1974) *My Best Men are Women*. London, Hodder.

Lehmann, H. T. and Pelikan, J., (1955–86) *Luther's Works*, esp. vols. I and XLI. St. Louis, Concordia Publishing House, and Philadelphia, Fortress.

Leonard, G., (1984) 'The ordination of women: theological and biblical issues (2)' in *Epworth Review* 11, pp. 42–9. See also *s.v.* Amiel.

Lewis, A. E., ed., (1984) *The Motherhood of God* (Report of the Woman's Guild/Panel on Doctrine Study Group [of the Church of Scotland]) Edinburgh, St Andrew Press.

Li, F. Tim Oi and Harrison, T., (1985) *Much Beloved Daughter*. London, DLT.

Lienhard, J. T., (1984) *Ministry* (Message of the Fathers 8). Wilmington, Del., Glazier.

Lightfoot, J. B., (1894) 'The Christian Ministry' in *St. Paul's Epistle to the Philippians*, pp. 181–269. Rev. edn, London, Macmillan.

Lips, H. M. and Colwill, N. L., (1978) *The Psychology of Sex Differences*. Englewood Cliffs, NJ, Prentice-Hall.

Lloyd, T., ed., (1977) *Lay Presidency at the Eucharist?* Bramcote, Notts., Grove Books.

Loades, A., (1987) *Searching for Lost Coins: Explorations in Christianity and Feminism*. London, SPCK.

Loewe, R., (1966) *The Position of Women in Judaism*. London, SPCK.

Lohfink, G., (1985) *Jesus and Community*. ET, London, SPCK.

Longenecker, R. N., (1975) *Biblical Exegesis in the Apostolic Period*. Grand Rapids, Eerdmans.

Lumen Gentium, see s.*v.* Abbott and Gallagher.

Lutge, H. K., (n.d.) *Sexuality – Theology – Priesthood*. San Gabriel, Ca., Concerned Fellow Episcopalians.

Luther, see s.*v.* Lehmann and Pelikan.

Maccoby, E. E. and Jacklin, C. N., (1974) *The Psychology of Sex Differences*. Stanford University Press.

McMillan, C., (1982) *Women, Reason and Nature*. Oxford, Blackwell.

McNamara, J. A., (1983) *A New Song: Celibate Women in the First Three Christian Centuries*. New York, Hawarth Press.

Macquarrie, J., (1977) *Principles of Christian Theology*. Rev. edn, London, SCM.

Macquarrie, J., (1986) *Theology, Church and Ministry*. London, SCM.

Maitland, S., (1983) *A Map of the New Country: Women and Christianity*. London, Routledge & Kegan Paul.

Marshall, I. H., (1977a) *I Believe in the Historical Jesus*. London, Hodder.

Marshall, I. H., ed., (1977b) *New Testament Interpretation*. Exeter, Paternoster.

Marshall, I. H., (1978) *The Gospel of Luke*. Exeter, Paternoster.

Marshall, I. H., (1980a) *Last Supper and Lord's Supper*. Exeter, Paternoster.

Marshall, I. H., (1980b) *Acts: An Introduction and Commentary*. Leicester, IVP.

Martimort, A. G., (1982) *Deaconesses: An Historical Study*. ET, San Francisco, Ignatius Press.

Mascall, E. L., (1977a) *Women Priests?* Rev. edn, London, Church Literature Association.

Mascall, E. L., (1977b) *Theology and the Gospel of Christ*. London, SPCK.

Mascall, E. L., (1978) 'Some Basic Considerations' in Moore (1978) pp. 9–26.

Mead, M., (1962) *Male and Female*. Harmondsworth, Penguin. (Original edn, 1949.)

Metz, J.-B., and Schillebeeckx, E., (1981) *God as Father? (Concilium* 143). Edinburgh, T. & T. Clark.

Mickelsen, A., ed., 1986 *Women, Authority and the Bible*. Downers Grove, Ill., IVP.

Miller, J. W., (1986) 'Depatriarchalizing God in Biblical interpretation: a critique' in *CBQ* 48, pp. 609–16.

Mitchell, J., (1971) *Woman's Estate*. Harmondsworth, Penguin.

Moberly, R. C., (1899) *Ministerial Priesthood*. Rev. edn, London, John Murray.

Mollenkott, V. R., (1977) *Women, Men, and the Bible*. Nashville, Abingdon Press.

Moloney, F. J., (1985) *Woman: First Among the Faithful*. London, DLT.

Moltmann, J., (1985) *God in Creation*. ET, London, SCM. See also *s.v.* Küng.

Moltmann-Wendel, E., (1982) *The Women around Jesus*. ET, London, SCM.

Moltmann-Wendel, E. and Moltmann, J., (1983) *Humanity in God*. ET, London, SCM.

Montefiore, C. G. and Loewe, H., (1938) *A Rabbinic Anthology*. London, Macmillan.

Moore, P., ed., (1978) *Man, Woman, and Priesthood*. London, SPCK.

Morley, J., (1984) *In God's Image?* London, MOW.

Morley, J., (1988) *All Desires Known*. London, MOW and WIT.

Morley, J. and Ward, H., eds., (1986) *Celebrating Women*. London, MOW and WIT.

Morris, J., (1973) *The Lady was a Bishop*. London, Macmillan.

Moulton, J. H. and Milligan, G., (1930) *The Vocabulary of the Greek Testament*. London, Hodder.

Movement for the Ordination of Women, see *s.vv.* Morley; Morley & Ward; Muddiman; Tomkins.

Muddiman, J. & G., (1984) *Women, the Bible and the Priesthood*. London, MOW.

Mulieris Dignitatem (Apostolic Letter of the Supreme Pontiff John Paul II). (1988) London, CTS.

Murphy-O'Connor, J., (1976) 'The non-Pauline character of 1 Cor. 11:2–16?' in *Journal of Biblical Literature* 95, pp. 615–21.

Murphy-O'Connor, J., (1980) 'Sex and logic in 1 Cor. 11:2–16' in *CBQ* 42, pp. 482–500.

Murray, R., (1975) *Symbols of Church and Kingdom: A Study in Early Syriac Tradition*. CUP.

Neusner, J., (1973) *The Idea of Purity in Ancient Judaism*. Leiden, Brill.

Newbigin, L., (1983) *The Other Side of 84: Questions for the Churches*. London, British Council of Churches.

Nunally-Cox, J., (1981) *Foremothers*. New York, Seabury Press.

Oakley, A., (1981) *Subject Women*. Oxford, Robertson.

Oakley, A., (1985) *Sex, Gender and Society*. Rev. edn, Aldershot, Gower Publishing Company.

O'Connor, D. J., (1967) *Aquinas and Natural Law*. London, Macmillan.

Oddie, W., (1984) *What Will Happen to God?* London, SPCK.

Ogilvie, R. M., (1969) *The Romans and their Gods*. London, Chatto & Windus.

Orthodox Churches: see *s.v.* Tarasar & Kirillova.

Padgett, A., (1984) 'Paul on women in the Church: the contradictions of coiffure in 1 Cor. 11:2–16' in *Journal for the Study of the New Testament* 20, pp. 69–86.

Padgett, A., (1987) 'Wealthy women at Ephesus: 1 Tim. 2:8–15 in social context' in *Interpretation* 41, pp. 19–31.

Pagels, E., (1976) 'What became of God the Mother? Conflicting images of God in early Christianity' in *Signs* 2; reprinted in Christ & Plaskow (1979) pp. 107–19.

Pagels, E., (1979) *The Gnostic Gospels*. London, Weidenfeld & Nicolson.

Parvey, C. F., see *s.v.* World Council of Churches.

Payne, P. B., (1986) '*Oude* in 1 Tim. 2:12' (paper given to the Evangelical Theological Society, Nov. 1986).

Pelikan, J., see *s.v.* Lehmann.

Percival, H. R., (1900) *The Seven Ecumenical Councils of the Undivided Church* (Nicene and Post-Nicene Fathers, 2nd. series, 14). Oxford, Parker.

Perrin, N., (1967) *Rediscovering the Teaching of Jesus*. London, SCM.

Perrin, N., (1970) *What is Redaction Criticism?* London, SPCK.

Pomeroy, S. B., (1975) *Goddesses, Whores, Wives, and Slaves: Women in Classical Antiquity*. New York, Schocken Books.

Pomeroy, S. B., (1984) *Women in Hellenistic Egypt*. New York, Schocken Books.

Pope, M. H., (1977) *Song of Songs* (Anchor Bible). Garden City, New York, Doubleday.

Priesand, S., (1975) *Judaism and the New Woman*. New York, Behrman House.

Prohl, R. C., (1957) *Woman in the Church*. Grand Rapids, Eerdmans.

Rahner, K., (1968) *Servants of the Lord*. ET, London, Burns & Oates.

Raming, I., (1976) *The Exclusion of Women from the Priesthood: Divine Law or Sex Discrimination?* ET, Metuchen, NJ, Scarecrow.

Ramsey, G. W., (1988) 'Is name-giving an act of domination in Genesis 2:23 and elsewhere?' in *CBQ* 50, pp. 24–35.

Ramsey, M., (1985) *The Christian Priest Today*. Rev. edn, London, SPCK.

Raven, C. E., (1928) *Women and Holy Orders*. London, Hodder.

Rawlinson, A. E. J., (1949) *St. Mark*. Rev. edn, London, Methuen.

Rengstorf, K. H., ed., (1983) *Die Tosefta, Seder 1: Zeraim*. Stuttgart, Kohlhammer.

Robinson, J. M., ed., (1977) *The Nag Hammadi Library in English*. New York, Harper & Row.

Roman Catholic Church: see *s.v.* Abbott and Gallagher; Anglican-Roman Catholic International Commission; Catholic Biblical Association; Joint Study Group; *Mulieris Dignitatem*; Sacred Congregation.

Ruether, R. R., (1974) *Religion and Sexism*. New York, Simon & Schuster.

Ruether, R. R., (1981) 'The Female Nature of God: A Problem in Contemporary Religious Life' in Metz and Schillebeeckx (1981) pp. 61–6.

Ruether, R. R., (1983) *Sexism and God-Talk: Toward a Feminist Theology*. London, SCM.

Ruether, R. R., (1985) *Women-Church: Theology and Practice of Feminist Liturgical Communities*. San Francisco, Harper & Row.

Runcie, R., (1988) *Authority in Crisis? An Anglican Response*. London, SCM.

Russell, A., (1980) *The Clerical Profession*. London, SPCK.

Russell, G. and Dewey, M., (1978) 'Psychological Aspects' in Moore (1978) pp. 91–100.

Sacerdotium Ministeriale see next entry.

Sacred Congregation for the Doctrine of the Faith:
Declaration on the Question of the Admission of Women to the Ministerial Priesthood. (1976), London, CTS, (= *Inter Insigniores*). *Sacerdotium Ministeriale* (Letter to the Bishops of the Catholic Church on Certain Questions Concerning the Minister of the Eucharist). (1983). London, CTS.

Saward, J., (1978) *The Case Against the Ordination of Women*. Rev. edn, London, Church Literature Association.

Sayers, D. L., (1971) *Are Women Human?* Grand Rapids, Eerdmans. (Original edn, 1946.)

Scanzoni, L., (1982) 'The Great Chain of Being and the Chain of Command' in *Reformed Journal* 26 (1976) pp. 14–18, reprinted in Hestenes (1982) pp. 76–9.

Schaps, D. M., (1979) *Economic Rights of Women in Ancient Greece*. Edinburgh University Press.

Schelkle, K. H., (1979) *The Spirit and the Bride*. ET, Collegeville, Minn. Liturgical Press.

Schillebeeckx, E., (1981) *Ministry: A Case for Change*. ET, London, SCM.

Schillebeeckx, E., (1985) *The Church with a Human Face*. ET, London, SCM.

Schnackenburg, R., (1980–82) *The Gospel according to St. John*. 3 vols., ET, New York, Seabury Press.

Schneir, M., ed., (1972) *Feminism: The Essential Historical Writings*. New York, Vintage Books.

Schweizer, E., (1961) *Church Order in the New Testament*. ET, London, SCM.

Schweizer, E., (1971) *The Good News according to Mark.* ET, London, SPCK.

Schweizer, E., (1976) *The Good News according to Matthew.* ET, London, SPCK.

Scottish Episcopal Church: see *s.vv.* Joint Study Group; Group for the Ministry of Women.

Sedgwick, P., (1988) 'Recent criticisms of the concept of authority in the Church of England' in *Theology* 91, pp. 258–66.

Shahar, S., (1983) *The Fourth Estate.* ET, London, Methuen.

Sheerin, D. J., (1986) *The Eucharist* (Message of the Fathers 7). Wilmington, Del., Glazier.

Sigurbjörnsson, E., (1974) *Ministry Within the People of God.* Lund, Gleerup.

Smith, M. S., (1988) '"Seeing God" in the Psalms: the background to the beatific vision in the Hebrew Bible' in *CBQ* 50, pp. 171–83.

Southern, R. W., (1970) *Western Society and the Church in the Middle Ages.* Harmondsworth, Penguin.

Spencer, S. I., ed., (1984) *French Women and the Age of Enlightenment.* Bloomington, Indiana University Press.

Stanton, E. C., ed., (1985) *The Woman's Bible.* Edinburgh, Polygon Books. (Original edn, 1895–98, New York, European Publishing Co.)

Storkey, E., (1985) *What's Right with Feminism,* London, SPCK.

Streeter, B. H., (1929) *The Primitive Church.* London, Macmillan.

Stroup, G., (1981) *The Promise of Narrative Theology.* London, SCM.

Swidler, A., (1981) 'The Image of Woman in a Father-Oriented Religion' in Metz & Schillebeeckx (1981) pp. 75–80.

Swidler, L., (1976) *Women in Judaism.* Metuchen, NJ., Scarecrow.

Swidler, L. & A., eds., (1977) *Women Priests: A Catholic Commentary on the Vatican Declaration.* New York, Paulist Press.

Sykes, S. W., (1978) *The Integrity of Anglicanism.* London & Oxford, Mowbray.

Sykes, S. W., (1987) *Authority in the Anglican Communion.* Toronto, Anglican Book Centre.

Tarasar, C. J., & Kirillova, I., eds., (1977) *Orthodox Women* (Report of the Agapia Consultation). Geneva, WCC.

Tavard, G. H., (1977) 'The Scholastic Doctrine' in Swidler (1977) pp. 99–106.

Taylor, V., (1966) *The Gospel according to St. Mark.* Rev. edn, London, Macmillan.

Terrien, S., (1985) *Till the Heart Sings: A Biblical Theology of Manhood and Womanhood.* Philadelphia, Fortress.

Tetlow, E. M., (1980) *Women and Ministry in the New Testament.* Lanham, New York, University Press of America.

Theissen, G., (1978) *The First Followers of Jesus*. ET, London, SCM.

Theodorou, E., (1977) 'The Ministry of Deaconesses in the Greek Orthodox Church' in Tarasar and Kirillova (1977) pp. 37–43.

Thompson, D'A. W., (1936) *A Glossary of Greek Birds*. Rev. edn, OUP.

Thrall, M. E., (1958) *The Ordination of Women to the Priesthood*. London, SCM.

Tomkins, O. S., (1984) *A Fully Human Priesthood*. London, MOW.

Toon, P. and Spiceland, J. D., eds., (1980) *One God in Trinity*. London, Bagster.

Trible, P., (1978) *God and the Rhetoric of Sexuality*. Philadelphia, Fortress.

Trible, P., (1979) 'Eve and Adam: Genesis 2–3 Reread' in Christ and Plaskow (1979) pp. 74–83.

Van der Meer, H., (1973) *Women Priests in the Catholic Church?* ET, Philadelphia, Temple University Press.

Visser 't Hooft, W. A., (1982) *The Fatherhood of God in an Age of Emancipation*. Geneva, WCC.

Vogt, K., (1985) '"Becoming male": One Aspect of an Early Christian Anthropology' in Fiorenza and Collins (1985) pp. 72–83.

Von Allmen, J.-J., (1963) 'Is the Ordination of Women to the Pastoral Ministry Justifiable?' in Lutge (n.d) pp. 21–42. (Original French publication in *Verbum Caro* 17, no. 65.)

Ward, B., ed., (1973) *The Prayers and Meditations of St. Anselm*. Harmondsworth, Penguin.

Ware, K., (1978) 'Man, Woman and the Priesthood of Christ' in Moore (1978) pp. 68–90; also reprinted in Hopko (1983) pp. 9–37.

Warmington, E. H., (ed.), (1940) *Remains of Old Latin*, vol. 4 (Loeb Classical Library), London, Heinemann.

Warner, M., (1976) *Alone of all her Sex: the Myth and the Cult of the Virgin Mary*. London, Weidenfeld & Nicolson.

West, M. L., ed., (1978) *Hesiod: Works and Days*. OUP.

Whale, J. S., (1957) *Christian Doctrine*. London, Fontana (Collins). (Original edn, 1941.)

Wijngaards, J., (1977) *Did Christ Rule out Women Priests?* Great Wakering, Mayhew-McCrimmon.

Williams, A. L., ed., (1921) *Tractate Berakoth: Mishna and Tosephta*. London, SPCK.

Williams, D., (1977) *The Apostle Paul and Women in the Church*. Ventura, Ca., Regal Books.

Witherington, B., (1984) *Women in the Ministry of Jesus* (*SNTSMS* 51). CUP.

Witherington, B., (1988) *Women in the Earliest Churches* (*SNTSMS* 59). CUP.

Woollcombe, K. J. and Taylor, J. V., (1975) *No Fundamental Objections*. Midhurst, Sussex, Anglican Group for the Ordination of Women.

World Council of Churches:

Baptism, Eucharist and Ministry (Faith and Order Paper no. 11) (1982) WCC, Geneva. (= *Lima Report, BEM*).

The Community of Women and Men in the Church: *The Sheffield Report*, ed. C. F. Parvey. (1983). WCC, Geneva.

Concerning the Ordination of Women. Department of Faith and Order, (1964). WCC, Geneva.

Ordination of Women in Ecumenical Perspective ed. C. F. Parvey (Faith & Order Paper 105) (1980). WCC, Geneva.

Wright, F., (1980) *The Pastoral Nature of the Ministry*. London, SCM.

Zizioulas, J. D., (1985) *Being as Communion*. London, DLT.

Index of Biblical References

Genesis
1—3 91, 145, 150
1— 30, 147, 150, 167
1.2 136
1.26f. 30, 91, 92, 124,
   145, 150, 165, 183, 187
1.27 55
1.28 60
2—3 68, 165
2— 30, 65, 146, 147
2.7f. 146
2.15f. 146
2.18 60, 147
2.19–23 146
2.20 30
2.21–4 165
2.23–5 146
2.23 147
3— 116, 148
3.8 133
3.16 148, 187
3.17 145
3.20 139, 157
3.21 145
5.1f. 165
6.1–4 65
18— 25
19.6–8 24
21— 24
22— 26
27— 31
29.14 157
31— 31
31.54 26
38— 24
46.1 26

Exodus
15.3 134
15.20 26, 31
15.21 31
18.4 30
20.12 139
20.17 27, 37
21.7 24
23.17 27
33.23 133

Leviticus
12.1–5 27
12.6f. 26
15.1–18 27
15.19–33 27

15.29f. 26
27.1–8 27

Numbers
5.11–31 24
5.18 71
12— 32
23.19 138
27.1–11 24

Deuteronomy
4.9 25
22.28f. 25
24.1 25
24.16 31
32.6 139
32.18 134
33.7 30

Joshua
7.24f. 31

Judges
4.9 28
5— 32
5.24–7 28
5.30 37
9.2 157
9.49 101
9.53f. 28
11.30–40 24
13.2–22 31
19— 24
21.14–23 37

Ruth
4— 24

1 Samuel
1— 31
2.1–10 31
2.19 139
15.29 138
18.6f. 26
18.21 37
25.3 31
25.23–5 31
25.33 31

2 Samuel
3.7 37
13.1–20 37
16.21f. 37

1 Kings
1.11–40 32

3.27 139
17.23 139
18— 21

2 Kings
4.20 139
8.18 32
11.1–16 32
22.15, 18 32

Nehemiah
5.4 24
6.14 32
8.3 25

Job
10.18f. 134

Psalms
1.1 37
17.8 135
22.7 134
28.1 138
34.8 37
37.7 135
62.2 138
68.5 139
71.6 134
84.12 37
90.2 134
103.13 139
112.1 101
128.3 26

Proverbs
3.11f. 139
5.18f. 33
8—9 137
19.14 26
31.10–31 26
31.13–24 25
31.20, 26 33

Ecclesiastes
7.26 30
9.9 33

Song of Songs
1.2 33
2.1 33
3.1–4 33
8.3 33

Isaiah
2.9 101

Isaiah (cont.)
5.12 138
8.3 32
19.16 28
22.22 78
31.5 135
42.14 134, 138
46.3 134
49.15 134
52.13 83
54— 169
60.17 96
66.13 134, 137

Jeremiah
2.24 138
31.9 139
51.30 28

Daniel
6.24 31
13— (= Susanna) 31

Hosea
2.16 169
5.14 138
11.9 195
11.13 135

Joel
2.28f. 197

Micah
6.4 32

Nahum
3.13 28

Zechariah
9.9 169

Malachi
1.6 139
2.10 139
3.20 (= 4.2) 138

Tobit
2.11 25
8.6 50

Judith
8.6-8 31
8.28-31 31
14.18 28
15.12—16.17 26

Wisdom
7— 137

Ecclesiasticus
24.1-22 137
25.16-26 29
25.24 148
26.1-4 26
26.6-12 29

26.14-18 26
42.12-14 29

Baruch
4.8 135

Susanna see Daniel
2 Maccabees
7.21 28

Matthew
5.9 48, 49, 140
5.16 49
5.21 48
5.22-4 48, 70
5.28 48
6.9 49, 134
6.15 141
6.26, 32 141
7.4f. 48
7.11 141
7.24-7 48
8.15 83
8.19-22 45
10.1-15 84
10.1 46
10.2 79
10.5 182
10.9f. 61
10.37 43, 49
10.40 78
10.42 46
11.19 par. 137
11.25 134
12.49f. 47
14.21 43
15.32 43
15.38 43
16.17-19 73
16.19 77
18.1-5 84
18.5 166
18.15 70
18.18 78
18.19 78
18.35 141
19.28 79
20.20 50
20.26-8 84
21.22 78
21.31f. 47
23.8-12 77
23.10 83
23.11 84
23.37 135
25.2 48
25.40 166
26.6-13 42
27.55 45
27.61 46
28.1-10 46
28.16-20 73, 76, 78

Mark
1.10 136, 142
1.29-31 40
1.31 par. 41
2.14 45
2.19f. par. 169
2.19 170
3.13-19 73
3.14 85
3.32-5 47, 77
5.24-34 40
5.35-43 40
5.41 50
6.7-13 84
6.30 79, 85
7.10 139
7.24-30 40
8.29 par. 45
9.35 84
9.37 78, 166
10.6f. 165
10.10-12 49
10.13-16 par. 43
10.28-30 48, 52
10.29 49
10.45 84, 191
11.24f. 78
12.31 par. 176
12.40 par. 47
12.41-4 47
12.49f. 47
13.17 47
14.3-9 42
14.15 84
14.36 134
14.50 50
15.40f. 45, 46
16.1-8 46
16.9 53

Luke
1.38 83
1.41-5 51
1.48 83
2.36-8 51
2.51 139
4.18 83
7.13 41
7.35 137
7.36-50 41f.
8.1-3 45
8.1 46
8.3 83
8.21 47
9.1-6 84
9.46-8 84
9.48 166
10.1-20 73
10.1 49
10.4 61
10.16 78

Luke (*cont.*)
10.38–42 41, 44
11.27f. 44
13.10–17 41
13.21 50
13.34 135
14.25–7 49
14.26 43
15.8–10 47
15.11–32 141
18.15 43
22.24–6 77, 191
22.26f. 84
22.27 83, 191
22.30 79
22.31f. 73
22.32 70
23.28 47
23.49, 55f. 46
24.1–11 46
24.10f. 46
24.22f. 46
24.33 76
24.36–49 73
24.47 78

John
1.13 170
1.14 167
1.29 138
3.3, 5 137, 170
3.29 169, 170
4— 44
4.24 195
4.29 45
4.39 44
7.53—8.11 41
11.27 45
12.1–8 42
12.2 41, 83
13.4–16 84
13.14 191
13.16 79
13.20 78
14.26 142
15.4, 7 196
15.17 176
15.26 142
16.8, 13, 14 142
16.13 182
18.36 191
20.1 46
20.11–18 46
20.17f. 46
20.19–23 73, 76
20.21 191
20.22f. 77, 78
21.15–17 73

Acts
1.8f. 78
1.8 191

1.11 84
1.14 76
1.15ff. 82
1.16 73
1.20 85
2.14 73
2.17f. 78, 197
2.18 83
2.42f. 46 75
3.13, 22 83
4.27 83
6—8 75
6.1–6 75, 81
6.2f., 4 83
8.12 56
9.1–22 74
9.36 52, 73
10— 182
10.34 187
11.1–18 182
12.2 79
13.2f. 75
14.3 102
14.23 75, 85
15— 182, 184
15.22 82
17.17 16
18.24–8 57, 73
20.17, 28 85
21.8 75
21.9 73, 99

Romans
1.1 83
1.13 70
3.24 55
5.1f. 55, 66
5.2 194
5.12–21 55, 168
6.4 55
6.10 74
6.14 56
7.1–6 57
7.2 64
8.14–17 140
8.14f. 194
12— 73
12.1 70, 194
12.4–13 82
12.4–8 56
12.10 63, 176
13.1–7 63
13.9 176
13.11f. 60
13.14 196
15.31 83
16— 57, 59, 74, 82
16.1f. 57, 58, 81, 83
16.2 82
16.3f. 57
16.5 75

16.6 57
16.7 58, 99
16.12, 13 57
16.15f. 57

1 Corinthians
1.10 70
1.11 57
1.14–17 75
1.22–4 137
1.26 174
1.30 137
3.4–11 183
3.5–4.1 191
3.5f. 192
5.4f. 82
6.2 79
6.14–20 61
7— 60–2, 67–9, 93
7.1f. 60
7.3–5 61, 94
7.7, 8f. 60
7.15 57
7.24, 26 60
7.29f. 60
7.31, 37f. 60
7.39 64
8.6 137
8.7–13 66
9.15 57
10.23–33 66
11— 67, 69, 99, 116, 165
11.1 65
11.2–16 64–6, 70, 71, 98, 148, 149, 165
11.3 187
11.6 111
11.7 91, 92
11.10 107
11.11f. 66, 165
11.34f. 67
11.40 67
12—14 64
12— 73
12.4–11 56, 82
13— 176
13.11 101
14.26–40 66f.
14.27, 31 64
14.34f. 69, 98, 102
14.35 21
14.40 199
15.10 57
15.22 55
16.19 75

2 Corinthians
3.17 56
5.17 55, 149, 165
5.18, 20 83
11.2 170
11.3 70

Galatians
2.11–18 184
3.27 55, 196
3.28 55, 69, 110f., 124,
    149, 165, 187
4.19 142
4.21–31 56
4.24–6 169
5.1 56
5.13–25 56
6.2 176
6.15 165

Ephesians
1.22f. 183
2.18 66
2.20 79
3.20 191
4.2 176
4.11–13 56, 73, 82
4.13 92, 115
4.24 55, 149
5— 165, 170
5.1 196
5.21 176
5.22—6.9 62–4
5.22–33 169
5.22 174
5.28 63
6.20 83
6.21 58

Philippians
1.1 73, 81
2.6f. 173
2.7f. 83, 168
4.2f. 57

Colossians
1.7 58
1.15–20 137
1.16–18 183
1.23, 25 58
1.28 101
3.10 55, 149
3.11 183
3.18—4.1 62
4.7 58
4.15 57, 75

1 Thessalonians
1.6 196
2.7 142

4.15 60
5.12 73, 82
5.19 199

1 Timothy
2— 68, 165
2.1f. 68
2.8–14 67–9
2.9–15 148
2.9 18
2.11–15 98
2.12 108, 161
2.13f. 68, 148, 149
2.15 68, 194
3.2 85
3.11 81, 85
4.14 75, 85, 102
5.1f. 57, 62
5.5 163
5.9f. 113
5.14 68
5.17 82, 85
6.1f. 62
6.20 102

2 Timothy
1.6 102
3.6 69
4.11 83

Titus
1.5 85, 102
1.7 85
1.10f. 69
2.2–10 62
2.3 80
2.7f. 63
3.1 63

Philemon
2 57, 75
9 83

Hebrews
2.14–18 168
3.1 82, 193
4.14—10.22 74
5.16 194
7.25 194
7.27 74
9.12 74
9.15 194
10.19–22 194

12.2 183
12.29 138
13.7 82
13.15 74
13.17, 24 82

James
1.1 83
1.8, 12, 23 101
2.8 176
3.1 73
3.2 101
5.14 73

1 Peter
1.3 170
1.16 163
1.22 176
1.23 170
2.5, 9f. 74
2.13–17 63
2.18–3.7 62
2.25 83
3— 165
3.1–5 18
3.1f. 63
3.7 28
5.1–4 191
5.1 73
5.5 196

2 Peter
1.1 83
1.4 196

1 John
1.5 138
2.27 83
4.7–11 176

2 John
1 73

3 John
1 73

Revelation
1.1 83
1.6 74
5.10 74, 79
5.12 138
21— 170
21.2 169
21.14 79

Index of Names and Subjects

abbesses 105, 108f., 110, 161
Abelard 70
Abigail 31
abortion 121, 128
Abraham 24, 26, 41
Adam, 'Adam 30, 55, 68, 91f., 107, 110, 145–9, 168; in art 194
adultery: 15, 20, 24, 29, 48, 170; woman taken in 41
Aegidius of Rome 70
Aelred of Rievaulx 136
Africa, southern 183
aggression 121, 154, 162, 190
allegorizing 34, 97, 148, 170
Ambrose 92, 101, 103, 116, 174
Ambrosiaster 65, 90, 101, 174
American Episcopal Church (ECUSA) 126f., 178
Ananias (disciple) 74
angels 65, 107
Anglican Communion 123, 128, 161, 178
Anglicanism: authority in 5, 6, 111; and women's ministry 1, 124f., 126–8, 161, 174f., 180, 192
Anna (prophetess) 51
anointing: 100, 162, 183; of Jesus 42f., 50, 52, 95
Anselm 135, 142
Antioch 75
Antoninus Pius 20
Aphrahat 136
Apollos 57
apostles 46, 72f., 75, 76–80, 82f., 84, 96, 97, 177f., 193; meaning of term 85; women as 46, 79, 99
'apostolate of the laity' 128, 130
Apostolic Church Order 97
Apostolic Constitutions 95, 201
Apostolic Letter *see Mulieris Dignitatem*
apostolic succession 96, 123, 177, 183, 193
Aquila *see* Priscilla
Aquinas, Thomas 17, 107–10, 112, 115, 147, 174f., 191
Aristeas, Letter of 29
Aristotle 16f., 62, 90, 109, 116, 117, 119, 140
Arsinoe II 17
Artemisia 17
Articles, Thirty-Nine 143, 184
asceticism 61, 90, 93f., 112
Asia Minor, women in 17

Association for the Apostolic Ministry 155
Assumption (of Virgin Mary) 102, 182
Assyria, women in 22
Astarte 196
Athaliah 32
Athens, women at 14–17, 19f.
Augustine 91–4, 100, 101, 107, 116, 194
Augustus 20, 21
authority: men's and women's 65, 80, 82, 90, 96, 105, 108, 110, 139, 162, 165, 174, 190, 192, 197; of abbesses 105, 108f., 110; of Christ 191; of Church Fathers 89, 150; of deacons, 180, 184; papal 128; sources of 4–8; 34–7; structures of 76, 123 *see also* Church; hierarchy; Jesus; Scripture; subordination; Tradition

Baal 196
ba'al (husband) 24.
Babylon, women in 22
Bacchus *see* Dionysos
Baker, Bishop J. A. 169
Balch, D. L. 63
baptism: by disciples 74, 97; by women 80, 98, 100, 106, 162; of women 54, 65, 95, 184; rebaptism 103; theology 55f., 65, 171f., 193
Bar Mitzvah 27
Barnabas 75, 102
Barth, Karl 152, 157
Basil, 100
Bathsheba 32
'begetting' (fatherhood), as theological metaphor 139f., 170f., 195
Beguines 105
Ben Sirach 29, 148
Bernard of Clairvaux 136
Bible *see* Scripture
biological factors 92–5, 109f., 118, 119f., 139f., 150–4, 157, 188f.
birth control 120, 128, 155
Birth narratives 50f.
bishops: 77, 80, 96, 97, 105, 107, 177–81, 183; women as 1, 98, 110, 127, 171, 178, 192 *see also* episcopate
blessing, pronouncement of 28, 193
Bonaventure 110, 167, 171
Book of Common Prayer (BCP) 84, 184
Booth, C. and W. 125
Bosanquet, Mary 123
bride, image of *see* Church

Bridget of Sweden 105
Brown, R. E. 51
Bucer, Martin 113

Caird, G. B. 138f.
Calvin, John 102, 113f.
Canaanite gods 137, 143
Canada, Anglican Church of 126f.
Canham, Elizabeth 163
Canon Law 100, 103, 106, 123, 128, 191, 199
Cathars 106, 115
Catherine of Siena 105, 115
Catholic Biblical Association of America 132
Cato 21
celibacy: 60f., 93f.,; clerical 106, 128, 158, 162, 167, 173, 181
character, sacramental 109, 164, 171f., 193
'charismatics' 64, 98, 165
child-bearing, childbirth: 2, 27, 68, 95, 105, 111, 120, 140, 156; image of God's activity 134; seen as a curse 102, 148f.
Christology: Christ as bridegroom 63f., 169–71; High Priest 74, 82, 192f.; mediator 66, 110, 194; mother 135–8, 195f.; new Adam 55, 168; sacrifice 96; servant 134, 173, 191, 202; Son 134, 140; wisdom 137; relation to Church 64, 178, 183, 196 see also incarnation; Logos; redemption; resurrection
chromosome abnormalities 152
Chrysostom, John 16, 58, 99, 100, 113, 155, 169, 183
Chrysostomos, Archbishop (of Athens) 132
Church: authority of 4, 34, 117f., 122f., 191–3; as bride/woman 63f., 169, 174; as family 95f.; as people of God 31, 74f., 164, 193 see also Councils, Creeds, Fathers; hierarchy
Church in Wales 127, 184
Church of England: 1f., 126, 127, 166; Articles of Religion 143, 184; Reports 8, 132, 167, 174, 183 see also Anglicans
Church of Scotland 126, 131
Church of Sweden 125f.
Church Union 156
circumcision 27, 56, 156, 182, 194
Clark, Elizabeth 94
Clark, S. B. 144, 150, 153, 157
Claudius 20
Clement of Alexandria 94, 100, 102, 135f., 142
Clement of Rome 96
Collyridian heresy 99
Communion, Holy 95, 97, 128 see also Eucharist; Lord's Supper

complementarity of the sexes 173f., 188–90
conception: 109f., 140; Immaculate 102, 182
Condorcet (philosopher) 118
Confirmation 162, 171f., 178, 179, 183
Congregationalists 124
conscience: authority of 5f.; clauses 126, 127
Cornelia (mother of Gracchi) 19
Cornelius 182
Councils: 5, 103, 181f., 184, 200; Nicea 103, 182; Oecumenical 89, 101, 103, 181, 184; Toledo 141; Trent 84, 105, 171; Vatican II 38, 84, 126
courtesans 16
Cranmer, Thomas 176
Creation: narratives 91, 144–50; of humanity 30, 55, 107, 113, 133, 145–7, 165, 188, 194; of women 90f., 'Order' 144f., 149, 188, 196 see also Adam; Eve; God
Creeds: 5, 101; Apostles' 175; Athanasian 201; Nicene 138
criticism, biblical 3, 39f., 122, 130
Cyril of Jerusalem, 102

Daly, M. 132
deaconesses 58f., 103, 113, 123, 124f., 126, 127, 131, 157
deacons: 73, 76, 80f., 96, 100, 102, 103, 113, 180f., 184; female 58, 81, 100f., 113, 115, 126, 132, 161, 179, 192 see also diaconate; diakonos; Seven
Deborah 32, 36, 108, 163, 199
Decalogue 27, 47
Decretals 106f.
Demeter 17, 143
Demosthenes 16
Dempsey-Douglass, J. 113
Dentière, Marie 113
deutero-Pauline writings 54, 62–4, 69 see also Paul
Devil 5, 91, 99
Dewey, M. 162f.
diaconate 106, 180f., 184, 201 see also deacons
diakonia 83 see also service
diakonos: 96, 180; meaning of 58f., 73, 80f., 100f.
Didache 96
Didascalia 100, 201
didaskalos 98 see also teacher
Dionysos (Bacchus) 21, 143, 175, 196
disciple, baptism by 74, 97
disciples, women 42, 43–7, 51–3
discipleship 45–7, 72–9 passim, 82
discipline, exercise of 159, 161, 178, 193, 196

divorce 15, 19f., 25, 48f., 52, 128
Doctors, Church 107, 111, 150, 165, 187
  see also Aquinas; Bonaventure;
  Catherine
domestic duties see household duties
Domitian 13
dove-imagery 136, 142
dowries 15, 25
dress, female 18, 68 see also veiling
'duality' (in Creation) 151, 194
Duns Scotus 110f., 115
Durandus of Pourçain 111, 115

Eames, Archbishop 128
education: of women 2, 15, 25, 69, 105,
  112, 114, 119, 160f., 187, 197–9, 200
Egypt, women in 17f., 22
elders: 2, 75, 80f., 82, 197; female 37, 80;
  male 28, 113
Eliezer, Rabbi 29
Eliot, George 198, 201
Elizabeth (NT) 51
Elyot, T. 114
Enlightenment 117f., 130
Ephrem 136
epiclesis 136
Epicurus 18
Epiphanius 99, 100
Episcopal Church of the USA (ECUSA)
  126f., 178
episcopate 177–9, 180f. see also bishops
episkopos, meaning of term 73, 76, 80f.,
  85, 96, 177, 179
equality: racial 183, 187; religious 30–4,
  36, 47, 55–9, 91f., 111, 164; sexual 64,
  120–2, 124, 144–58 passim, 187f., 193,
  200
Equal Opportunities legislation 119
Equal Pay Act 131
Erasmus 115
Esther, Queen 31
Eucharist 76, 95, 96f., 128, 133, 136,
  166–9, 175, 178, 179, 180, 193 see also
  Lord's Supper; presidency, eucharistic
Eumachia 20
Euripides 16, 22
Eustochium 94
Evangelical Revival 123
Eve: creation of 68, 91f., 110, 146–8; as
  mother 139; naming of 147, 157; sin of
  55, 68, 91, 83f., 112, 148f.
experience, evidence of 6f., 163f., 185,
  197
exposure (of infants) 19
'extraordinary ministers' 2, 184, 199
'ezer (helper) 30, 38, 147

faith, women as paradigms of 44f., 46,
  50f.

'Fall' 68, 93f., 112, 145, 147f. see also
  Adam; Eve
family: Church as 46f., 77, 178, 181,
  196; solidarity of 30f., 147; women's
  roles in 192
fatherhood see begetting; God; procreation
Fathers, Church: 29, 59, 65, 66, 89–103,
  141, 144, 165, 199; authority of 5, 89,
  107, 150, 187 see also under individual
  Fathers.
femininity, characteristics of: 94, 141,
  142, 144f., 150–7, 160–3, 173f., 189,
  198f. see also 'inferiority'; 'passivity';
  'weakness'
feminism, feminists 6, 33, 42, 48, 52, 54,
  69, 120–2, 124, 129f., 131
Fiorenza, E. S. 42, 49
Fliedner, T. 124
forgiveness of sins: 55; declaration of 80,
  162, 178, 179, 193; power to 'bind and
  loose' 73, 76–8, 110
freedom: Christian 56, 98, 198; human
  129
Friedan, Betty 121
Fulvia (wife of Mark Antony) 20

Gaius, Institutes 22, 90
Galen 119
Galot, Jean 46, 76–8
gender see femininity; masculinity; sex
Gentiles 40, 182f., 184
Gibson, John 148f.
glossolalia 64
Gnosticism, 'gnostics' 63, 68, 93, 94,
  98, 137, 142
God: as Creator 30, 91, 95, 139; as
  Father (or male) 49, 96, 134, 140, 171,
  175, 194f.; as Mother (or female) 6, 49,
  131, 135–9, 141, 142f., 170, 194–6;
  doctrine of 130, 133–43 passim, 195,
  201; images of 133f., 138 see also
  grace; imago dei; love
goddess cults 121, 131, 141, 196
Gortyn Law Code 17
Gospel of Thomas 93
grace: 197f.; eucharistic 168f.; in Paul's
  theology 56, 68; in ordination 108, 198
Graeco-Roman world, Greece: 80;
  women in 14–22, 26, 28, 32, 36, 66
Gratian 106f., 111, 194
Greer, Germaine 121
Gregory the Great 95
Grimké, Sarah 124

Hagar 24, 56, 169
Hall, Bishop R. O. 126, 182f.
Hanilai, Rabbi 38
Hannah 31
Hanson, Richard 81

Harris, Bishop Barbara   132
Hayter, Mary   35f., 147
'headship', male   51, 65f., 164–6, 173f.,
   178, 195   see also hierarchy;
   subordination
healing   40f., 51, 98, 193
Hecate   20
Hegesippus   96
Hengel, Martin   13, 52
Herakles   140, 143
heresy, heretics   90, 98, 99, 161, 165
Herod (Antipas)   79; the Great   13
Herzel, Susannah   155
hetairai   16
hierarchy: in Church   77, 82, 95–7, 106,
   128, 130, 174, 188, 192; in 'Creation
   order'   65f., 114, 144
hiereus   74, 97
Hilda (abbess)   105
Hildegard (mystic)   105
Hipparchia   18
Hippolytus (Church Father)   100
Hodgson, L.   171f.
Holy Spirit   see Spirit
Homer   22
homo, meaning of   194   see also 'man'
homosexuality   16, 24, 70
Hong Kong   126, 127
Hood, Margaret   155
Hooker, Morna   65
Hooker, R.   176
hormones   154
household: duties, management   15, 44,
   47, 112, 120, 121, 181, 189, 198; Codes
   62–4, 68f., 165
Huldah (prophetess)   32, 36

iconic factors   see 'representation'
Ignatius of Antioch   96, 102, 183
imago dei (image of God)   55, 63, 90, 92,
   110, 145f., 156, 173, 187, 189
incarnation   5, 37, 110, 167f., 173f.
'inclusive language'   see language
'inferiority', female   69, 107, 112, 118f.,
   144, 156f., 186–8
inheritance, women's rights to   15, 17,
   23f.
Inter Insigniores (Vatican Declaration)
   129, 167, 175
Irenaeus   96, 98
Isaac   26, 33
Isaiah's wife   32
'ish, 'ishshah, meaning of   27, 37, 101,
   147, 157
Isis   21
Islam   1, 117

Jacob   33
Jael   32

Jairus' daughter   40, 50
Japan   127, 153
Jephtha's daughter   24
Jeremias, J.   43; 142
Jerome   70, 93, 102, 183
Jerusalem   13, 47, 72, 75, 76, 80, 82,
   135, 168
Jesus of Nazareth: attitudes to women
   40–3; 47, 49, 50f., 94, 95, 130, 165;
   calls God 'Father'   29, 140–2;
   commissions to followers   74–9, 83, 178,
   182; masculine orientation   48f.;
   teaching   8, 35, 39f., 43–51, 78, 165, 166
   see also Christology
Jezebel   32
Joan of Arc   106, 115
John Paul II, Pope   129, 175, 188, 192
Johnson, Elizabeth   138
Jose b. Johannan, Rabbi   37
Josephus   62, 71
Josiah   32
Judaism: ancient 23–38 passim, 151;
   modern 126, 132
judges, female   32, 108, 165
Judith   31
Julian of Norwich   105, 136
Junia (apostle)   58, 70, 81, 100
jurists, Roman   19, 22, 90
Justinian   22, 90
Juvenal   21

Kabbalistic tradition   137
kephalē, meaning of   65f., 148
Klein, V.   154
Knox, John   114, 116, 148
koinē Greek   14
kyrios   14f., 24

Lambeth Conference 1989   127f.
language: analogical 133; 'exclusive'
   168; 'inclusive' 37, 55, 70, 80, 101,
   128, 145–7, 175, 200; metaphorical
   133f., 142, 168–71, 175   see also 'man'
Las Huelgas   105
Last Supper   76f., 84, 97, 167
Latin America   6, 128f.
Law: Church 101, 107, 199; Divine 122;
   Jewish 25, 27, 41, 56f., 66f., 98, 165
   see also Canon Law; jurists, Roman;
   Natural Law
laying on of hands   74f., 100, 103, 124,
   193
Leander of Seville   94
Leonard, Bishop G.   144, 150, 151, 163,
   171, 175, 201
lesbianism   121
Li, Florence T. O.   126, 163, 183
Liberation Theology   129, 132
Lightfoot, J. B.   81

liturgy: 194; Divine 180; feminist 6, 130
Livy 21
Logos 135, 137f., 167
Lohfink, G. 43, 77
Lombard, Peter 92, 107, 110
Longenecker, R. N. 149
Lord's Supper 75, 80, 84, 94, 96, 168f., 193 *see also* Eucharist; presidency, eucharistic
Lot's daughters 24
love: Christian 174, 176, 190; heterosexual 16, 33; homosexual 16; marital 33f., 62–4, 156; of Christ 63f.; of God 160, 170, 196, 200; priestly 176
Lumen Gentium 175, 183
Luther, Martin 35, 112, 113f., 148
Lutheran Churches 125f., 177

Macarius 136f., 142
magisterium, Church's 34
magistrates, women 18, 165
'man': doctrine of 130, 194f.; vocabulary for 27, 37, 49, 92, 101, 175
Manoah's wife 31
Marcion 98
Margaret, Queen of Scotland 114
marriage: 121, 124; Christian teaching on 52, 56, 60–4, 92–5, 112, 156, 162, 165, 188f.; Greek 15, 16f.; Jewish 23–6, 33, 37; Roman 19f.
Married Women's Property Act 124
Martha 41, 44f., 51, 52, 199
martyrs: Maccabean 28; women 90, 110
Marxism 118, 121, 129
Mary Magdalene 45f., 50, 83, 93, 100
Mary, mother of Jesus 44, 46, 51, 53, 76, 83, 94, 99, 100, 102, 182, 189, 201
Mary of Bethany 44f., 51, 52, 199
Mascall, E. L. 151, 152, 168
masculinity, characteristics of 94, 141, 144f., 150–4, 162, 173f., 189f. *see also* aggression; reason
matrimony 162 *see also* marriage
medieval period 63, 101, 104–16, 171, 193
Mennonites 123
menstruation 27, 93, 94, 95, 102, 151, 156
Methodists 123, 201
methodology 4–8, 34–7, 165, 187
Michal 37
Michelangelo, 'Creation of Man' 146, 194
Mill, John Stuart 118
ministry: 'every member' 130, 193; functions of 159–74, 177–84 *passim*, 196; non-stipendiary 2, 158, 181; ordained 141f.; theology of 2, 7, 72–84 *passim*, 89, 95–101, 130–2, 177–84,

197–9 *see also* Orders; ordination; priesthood
Min (Egyptian god) 175, 196
Miriam 31f., 36, 163
misogyny 22, 29f., 65, 61, 91, 114, 129, 148
mission: charges 73, 78, 84; women's share in 44, 49, 128, 161
Moberly, R. C. 172
Moloney, F. J. 50
Moltmann-Wendel, E. 42
monasticism 93
Montanists 98
Montesquieu 122
Moravians 123
Morély, Jean 113
Morris, Dinah 198, 201
Moses 23, 31, 32, 91
Mother, God as 6, 49, 131, 134–8, 141, 142, 143; Jesus as 135f.; Holy Spirit as 136f., 142, 170
motherhood: 112f., 114, 136, 139; and ministry 154–6, 158, 181, 192; Jesus' teaching on 44, 46f. *see also* childbirth; conception
Mott, Lucretia 126
Movement for the Ordination of Women (MOW) 163
Mulieris Dignitatem 129, 175, 188, 200, 201
mystery religions 21, 97
myth 147, 148

'naming formula' 157
Natural Law 90, 92, 94, 107, 110, 111, 112, 114, 117, 122, 130, 155
nature, arguments from 15f., 116, 150–7 *see also* Natural Law
Nektarios (Kephalas) 132
Neopythagoreans 18, 62
Nero 13, 21
New Zealand, Anglican Province of 126
Noadiah (prophetess) 32
non-stipendiary ministry 2, 158, 181
nuns 100, 105, 106, 110, 112, 128, 192
Nympha 57, 75

Odes of Solomon 136
Oecumenical Councils *see* Council
Old Catholics 126, 174, 180
ontological factors 160, 164–74, 193
Oppian Law 21
Order, ministerial 96, 177, 180
Orders, Holy 1, 103, 108–11, 124, 129, 132, 171f., 192
Ordinals 84, 174, 180, 184, 199
Ordination: of women 99, 101, 105, 106–11, 114, 125–9, 132, 136, 144, 156, 157, 173–93 *passim*, 197–9; role of Holy

Ordination (*cont.*)
   Spirit 136, training for 160   *see also*
   ministry; Orders; priesthood
Origen 70, 99, 100, 102
Orthodox Churches 1, 5, 122, 126, 132,
   144, 177, 182
Oxford Movement 123

Pandora, myth of 148
papyri 17, 85, 98
papacy 93, 104, 112, 128   *see also* Popes
parables 47f., 166
Paraclete 136f., 142
Parsons, Anne 194
'passivity', feminine 109, 139, 162, 174,
   189, 201
pastoral care 160, 161, 178, 178–80
Pastoral Epistles 67–9, 73, 81
patriarchy 23f., 33, 129, 140
Patristic Age 89–103, 180, 193   *see also*
   Fathers, Church
Paul: as mother 142; attitudes to
   sexuality and marriage 59–64, 93;
   attitudes to women and their ministry
   54, 57–9, 64–72, 80, 82, 91, 98, 108,
   113, 130, 147f., 149; conversion 74f.,
   102; on his own ministry 74f., 79, 170,
   191f.; theology of 55–7, 67, 69, 98, 99,
   110f., 165, 166, 168, 189
Paulianist heresy 103
Peloponnesian War 15
Pentecost 78
penance, sacrament of 77, 162   *see also*
   forgiveness
people of God   *see* Church
Pericles 15
Perictione 18
Peripatetics 18
Persis 57
Peter: 45, 73, 77, 79, 84, 182f., 184,
   194; mother-in-law of 40
Pharisees 41, 47, 84
Philip the Evangelist: 75; daughters of
   99
Philo 28, 62, 71
Phoebe (deacon) 58f., 70, 81, 83, 113,
   199
Photian schism 182
Photius, *Nomocanon* 103
Plato, Platonists 16, 62
polygyny 24
Pompey 13
Popes: John Paul II 129, 175, 188, 192;
   Paul VI 132; Pius IV and V 106; Soter
   107
potestas (sacred power) 112, 172
prayer: Christian 68, 75, 76, 130, 141f.,
   160; by women 31, 47, 66f., 76, 114,
   160, 163; Jewish 22, 55

preaching: 159, 179; men's 46, 49;
   women's 99, 112, 113, 123, 125, 160,
   201
presbyter, *presbyteros*: 76, 80f., 97, 100,
   102, 183; meaning of 73, 80
presbytera, presbytis (?woman elder) 80,
   85, 98, 100
presbyterate   *see* priesthood
presidency, eucharistic 75, 80, 81f., 84,
   96, 97f., 178, 179, 193
priesthood (Christian): 95f., 106–11,
   151, 153, 163f., 166–74, 179–81; of
   Jesus Christ 74, 82, 192f.; of women
   129, 130, 155–7, 162; 'royal' (of
   believers) 74, 85, 192; sacerdotal 97f.,
   106, 112, 193, 197   *see also* priests
priests (Christian): as 'begetters' 170–4;
   as mediators 97; functions of 179f.;
   qualities of 160–4, 172, 176; shortage
   of 129; as successors of apostles 77,
   80f., 96, 183; women priests 1, 98, 103,
   106, 107, 125–7, 133, 141f., 163, 171,
   192, 195, 199
priests and priesthood, Jewish 26, 97,
   106, 141, 143, 151, 192
priests and priestesses, pagan 20, 22, 74,
   96, 143, 196
Primasius 103
Priscilla (Prisca) 57f., 70, 75, 163, 197
Priscillian 98
procreation 92f., 109, 157   *see also*
   begetting; sex
professions, women in 1, 2, 17, 105,
   119f., 131, 155, 163, 181, 198
prophetesses   *see* prophets, female
prophets and prophecy: 66f., 74, 75, 96,
   108; female 22, 31f., 51, 65, 73, 98, 99,
   163
prostatis, meaning of 59, 82
prostitutes, prostitution 20, 22, 41, 47,
   50, 143
Protestants 5, 104, 111, 114, 123, 124,
   125, 172, 173
psychological factors 144f., 150–7, 162f.,
   185f., 188–90, 198f.
purity, ritual 27, 35, 38, 40, 41, 94f., 97,
   102, 143, 156
Pythagoras 17

Quakers (Society of Friends) 6, 123, 124
queens   *see* royal women
Qoheleth 29f.

rabbis: 28f., 37f., 41, 43, 52, 65; title of
   77; women as 126
Rachel 21, 25, 31, 33
Raming, Ida 107
rank, clerical 96f., 191   *see also* hierarchy
rape 24f., 35, 37

Raven, Charles 126, 132
Readers, lay 2, 126
reason: authority of 5–7, 150, 163f., 182, 185; male 'superiority' in 107, 110f., 152f.,; women's 'intuitive' 153, 158
Rebekah 31, 33
redemption 37, 55, 149, 156, 168, 193
Reformation 104, 111–14, 123, 181f., 187
Reformed Churches 113, 123, 125, 172, 195
Reform Judaism 126
'representation'; of Christ or God 63f., 110, 133, 142, 166–71, 173f., 195f., 201; of humanity 194–6; of women by men 195f.
resurrection 46, 49, 76, 115
Reuben, Testament of 29, 65, 156
revelation, divine 6, 8, 163, 185, 197
Revolution, French 118
rights: civil 118, 119; human 63, 128, 129, 131; paternal 19, 24; women's 120–2, 131, 184
Roman Catholicism: 1, 5, 6, 34, 38, 77, 84, 98, 106, 108, 115, 122, 128–30, 158, 162, 163, 167, 171, 176, 182, 184 *see also* papacy; Popes
Rome and Roman Empire 13f., 18–22 *passim*, 24, 26, 52, 63, 66, 89, 95, 102, 104, 108
royal women 17, 32, 102, 105, 114, 166
Ruether, R. 201
Runcie, Archbishop R. 191
Russell, G. 162f.
Ruth 24, 25, 31

Sacerdotium Ministeriale 175
sacraments: 159, 161f., 171, 193, 195, 196; administered by women 2, 95, 106, 108, 184, 186, 199; lay celebration of 193 *see also under individual sacraments*
Sacred Congregation for the Faith 129, 132
sacrifice 26, 74, 194; of Christ 97
saints, women 106, 115, 153, 163
St Joan's International Alliance 163
Salome Alexandra (Jewish queen) 32
Salvation Army 125
Samaritan woman 44, 45, 51, 99
Sanhedrin 28, 80
Sappho (woman poet) 17
Sarah 24, 26, 31, 56, 169
Saward, John 139f., 155, 168
Sayers, Dorothy L. 194
scholarship, biblical: 3, 39f., 122; women's 90, 160
Schweizer, E. 72
Scottish Episcopal Church 127, 131, 184

Scripture, authority of 3–8, 34, 112, 117, 164f., 182, 185, 187f. *see also* criticism, biblical
servanthood, service (Christian) 52, 77f., 83, 84, 85, 174, 191–2, 196
'servers', women 128
Seven, the 75, 76, 81
Seventy, the 49, 61, 72, 73
sex, sexuality: and grammatical gender 46, 134; attitudes 34, 47, 59–64, 93–6, 101, 106, 119f., 130, 186; differentiation 113, 144–58, 159–66 *passim*, 162, 171, 173f., 178–81, 187–90, 197f.; intercourse 60, 93–5, 120, 139, 140, 170, 188f.; morality 16, 48, 82, 128, 185 *see also* femininity; masculinity
silence, women's 26, 66f., 68, 98, 124, 199
slavery: abolition of 119, 123f., 183; Christian attitudes 56, 62f., 74, 83, 149, 165, 173; Graeco-Roman 14, 15, 55, 62; Jewish 24, 55, 62
Society for New Testament Studies 160
Solomon 33
Song of Songs (Canticles) 38, 170, 189
Sophia christology 138 *see also* Wisdom
Sophocles 15
soul 91f., 108, 172, 175
Soviet Union 117, 153
Sparta 17
Spirit, Holy: 3, 5, 7, 64, 112, 182, 185–99 *passim*; as Mother (or female) 136f., 142, 170, 195; as male 134; received by women 78, 98, 113, 123
spiritual gifts 56, 73f., 165, 188, 197f.
Stanton, Elizabeth C. 124
Stephen 75
Stoics 18, 62
Storkey, Elaine 121
Stone, Lucy 123f.
subordination (of women) 1, 14–37, 62–9, 90–101 *passim*, 105, 106, 107–24 *passim*, 144–64, 171f., 178, 184, 187f., 200
Susannah (OT) 31
synagogue, women's roles in 26, 28, 37, 46, 80
synergoi (fellow-workers) 56f., 82
Synesius, bishop of Cyrene 136
synods *see* Councils
Sweden, Church of 125f.
Syrian Church 100, 136f.
Syro-Phoenician woman 40, 50

Tamar: daughter-in-law of Judah 24; daughter of David 37
teachers, teaching: apostolic 75, 122; by women 68f., 80, 85, 91, 98, 161, 197

Temple, Jerusalem 26, 38
Teresa of Avila 115
Teresa, Mother (of Calcutta) 161
Tertullian 65, 91, 98, 101, 102, 116,
  148, 175
Testament of Reuben 29, 65, 156
Theodore of Mopsuestia 102
Theodore of Tarsus 95
Theodore the Studite 166
Theophylact 70, 99
Thirty-Nine Articles 143, 184
threefold ministry 4, 96, 125–9, 177–84,
  192 *see also* bishops, deacons, Orders,
  priests
Thucydides 15
tongues, speaking with 64
tonsure 108, 111, 171
Tradition: authority of 5–7, 34, 131,
  182, 185, 187; traditions 106, 123, 183
transsexualism 151f.
Trent, Council of 84, 105, 171
Trible, Phyllis 142, 146, 147
Trinity, Holy 5, 130, 134, 173, 182, 196,
  201
Twelve, the 46, 49, 51, 58, 61, 72f., 74,
  76–80, 96, 97, 102, 178, 182

Ulpian 22, 90
'uncleanness' *see* purity
unction 162 *see also* anointing
unity, church 178, 182f., 192
USA 1, 123f., 127, 153

van der Meer, H. 98
Vatican Declaration (1976) 108, 115,
  129, 132, 167
Vatican II (Second Vatican Council) 38,
  84, 128
veiling of women 28, 64–6, 71
Venus 20

Verginia 24
vessels, sacred, women's handling of 95,
  106
Vesta 21, 143
Vincent of Lérins 181, 184
virgin birth 140
virginity, virgins: 22, 24, 60, 67, 90,
  93f., 100, 101, 102, 114; Vestal Virgins
  20 *see also* Mary, mother of Jesus
vocation 155, 160, 163, 185f.
von Allmen, J.-J. 76, 155
von Grumach, Argula 113
vote, women's right to 124, 125

Wales, Church in 127, 184
Ware, Bishop K. 144f., 150, 166f., 201
Warner, Marina 94, 102
'weakness', feminine 19, 22, 90, 94, 107,
  111, 144, 148, 171, 192
Wesley, John 123
Westminster Confession 143
widows: 24, 31, 47, 68, 75, 90, 100, 103,
  112, 113, 163; widow of Nain 41
Wisdom, Divine, as female 137f., 143
witnesses, women as 44, 91
Wollstonecraft, Mary 118
womb, vocabulary for 134f., 170
Women's Movement 120–2, 129
World Council of Churches (WCC) 131,
  174, 177
World War: I 125; II 125, 126

Xenophon 15, 112

Yahweh: 27, 30, 133f., 141; consort of
  137

Zell, Katherine 113
Zeus, 140, 175
Zion, imagery for 169